iPhone® 3D Game Programming All in One

Course Technology PTR

A part of Cengage Learning

COURSE TECHNOLOGY
CENGAGE Learning

Australia • Brazil • Japan • Korea • Mexico • Singapore • Spain • United Kingdom • United States

COURSE TECHNOLOGY
CENGAGE Learning™

iPhone® 3D Game Programming All in One

Jeremy Alessi

Publisher and General Manager, Course Technology PTR: Stacy L. Hiquet

Associate Director of Marketing: Sarah Panella

Manager of Editorial Services: Heather Talbot

Marketing Manager: Jordan Castellani

Senior Acquisitions Editor: Emi Smith

Project Editor: Marta Justak

Technical Reviewer: Michelle Menard

Copy Editor: Gene Redding

Interior Layout Tech: MPS Limited, A Macmillan Company

Cover Designer: Matt Donlan

Cover Producer: Mike Tanamachi

CD-ROM Producer: Brandon Penticuff

Indexer: Kelly Talbot

Proofreader: Michael Beady

For product information and technology assistance, contact us at
Cengage Learning Customer & Sales Support, 1-800-354-9706

For permission to use material from this text or product, submit all requests online at **cengage.com/permissions**

Further permissions questions can be emailed to
permissionrequest@cengage.com

Apple, iTunes, iPhone, iPod Touch, and Xcode are registered trademarks of Apple Inc. 3D Studio Max and Mudbox are registered trademarks of Autodesk Inc. PhysX is a registered trademark of NVIDIA Corporation. Windows is a registered trademark of Microsoft Corporation. Photoshop is a registered trademark of Adobe Systems Incorporated. Wii Sports Resort is a registered trademark of Nintendo. Google and Google Earth are registered trademarks of Google. All other trademarks are the property of their respective owners.

All images © Cengage Learning unless otherwise noted.

Library of Congress Control Number: 2009942391

ISBN-13: 978-1-4354-5478-1

ISBN-10: 1-4354-5478-2

Course Technology, a part of Cengage Learning
20 Channel Center Street
Boston, MA 02210
USA

Cengage Learning is a leading provider of customized learning solutions with office locations around the globe, including Singapore, the United Kingdom, Australia, Mexico, Brazil, and Japan. Locate your local office at: **international.cengage.com/region**

Cengage Learning products are represented in Canada by Nelson Education, Ltd.

For your lifelong learning solutions, visit **courseptr.com**

Visit our corporate website at **cengage.com**

Printed in the United States of America
2 3 4 5 6 7 12 11 10

This book is dedicated to my mother, my father, and my wife. Mom, thanks for always believing in me. Life's not the same without you. Dad, thanks for teaching me the value of hard work by making me lift those five-gallon buckets when I was three years old. Finally, thank you, Hilary, for putting up with all the late nights and long hours that go into game development. Your love and support are mind-boggling!

ACKNOWLEDGMENTS

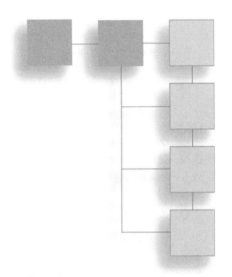

I would like to thank all of my friends and family who helped me along the broken road of game development. In no particular order, thanks to Kacey, Luke, Evan, Stephanie, Frank, Joe, Kerri, Greg, Ease, John, Stacey, Steve, Jeremy, Chris, Match, Michael, Emily, Nick, Rich, and Leroy. You all listened when I needed an ear and played when I needed a spare set of thumbs.

I would also like to thank all the folks at Unity Technologies. David Helgason and Joachim Ante, I'm your biggest fan! Thank you for believing in my writing and trusting me with your engine. Unity3D is a masterpiece of game development technology—thanks for empowering my imagination.

Of course, we wouldn't have a book at all if it weren't for all the great people involved. Thank you, Marta Justak—you are just plain awesome. This book never would have come together without your calls (phone or otherwise). Thank you, Michelle Menard, for staying sane and keeping me logically honest. Thank you, Gene Redding, for whipping the book into shape and for really doing your homework on the subject at hand. Thank you, Brandon Penticuff, for getting all that data on the CD (it fit, right?). Thanks a million, Matt Donlan, for creating beautiful cover art at a moment's notice. Finally, thanks, Emi Smith, for giving me the chance to write about making iPhone games in the first place; it's not often that a person gets to partake in a passion on this level. I appreciate it to the fullest.

I also need to thank some industry folks. Thanks to Brenda Brathwaite for talking to me about Skyline Riders at Dave and Busters in Bethesda, Maryland, way back in early 2002. In some ways, that was the beginning of my professional game development career. Thank go to Jeff Tunnell for guiding me through the development of my first published game, *Aerial Antics*. Without the indie movement, I don't know where the industry would be today. Thanks to Adrian Tysoe for taking a shot with me on *Aerial Antics*. The visuals still stand strong today. We made a killer game (even if the music sucks). Thanks to the Gamasutra guys, Simon Carless and Christian Nutt, for all the help with the *Games Demystified* series and beyond. Thank you Mario and GLaDOS, without gravity and portals, this book would not be possible. Thank you Ori Cohen for helping me produce *Skyline Blade.* When that game hit the App Store, I finally saw the light at the end of the tunnel. Thank you Fraser McInnes at Pocket Gamer for making me realize just how much more of the tunnel I have left to traverse before I reach the light. Thank you Rich Smith, you worked alongside me during the hardest time of my life, and that office was depressing without you. Finally, thank you to all the players for downloading the heck out of *Crash For Cash.* You answered a prayer of mine by taking the game all the way to a #1-ranked position. It's hard to feel down about anything when your game has been played nearly two million times.

In addition, I'd like to thank my new family-in-laws. The past year has been tough, and there's no rest for the weary. Luckily, there was a lot of laughter, good company, and good food (always good food). I'm a family person and without you all I would have been awfully lonely this year. I cannot possibly thank you enough for all that you've done!

Lastly, thanks Apple for developing a revolutionary gaming platform to write about. I can't wait to see what's next!

About the Author

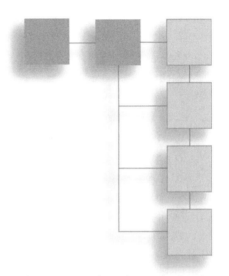

Jeremy Alessi has been developing video games for over a decade. Scholastic, Garage Games, and Reflexive Entertainment have published his work. His first independent title, *Aerial Antics* (2004), was nominated for Sim Game of the Year by Game Tunnel, was listed as a top-five physics download by Computer Gaming World, and was featured on the G4 Network TV show *Cinematech*. Jeremy has produced numerous titles for the iPhone through independent studio Midnight Status. Several of his iPhone titles have held top 100 positions in the App Store, including *Crash For Cash,* a #1-ranked title that has been played nearly two million times. Jeremy is also a freelance tech writer, having created the popular *Games Demystified* series of articles that appear on Gamasutra. Last, but not least, Jeremy works part-time programming serious games for L3 Communications, the sixth largest defense contractor in the United States.

Contents

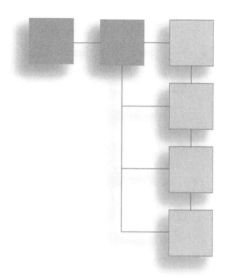

INTRODUCTION

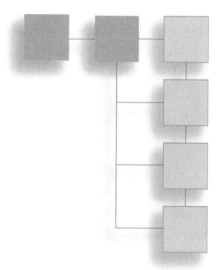

The iPhone platform is the newest and most revolutionary game platform in existence today. Developers, both large and small, are finding critical and financial success while game players are now able to have fun with more experiences for less money than ever before. This book focuses on 3D game development for the iPhone and iPod Touch utilizing Unity (unity3d.com). Unity is an excellent tool capable of PC, Mac, Xbox 360, and Wii development, as well as iPhone and iPod Touch deployment. Unity can be acquired free via the "indie" version, although more experienced users may want to opt for the advanced version of Unity to unlock professional-level features.

Aside from covering Unity, this book will cover certain aspects of Xcode, concept art, basic 3D modeling, math, physics, game prototyping, and the business aspects to help you become successful on the App Store. Creating games isn't just a technical challenge. Smart design, clever marketing, and a clear understanding of the business can make or break a game just as easily as a poor algorithm or unattractive visuals.

There has never been a better time to jump into game development. The tools are great, the market is hot, and the iPhone technology represents the cutting edge of the game industry on many fronts. Never before has such great technology been so widely accessible. In the past, the best technology and development tools were reserved for large publishers with deep pockets. Now it's possible for an independent game developer to emerge on top, armed with the best tools the industry has to offer. Let's get started!

What You'll Find in This Book

This book covers the creation of *Tropical Tailspin* (a casual flight simulator for the iPhone) from conception to completion as a published product on the App Store. The development process begins with a high-level analysis to determine what game to make. Once the game concept is determined, the iPhone hardware is examined to figure out the best way to support the game concept with the iPhone's unique interface. From there, the book covers the creation of concept art, game prototyping, testing, and final production. The book ends with *Tropical Tailspin* uploaded to the App Store.

Who This Book Is For

This book is for novices and intermediate developers who want to learn about iPhone development. The book covers game development fundamentals, including programming principals, 2D image editing, 3D modeling, and more advanced 3D programming. The more complex aspects include the fixed-wing flight physics and the crunch associated with the delivery of the game to the App Store.

How This Book Is Organized

The book is divided into two parts, "Some Assembly Required" and "Game Makin'." The first part of the book focuses on the preparation required to begin developing a game, covering the tools in terms of both hardware and software development for iPhone games. The second part of the book covers the actual creative and engineering process necessary to create and ship a game.

Part I: Some Assembly Required

- **Ready, Fire, Aim!** covers the basics from the iPhone hardware to general programming. In this chapter, you'll learn about the hardware needed to test applications and the subtle differences between each revision released by Apple. Beyond the hardware, the first chapter highlights the software packages and general programming skills necessary to create a game.

- **Apple's Ring, Apple's Ropes** explores the boundaries Apple has created for developers to operate within and explains the registration, certificate, and provisioning processes involved in creating an iPhone game. By the completion of this chapter, you'll be a registered iPhone developer ready to dive into Unity and begin developing that dream game.

- **Unity Fundamentals** dissects the Unity iPhone interface. You'll learn about the Unity Editor's general functionality. You'll create a Unity 3D scene that could be deployed to the iPhone.

- **Creating the Perfect Concept** sets the stage for the creative endeavor that is involved in game development. In this chapter, you'll determine through logical analysis exactly what game you're going to develop. We'll lay out the groundwork for *Tropical Tailspin,* a game that will be released on the App Store.

Part II: Game Makin'

- **The Strengths and Weaknesses of the iPhone's Unique Input Interface** starts you on the journey of actually implementing your game. You'll learn about the code behind the most basic ways a player might interact with a game on the iPhone. You'll cover basic touch gestures, some graphics principles in 3D and 2D, and finally the use and calibration of the iPhone's accelerometer.

- **Concept Art** is the chapter in which we'll begin creating the imagery associated with *Tropical Tailspin.* This chapter covers both technical and design-oriented aspects of the basic art an iPhone game needs. We'll create concept sketches, a game icon, and the first 3D scene directly related to the *Tropical Tailspin* project.

- **Prototyping** builds on the 3D scene created at the end of Chapter 6. This chapter extends into the basic flight mechanics that will power the example game. By the end, we'll test our new mechanics in a playable fashion utilizing Unity Remote, a special tool that comes with Unity 3D and helps quickly run and debug the game over a network.

- **Play Testing and Iterating** covers the process of letting third parties test your game, offering feedback along the way. With the newly acquired input, we'll take our example game to the next level by changing our code, design, and art. By the end of this chapter, we will either have fixed all of our game's major issues or at least know what the major issues are that need to be addressed.

■ **Production Art** is the art that our game will ship with. In this chapter, we'll ditch the clumsy concept art and create art worthy of a download in the highly competitive environment that is the App Store. We'll model and texture an island chain, acquire, rig, and animate a seaplane, and set up our final scene in Unity including lights, skybox, and detail scenery.

■ **Tying Up Loose Ends** is a rough and wild ride. This chapter covers the crunch period in which many rapid solutions are developed in order to deliver *Tropical Tailspin*. By the end of this chapter, we'll have created a fully functional game and covered many new technical solutions to the problems encountered along the way.

■ **Shipping and Handling Extra** takes us beyond the development of *Tropical Tailspin* and onto the process of packaging the game for delivery to Apple. This chapter describes Xcode and the iTunes Connect Web site. By the completion of this chapter, *Tropical Tailspin* will be waiting in line for approval by Apple and be just one step away from players' hands.

About the CD-ROM

The *iPhone 3D Game Programming All in One* CD comes packed with the simple code samples that appear in Chapters 1-5, the full *Tropical Tailspin* game package, the seaplane model donated for educational use by Tomáš Dřínovský, a variety of media resources, and the Unity3D trial software. To use the *Tropical Tailspin* and sample code (also referred to in the text as the iPhone3DGamePro-grammingAllinOne project), simply create a new Unity project and then right-click in the Project View and use the Import Package option. Good luck!

CD-ROM Downloads

If you purchased an ebook version of this book, and the book had a companion CD-ROM, we will mail you a copy of the disc. Please send ptrsupplements @cengage.com the title of the book, the ISBN, your name, address, and phone number. Thank you.

PART 1

SOME ASSEMBLY REQUIRED

Creating iPhone games is a technical challenge. There are some fundamental aspects that you must think about before diving headfirst into a complex game project. First, you must have the proper hardware and software in place. In addition, there's a certain degree of math knowledge required. Creating a 3D game isn't a simple task, and it requires at least basic algebra skills. This book will cover the 3D math and physics necessary to make your game come alive from a top-down perspective. What this means is that we'll look at gameplay first and then move down, showing you how it is built. This method will help readers who aren't math savvy become just that.

Finally, beyond math and physics, we'll be learning how to program. Unity allows users to write code in C#, Boo (Python), and JavaScript. The reasons for providing three programming options are numerous. Chief among them is that different people have different tastes when it comes to programming syntax. Some users want a simpler interface even if it limits them, and some prefer a more complex interface because they are advanced users. In general, JavaScript is the language of choice among Unity users and within the Unity documentation.

This book will focus on JavaScript, which provides the simplest interface with Unity. One thing to note is that Unity is based on the Mono Project (www.mono-project.com). This means that Unity's specialized functionality is covered within Unity documentation, but its base functionality (such as string handling) is documented on the Mono Project Web site. For this reason, sometimes JavaScript calls can be excessively long if they reference a method deep within the Mono Project's code base. If the same code were written with C#, then a simple "using" call would be made at the top of the script so that long nested class calls could be avoided.

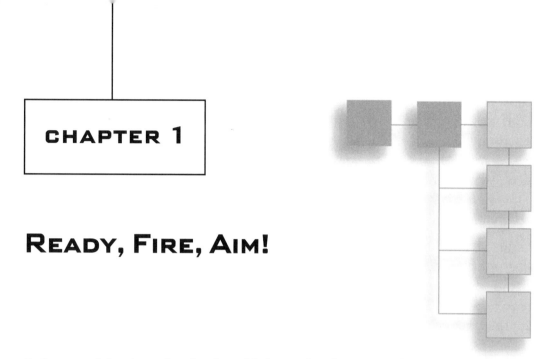

CHAPTER 1

READY, FIRE, AIM!

Before we delve into the depths of iPhone development, there are a few things you'll need. First and foremost, it's important to have an iPhone or iPod Touch to develop and test your games on. There are various revisions of each device on the market, and it's important to know the differences before developing your game.

The iPhone has three incarnations. The original iPhone that was released in 2007, the iPhone 3G, released during the summer of 2008, and the iPhone 3GS, released in June 2009. The original and 3G versions are pretty similar in terms of performance. The iPhone 3G is slightly but not noticeably quicker. The biggest difference between the two phones is the inclusion of GPS (global positioning system) in the iPhone 3G. If your game idea revolves around GPS, then you may have to exclude original iPhone owners.

The iPhone 3GS is a whole new ball game in terms of performance. The 3GS model is four times faster than the iPhone 3G and includes a new graphics chip, called the PowerVR SGX. This chip replaces the PowerVR MBX Lite included with the older iPhones. This new chip supports OpenGL ES 2.0, so not only will the iPhone 3GS outperform the frame rates of the older iPhones, but it can also handle next-generation shader effects.

The iPod also has three incarnations that offer similar gaming performance to their iPhone cousins, with a few exceptions, which should be taken into account when developing a game. The first-generation iPod, iPhone, and iPhone 3G all contain the Samsung ARM 1176JZ(F)-S v1.0 processor. The second-generation iPod contains an updated version of this processor, called the ARM 1176 v4.0. The original devices containing the v1.0 processor were all underclocked from 620MHz to 412MHz. The second-generation iPod Touch not only features an updated version of the ARM 1176 processor, but in addition it is clocked to 533MHz. This small update drastically improved the performance of the second-generation iPod Touch relative to the original hardware.

Figures 1.1 and 1.2 show the iPhone and iPod Touch, respectively. Cosmetically, they are almost identical, but there are a few differences. The iPod Touch is significantly thinner than the iPhone (0.46 inches for the original iPhone, 0.48 inches for the 3G/3GS, and 0.33 inches for the iPod Touch). Secondly, the volume and lock buttons on the iPod Touch are black plastic instead of metallic. In addition, the lock button is on the top right of the iPhone and on the top left of the iPod Touch. Finally, the speaker jack of the iPhone is located adjacent to the lock button, whereas it is next to the power input plug of the iPod Touch on the bottom of the device.

It's hugely important to test your games on multiple devices unless you are specifically targeting just one. In that case, it's possible to limit an application to

Figure 1.1
The iPhone.

Figure 1.2
The iPod Touch.

being downloaded only to a supported device via iTunes Connect, which we'll cover in depth later.

The final hardware variances are the inclusion of a camera on both of the iPhones, the exclusion of any sort of microphone on both iPods, and the exclusion of a speaker from the first-generation iPod Touch. These hardware variances are fairly subtle and do not affect most games. However, it is important that you pick the right device if you're developing a specialized game. Beyond that, it's also very helpful to test your game on multiple devices to consider the performance and tactile feedback differences caused by the subtle hardware upgrades Apple has executed over the lifetime of the platform. Here is a descending list of iPhone/iTouch hardware from most to least powerful.

- iPhone 3GS
- iPod Touch third generation
- iPod Touch second generation
- iPhone 3G
- iPhone
- iPod Touch first generation

With the various hardware configurations out of the way and with an i-Device in hand, it's time to pick up a development machine. The cheapest way to jump into iPhone development is with an Intel-based Mac Mini equipped with OS X Leopard ($599). It's important to note that older versions of OS X– and Power PC– (PPC) based Macs cannot be used for iPhone development. Whichever Mac you choose for development, make sure that it's equipped with OS X Leopard and an Intel-based processor. While there are some hacks available to develop using PPC processors, they will only carry you so far. It's best to begin with the proper tools if you're serious about developing and delivering a great iPhone game.

Note

A three-button mouse is also highly recommended. Without one, Unity's interface is not nearly as easy to navigate. Step 1 to streamlining Unity's interface is getting a three-button mouse.

After getting all of the necessary hardware in place, you'll need to load a number of software programs to begin developing your dream game. First up, of course, is Unity. The basic setup for developing iPhone games now consists of just a Unity iPhone Basic license. Previously, you needed to buy a copy of Unity Indie for $199 and then append an iPhone license on top of that. As of late October 2009, Unity Technologies removed the price tag from Unity Indie, which is now just Unity and is free for anyone to use. All in all, Unity iPhone Basic is a bargain at $399. The Unity development tools represent the current pinnacle of iPhone 3D game development. Developers both large and small use Unity to create hit games. *Zombieville USA*, seen in Figure 1.3, is a great example of a chart-topping "indie" iPhone game developed with Unity, while the new *Tiger Woods Online*, a desktop browser–based golf sim by EA, is an excellent example of what Unity can achieve in the hands of a larger company.

Beyond Unity, we'll cover some basic 2D and 3D graphics applications: Apple's Developer Connection interface and iTunes Connect. This book will cover some of the principles behind the 2D graphics that are used in a 3D game. I personally use Adobe Photoshop, but there are other options, and they will be covered briefly. In any case, it's the basic fundamentals of 2D graphics that are important, and those will be applicable in nearly all 2D graphics suites. The same will apply to our 3D graphics programs. There are many options out there, and each deserves its own book, so we will cover the basic principles for importing assets into Unity iPhone, but we won't be covering any one specific 3D application in depth. See the following lists for a few 2D/3D solutions.

Figure 1.3
Zombieville USA.

2D Graphics Applications

- Adobe Photoshop

- Corel PaintShop Pro

- GIMP (free)

3D Graphics Applications

- Autodesk 3DS Max

- Autodesk Maya

- Milkshape3D

- Wings3D (free)

- Blender (free)

The Apple Developer and iTunes Connect Web interfaces are both fairly self-explanatory, but we'll cover them in depth as clearly and concisely as possible because many developers have struggled with them.

Now you have an iPhone or iPod, a new Intel-based Mac running OS X Leopard, Unity iPhone, a 2D graphics editor, and a 3D graphics editor. With these tools in hand, you are ready to begin your journey to become the best game developer in the world, or at least one of them.

It hurts at first, but math is a primary component of game development. The good news is that this is really no big deal. I was terrible at math before learning how to program games. Before tackling this project, I wrote a series of articles for Gamasutra called "Games Demystified," which took a top-down approach to things like vector math by analyzing the coolest gameplay concepts and breaking them down into comprehensible chunks of math and physics. These articles have been enjoyed by players and developers alike. After reading this book, you'll see eye-to-eye with Einstein more than you ever thought possible.

Calculating a Trajectory for the Journey

The math required for game programming can be summed up pretty succinctly with the following equation:

Kinetic Energy $= \frac{1}{2}$ Mass $\times$ Speed^2

This is the equation for kinetic energy, the energy of motion. In all games, actions happen over a period of time. Basically, game programming is an art involving the arrangement of events over a period of time.

Can we actually create an equation for games?

Game $=$ (Fun^2) / Time

To create a good game, you have to know what to move and how long it should take to move it. Therefore, the basic rules of motion and time are the keys to a good game. If something doesn't move correctly, if it's too fast, or if it's too slow, the game goes down the tubes.

It's Not the Size of the Game, It's the Motion of the Air-to-Surface Missiles

Three-dimensional games involve gameplay occurring in three spatial dimensions. You may have heard whispers of these mysterious three dimensions in math class, but I'll bet you never applied them to a planet-devouring cluster bomb, right? If you want to shoot someone in a game, you have to know where to aim within the confines of good old X, Y, and Z. Those letters represent the three axes of motion within space, and they lay the guidelines for blowing stuff up. You're not a violent person? Still, if you want to run around a planet, travel through Einstein-Rosen portals, or race someone, you'll be doing that along these three axes of motion as well. See Figure 1.4 for the obligatory triple axis visual. These are the three axes of motion.

In Unity iPhone, things moving left and right are moving along the X-axis, things moving up and down are on the Y-axis, and things moving in and out are traveling along the Z-axis. Just for fun, let's skip ahead a bit to see how we'd actually move something in Unity. This is just a sample of what you'll actually be working with later on, so there's no need to whip out the old text editor yet.

This is how we'd create and move a ball up in Unity:

```
var ball : GameObject;
ball = GameObject.CreatePrimitive( PrimitiveType.Sphere );
ball.transform.position = Vector3( 0, 0, 0 );
ball.transform.position.y += 1;
```

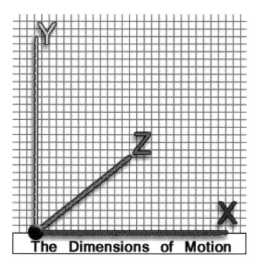

Figure 1.4
Obligatory triple-axis gizmo.

That wasn't so bad, was it? This code tells your iPhone to create a `GameObject` called `ball`, place it at the origin, and then move the ball up one unit along the Y-axis of motion. If you're not math savvy, variables like X, Y, and Z might be scary, but they're really just traits of some object that need a number assigned to them to be meaningful. Within the world of game programming, more meaning is applied with useful variable names such as `Ball.transform.position.y`. What this means is that we're dealing with the Y-axis of the position of the `transform` of an object known as `ball`. If you have no programming experience, this may still seem tricky, but you'll see stuff like that so many times by the end of this book that it'll be second nature to you!

A Long Time Ago (Like a Millisecond), Far, Far Away

As important as it is to know the three axes of motion, it's also important to control motion along those axes as well as the timing of other things within your game. Some would argue that timing is everything, and I have to agree. If a user touches his iPhone screen, he expects the appropriate reaction in a timely fashion. Behind the scenes of every game, there's a ton of code predicting how long a player will touch the screen. Typically, these little interactions can become "make or break" interactions by a matter of milliseconds, $1/1000^{th}$ of a second.

Time not only affects the speed of objects moving within your game world and the reaction of your game to player input, but the performance of your game as well. It's important to understand the implications of each line of code to your game's bottom line, which in many cases is time itself. The more you try to do with your code, the less time the CPU/GPU has to execute each event. Of course, as any good magician knows, the tricks of the trade can make a huge difference. Still, the laws of physics cannot be broken. There's only so much kinetic energy your iPhone can generate, and that has to be distributed between the bulk of your game code and the speed at which the player experiences the game.

Time is easily accessible in Unity. The ball won't move until two seconds have passed.

```
var ball : GameObject;
ball = GameObject.CreatePrimitive( PrimitiveType.Sphere );
ball.transform.position = Vector3( 0, 0, 0 );
var moveTheBallIn2Seconds = Time.time; //Time.time gives us the cur-
rent time
if ( moveTheBallIn2Seconds + 2 < Time.time );
{
    ball.transform.position.y += 1;
}
```

Both time and motion have been intertwined here in a rudimentary way. Creating actual game code will be more complex, but not by much. If these principles are making sense, then you are well on your way to becoming an expert game programmer.

What's a Vector, Victor?

Something you may have noticed in the previous code is the `Vector3( 0, 0, 0 )` call. This is hugely important in 3D game programming. A vector is a magnitude coupled with a direction. A Vector3 is a 3D vector, which could be the speed and direction of an airplane, the force and impact direction of a punch, or even a color. That's right—a 3D vector doesn't have to relate to an object moving through space in our 3D game, it could also be the color of a light in the 3D game. You may have heard of RGB color. This stands for red, green, and blue. In Unity, you'll find that many things, such as textures and lights, have color controls. The important thing to remember is that a vector is a magnitude coupled with a direction. A strong blue light could be described like this:

```
var streetlight = new GameObject( ''A Street Light'' );
streetLight.AddComponent( Light );
var red : float = 0;
var green : float = 0;
var blue : float = 1;
streetLight.light.color = Color( red, green, blue );
```

In this code sample, `Color (red, green, blue)` is actually nothing more than a Vector3 specifically created to handle colors within Unity. The basic principle is the same, though. There are three directions (red, green, and blue), and each one can have a magnitude or intensity. In the case of `Color()`, each component takes a floating-point (decimal point or fractional) value between 0 and 1, with 1 being full magnitude. In the previous sample, the `blue` direction has been assigned a maxed-out value, so our light will be very blue.

Talk the Talk

Beyond the basic concepts such as math, time, and vectors, 3D games are guided by a structure called a *programming language*. There are three language choices to pick from when developing iPhone games with Unity. This book will focus primarily on JavaScript.

The principles behind all programming languages are very similar. The basic concept is to ask the computer a series of questions and give it things to do according to the answers to the questions. Beyond the basic questions, there's another principle called a *loop*. A computer program is essentially a large questionnaire that repeats over and over again, or loops. Finally, the loop may ask and answer different questions, depending on what the user does. User actions are typically referred to as input, and the results of the questionnaire (usually displayed onscreen) are called output. There are a few symbols in this code that you may not be familiar with. Don't worry, we'll cover these basic notations shortly.

Some basic programming structures include:

```
if ( value1 == value2 )
  doSomething;
```

```
while ( value1 == value2 )
  keepDoingSomethingWhileValue1EqualsValue2;

for ( value1 = 0; value1 == 10; value1++ )
  keepDoingSomethingUntilValue1EqualsTen;
```

Computer programs become more complex when you nest these structures together. For example:

```
while ( value1 < value2 )
{
  If ( value2 >= value1 )
      value2--;
}
```

In this case, we'll keep subtracting 1 from `value2` so long as it's greater than or equal to `value1`. Then, as soon as `value2` becomes less than `value1`, we'll escape the `while` loop. When more than one line of code is to be contained within a programming structure, we use curly brackets { } to fence it in. If you have only one line of code to be executed within any of these control structures, then you don't need the curly brackets, but as soon as there's more than one line of code, you must contain the code within the curly brackets.

Beyond the basic questions and loops, a few additional programming conventions are very important. The first is the type of data we are asking questions about. In the previous examples, `value1` and `value2` are of type `int`, which is short for integer—any whole positive or negative number. In the color sample earlier, we used `float`, which is the type we use when we want access to numbers with decimal points or fractional values. There are many other types of data beyond `ints` and `floats`.

Before we cover additional data types, it's important to know the various operations we can perform on `ints` and `floats`. Some, but not all, of the following operations may also be applicable to additional data types.

Arithmetic Operators

- + Add

- − Subtract

- * Multiply

- / Divide

- ++ Increment

- —— Decrement

Obviously, add, subtract, multiply, and divide perform basic arithmetic on numbers or variables. Increment and decrement were used in the previous code samples; they simply add 1 or subtract 1 from a variable without having to state it explicitly.

Beyond arithmetic operators, there are assignment operators. They allow us to assign new values to variables.

Assignment Operators

- = Equal/Assign

- += Add/Assign

- —= Subtract/Assign

- *= Multiply/Assign

At the end of the following code, the Unity debugger would print 1:

```
var a : int = 1;
a += 1;
a -= 1;
a *= 2;
a /= 2;
print ( a );
```

Beyond these operators, there are other important data types, and the next best one to know is the string type. A string is technically an array of characters, but in layman's terms it is a word, such as those you are reading on this page. You could store a single word, a sentence, or even a whole book in a string if you wanted. Often, the information you want game players to read consists of string data, so it's important to know how to handle strings. Here's a quick lesson:

```
var aWord : String = ''Word'';
var anS : String = ''s'';
print ( ''A picture is worth a thousand '' + aWord + anS + ''.'' );
```

The print command displays "A picture is worth a thousand Words." Using the + operator on strings simply appends one string to the end of another. In a way, this works like adding various cars, such as a locomotive and a caboose, to a train.

Subtraction of strings is a different story. Typically, if you want to remove certain characters from a string, you would use the `Replace()` method:

```
var misspelledWord : String = ''Wourd'';
var correctlySpelledWord : String = misspelledWord.Replace(''u'',
'''');
print( correctlySpelledWord );
```

This code takes the misspelled `Wourd` and replaces the `u` with nothing. The end result is that `correctlySpelledWord` becomes equal to `Word`.

This brings us to a key aspect of programming with JavaScript. There are two functions of "equal." One is for assigning a value to a variable, and the other is for comparing values. If you want to assign a variable a certain value, you use the single =; if you want to compare two values to see if they are equal to each other, you use the double ==. You can use this method whether you're comparing or assigning ints, floats, strings, or even our next data type, the Boolean variable.

Computers read only 1s and 0s. Computers operate according to the presence or the absence of an electrical charge. Usually, we call this on or off. There's a data type for this concept called *Boolean*. Boolean logic is the logic of on or off, true or false. For example:

```
var value1 : boolean = false;
var value2 : boolean = true;
if ( value2 )
    value1 = true;
```

In this example, `value1` begins as `false` (off), and `value2` begins as `true` (on). The `if` statement asks the question "is `value2`?". In the absence of any other operators such as =, >, or <, the `if` statement is simply asking if a value is on or `true`, which is a Boolean logic question. In this example, `value2` is `true` (on), so the code also makes `value1` `true`.

It's possible to use other types in place of Boolean, but they use more memory. If you're only asking questions with yes or no answers, it's wise to use Boolean logic. There are also some other nifty ways to manipulate Boolean data types.

Boolean Operators

- &&   AND operator

- || OR operator

- !   NOT operator

These operators enable us to ask questions such as:

```
if ( value1 && value2 )
  doSomething;
if ( value1 || value2 )
  doSomething;
if ( !value1 )
  doSomething;
```

The first example will do something only if value1 and value2 are both true. The second example will do something if either value1 or value2 is true. The third snippet will execute the doSomething code only if value1 is not true. Sometimes, it's just as important to ask if something isn't on. For example, if the stove is not on, then touch it.

Conclusion

We've covered hardware, software, math, timing, and structure basics of iPhone game development. It's a great platform with countless intriguing functions. Before taking full advantage of this wonderful new device, there are a few boundaries to cover. Now let's move on to covering the first obstacle on your way to mastering iPhone game development.

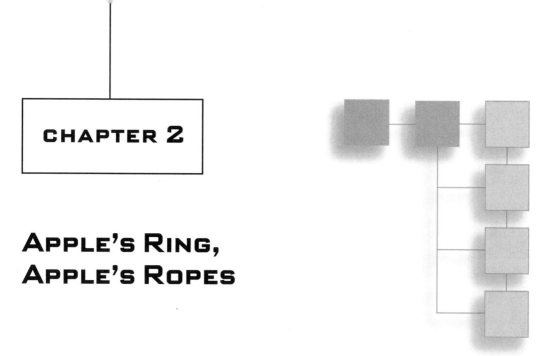

CHAPTER 2

APPLE'S RING, APPLE'S ROPES

If you're a boxer, there are limits to the extent you can punish your opponent or move to avoid being punished yourself. Those limits are the ropes. The ropes surround the ring, and they are there to help you. Of course, if you don't pay attention to the ropes, they can get in the way of victory. Apple has provided developers with a great set of ropes, beginning with the Apple Developer connection (developer.apple.com). Learn these ropes, and you'll be well on your way to App Store glory!

The Apple Developer connection is filled with information from tools and tutorials to developer testimonials. It's through this portal that you'll begin developing iPhone software.

The first step is to click on the iPhone Dev Center link.

Once you're there, you'll see links to Getting Started, the iPhone Reference Library, the iPhone Application Programming Guide, videos, and Coding "How-To's." You can peruse some of the documentation if you like, but most of it is aimed at Objective-C programmers. This book is aimed at developers looking to leverage Unity for the iPhone, so the most interesting link on the page for us is the Register link in the upper-right corner.

When you begin the registration process, the Developer Web site reminds you that you must have an Intel-based Mac running Mac OS X Leopard. Since you already read the first chapter and have an Intel-based Mac, go ahead and click Get Started.

The next screen you see asks you to create a new Apple ID or use an existing one. If you've never registered as an Apple Developer, you'll want to create a new Apple ID. However, if at some time in the past you registered in order to download Apple development tools, such as Xcode, you might want to use your existing Apple ID.

For this book, we'll assume that you're a completely new Apple Developer. Check the appropriate option and then click Continue.

The rest of the process involves filling out your personal profile, agreeing to the Apple Developer license, and verifying your email address.

$99

Before you can begin publishing iPhone games, you will need to pay a yearly fee of $99 to Apple through the iPhone Dev Center. Once you pay this fee, you'll gain access to the iPhone Developer program portal and iTunes Connect. These Web interfaces allow you to manage your software applications in full.

The iPhone Developer program portal is primarily used to control your App IDs, development/distribution certificates, and the provisioning files that let an app run on an iPhone or iPod Touch. Apple has implemented a special "code signing" system that is used to control piracy as well as updates, ensuring that each piece of software out there can be accounted for, linked to a developer, and updated in the proper sequential order. Code signing is required even for development purposes. Before you can deploy a Unity-developed game onto a test iPhone or iPod Touch device, you will need to pay your $99 and create a provisioning file for development and testing.

A Quick Look at iTunes Connect

The iTunes Connect Web site home page has several links, including:

- Sales/Trend Reports

- Contracts, Tax, and Banking Information

- Financial Reports

- Manage Users, Manage Your Applications

- Manage Your In App Purchases

- Request Promotional Codes

- Contact Us

The first stop you'll want to make after paying your $99 and signing into the iTunes Connect Web site is the Contracts, Tax, and Banking Information section. This is where you'll generate a contract between you or your business and Apple to handle transactions. The contract contains your contact information, your bank information, and your tax information. If you are a business, you'll need to supply Apple with the proper documentation to prove the business's existence. In addition, you'll also need to supply Apple with your bank information so that they can wire funds into your account. The information you'll need to supply consists of the bank name, account holder's name, account type, account number, branch ID (ask your local bank representative or see one of their business cards), ABA/routing transit number, and the bank Swift code. Once all of this information is provided, Apple can wire transfer money directly into your checking account, which makes things very easy. We'll be looking at iTunes Connect in more depth at the end of the book to upload our final product.

iPhone SDK and Xcode

It's not very important for you to fill out your contract information initially if you don't want to. It is a must that you download the iPhone SDK from the Apple Developer portal before you can delve into Unity development. The iPhone SDK provides developers with all the essential tools needed to develop for the iPhone and iPod Touch. The biggest component of the SDK is Xcode, which is Apple's primary development environment. We'll be developing games directly within the Unity engine, but Xcode is what Unity interfaces with to build and deploy apps for the iPhone. You absolutely will need Xcode and the iPhone SDK installed on your computer before beginning to develop with Unity. The installation process is simple, and advanced users can also append Objective-C code onto their Unity projects to gain additional functionality, which may not be provided by Unity out of the box.

We'll cover the details of Xcode and the various build configurations necessary for testing and releasing apps. For now, just be sure to download and install Xcode from the Apple Developer Portal.

OS X and iTunes Software Upgrades

Before you can begin deploying apps to your hardware using the account you purchased and the iPhone SDK, there are a number of steps that must be taken. The first step is to make sure that you're running the latest version of OS X. As of this writing, OS X version 10.5.4 or later is required. In addition, you must be running iTunes 7.7 or later. These requirements are part of the iPhone SDK. Next on your checklist should be the upgrade to iPhone/iPod OS 2.1 with iTunes. (This will cost $9.99 if you have an iPod Touch.) At this point, OS 3.1.3 is already available, and by the time this book is on the shelf, there will almost certainly be another upgrade. These three upgrades comprise the whole of the software upgrades you'll need for your development machine and development device.

Find Your Device Identifier

After upgrading these software components, there are just a few more steps before we can dive into Unity. Each iPhone or iPod Touch has a device identifier, which is a 40-digit hex code. You will need this code to register your device for development with Apple and to create provisioning files, which allow you to run and test your software on the actual iPhone/iPod hardware. To get the 40-digit code, launch Xcode and then connect your device to your workstation with the USB wire. Xcode will "automagically" detect your device and ask if you want to use it for development.

If Xcode fails to detect your device, you can also find your device manually by running Organizer (Main menu > Window > Organizer). The 40-digit code can also be acquired in iTunes by clicking on the Serial Number: text next to the picture of your iPhone/iPod. The serial number will transform into the Identifier (UDID) and will display the 40-digit code you need to register your device for development.

Adding Devices Using the iPhone Developer Program Portal

After you have the 40-digit identifier, it's time to log into the iPhone Dev Center (http://developer.apple.com/iphone). Once you have logged in, click on the iPhone Developer Program Portal link on the right side. The next step is to open the Devices link on the left side. The Add Devices page contains two fields: Device Name and Device ID. You can name the device whatever makes sense.

If you have a beta tester, you can enter that name here if you want. Whatever helps you keep this list of devices organized is beneficial. The device ID is not negotiable. Take the 40-digit hex code you found in iTunes or Xcode and enter it here. When you've added a device to this list, you can create a developer certificate and then a provisioning file.

Creating an iPhone Developer Certificate

Creating an iPhone developer certificate is slightly cumbersome. It involves generating a certificate signing request, the submission of the request for approval, approving the requests (for instance, if you have a team, you must approve additional developers), downloading and installing development certificates, and, finally, saving your private key and transferring to other systems.

Apple describes a digital identity as a way to identify an iPhone OS application electronically. This identity consists of a guarded or secret private key and a shared public key. The private key allows your applications to be signed by Xcode during the build process.

When you request and download a digital certificate, you are associating your real information with a digital identity. This is what allows applications to be controlled. A development certificate is restricted to development only and cannot be used for any other type of distribution. These certificates are valid only for a certain period of time, and the Apple certification authority may revoke a certificate at any time.

The first step toward generating a development certificate is to make a certificate signing request (CSR). This is done using the Keychain Access application built into Mac OS X Leopard. When a CSR is generated, a public and private key pair will be generated. This key pair will establish your iPhone developer identity. The private key will automatically be stored in the login keychain and can be viewed within the Keys category through the Keychain Access application.

Here's the step-by-step procedure to create a certificate signing request:

1. Launch Macintosh HD > Applications > Utilities > Keychain Access.

2. Select Main Menu > Keychain Access > Preferences.

3. Set Online Certificate Status Protocol (OSCP) and Certificate Revocation List (CRL) to Off.

4. Select Main Menu > Keychain Access > Certificate Assistant > Request a Certificate from a Certificate Authority.

5. Enter the email address that corresponds with the one you used to register as an iPhone Developer.

6. Enter your name in the Common Name field and be sure this matches your developer registration name.

7. Leave the CA Email Address field blank.

8. Click the Saved to Disk radio button and choose Let Me Specify Key Pair Information if asked; then click Continue.

9. Choose a filename for your key pair and save the file using 2,048 bits for Key Size and RSA for Algorithm.

10. The assistant will drop your new CSR file on the OS X desktop.

Uploading a Certificate Signing Request

Once a CSR has been created, there are a few steps to take in order to approve the request.

1. In the iPhone Developer Program Portal, go to Certificates > Development > Add Certificate.

2. Tap on the Choose File button and select the CSR generated on your OS X desktop.

3. The team administrator (who will be you if you opened your own developer account from scratch) will be notified by email that there's a certificate request waiting for approval.

Approving a Certificate Signing Request

Team agents and administrators have control over the approval of all iPhone development certificate requests. Before team administrators can approve or reject other team members' requests, they should submit their own CSRs and approve them first.

- When you navigate to the Certificates section of the Program Portal, there will be an Approve button to the right of any pending certificates. Click it to approve the certificate.

- Upon approval, the team member who requested a CSR will be notified by email that his certificate status has changed. The newly approved CSR may be accessed by both the requesting team member and any team administrators.

Downloading and Installing Development Certificates

After a CSR is approved, team members and administrators can download the resulting certificates from within the Certificates section of the iPhone Developer Program Portal. Once downloaded, these certificates allow Xcode to apply a digital signature to applications during the build process.

1. First, download the WWDR Intermediate Certificate from Certificates > Development. There is a box highlighting this feature with the text "*If you do not have the WWDR intermediate certificate installed, click here to download now."

2. Once the intermediate certificate is downloaded onto your local workstation, double-click it and install it with Keychain Access.

3. Next, find your newly approved certificate under the Certificates section of the program portal and click the Download button next to it to bring it over to your workstation. Once it has finished downloading, double-click the certificate to install it.

4. Team members can download their own personal development certificates. Team administrators can download the public certificates of all their team members. The private key for a CSR never leaves the original key pair creator and is always stored in the system keychain of that team member.

Creating an App ID

An app ID is an important component of the development and provisioning system. This unique ID allows an application to communicate with the Apple Push Notification service, as well as with an external hardware accessory. App IDs can also be used to share keychain data such as passwords within a group of applications.

Any single app ID is composed of a bundle seed ID and a bundle identifier. The bundle seed ID is a unique string consisting of 10 characters. This ID can also be used to share keychain access between multiple applications built with a single app ID. This ID can also be incorporated into various hardware accessories you may want to extend your iPhone app with.

The bundle identifier can be a unique application name, or it can be an asterisk (*) if you want to use a wildcard bundle ID. This is useful when you want to use a single app ID for multiple apps. For example, when I'm developing prototypes, I use an app ID called "test," which uses an asterisk for its bundle ID. This single ID is used on all of my development builds installed on my iPod and iPhone. One thing to note is that you cannot use Apple Push Notifications unless you're using an explicit app ID.

1. Using the iPhone Developer Program Portal, choose App IDs > Add ID.

2. Enter a simple name for reference within the program portal.

3. Enter a bundle identifier in the adjacent text field. Apple recommends the use of a reverse-domain name style string (com.domainName. applicationName). If you want to use this app ID for multiple applications, enter an asterisk or a reverse-domain name string with an asterisk in place of the Application Name. I use an asterisk only.

4. Click the Submit button, and the 10-character bundle seed ID will be generated and added to the bundle identifier. With the bundle seed ID appended, you now have your full app ID. You don't need to enter the bundle seed ID manually into Xcode.

Creating a Development Provisioning Profile

The last piece of the puzzle is creating a development provisioning profile. This is what allows your device to run test code by tethering a group of developers and devices to an iPhone development team. Each device used for testing during development must have a provisioning profile installed. Every profile contains a set of iPhone development certificates, the unique device identifiers of the devices authorized to run an app, and an app ID. The only developers who can run test code on their devices are those whose development certificates are included in the profile. One device can contain multiple provisioning profiles.

1. Within the iPhone Developer Program Portal, select Provisioning > Add.

2. Enter a provisioning profile name.

3. Select the devices to be associated with this particular provisioning profile.

4. Choose the iPhone development certificates to be hooked to the new provisioning profile.

5. Select an app ID for the provisioning profile. Only one app ID can be included with any single development provisioning profile. If you want to use the same keychain access for an entire group of applications, use an app ID, which contains the asterisk character. This creates what is called a *wildcard identifier.*

6. Finally, click the Submit button to create the provisioning profile.

Installing Provisioning Profiles

To run any test programs on your iPhone or iPod Touch, they must have a provisioning profile installed. Xcode and iTunes both have the capability to install provisioning files onto devices, but iTunes is somewhat sloppy as compared to using Xcode and Organizer. Before Xcode can use a provisioning file, the file needs to be located under Macintosh HD > Library > MobileDevice > Provisioning Profiles. Once a provisioning file is copied and pasted into the folder (after downloading from the iPhone provisioning portal), Xcode will be able to find it, and you can click the + button in Organizer to browse for it and install it on a device.

1. Go to the Provisioning section of the program portal.

2. Click on the Download button next to the provisioning profile.

3. Create a folder called Mobile Device under Macintosh HD > Library.

4. Within that folder, create a folder called Provisioning Profiles.

5. Drag and drop the freshly downloaded provisioning profile into the Provisioning Profiles folder.

6. You also can install these provisioning profiles by dragging them onto iTunes or Xcode, but I've found those processes to be somewhat messy. Creating the folder yourself works most efficiently.

7. Finally, within Xcode you can add development provisioning profiles to your development devices by clicking the + button under the Provisioning partition.

Conclusion

After you have your provisioning files, it's time to open Unity and begin developing your dream iPhone game. It's already been a long road, but there's still much more to learn before you can create that hit game. Don't worry, though; by the time you're done with this book, you'll have all the knowledge you need to release game after great game to the App Store!

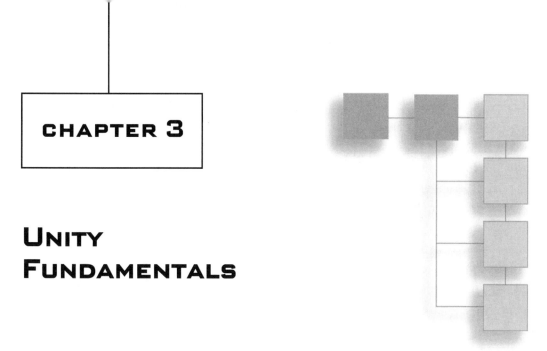

CHAPTER 3

UNITY
FUNDAMENTALS

Once you are a registered Apple developer and have paid your $99, downloaded the iPhone SDK/Xcode, and created your provisioning file for development, it's time to open up Unity. The Unity software package is a tremendous achievement in tool design. It not only has an excellent programming/script editor called *Unitron,* but it includes all manner of WYSIWYG (what you see is what you get) editors that allow you to design, organize, and maintain your game project.

And Now a Demonstration of This Fully Armed and Operational Game Development Tool

Initially, Unity may appear somewhat daunting, but at the end of your first day with the software you'll feel completely at home (see Figure 3.1). The basic components of the editor are a Game view, a Scene view, a Scene hierarchy, a Project hierarchy, and the Inspector. These components allow you to see what your game will actually look like, edit the current 3D scene, view each object in the scene in a hierarchal format, manage all the assets in your entire project, and edit individual objects down to the smallest detail.

Before going too crazy, let's learn the basic scene controls. Most of the menus are pretty cut and dried, but the Scene view requires a few extra key/mouse combinations to maneuver correctly.

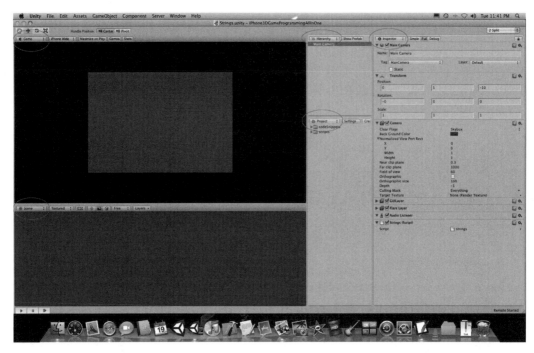

Figure 3.1
The Unity Editor.

Unity Scene Editor Controls	
Select an object	Left mouse button
Rotate camera (Orbit mode)	Option + drag mouse + left mouse button
Drag camera (Drag mode)	Option + drag mouse + middle mouse button
Zoom camera (Zoom mode)	Option + drag mouse + right mouse button
	or
	Scroll mouse wheel

When you open Unity for the first time, the Scene view will be empty. Before using any of the Scene Editor controls, you'll have to populate the scene. You can open the basicScene.unity file from the iPhone3DGameProgrammingAllInOne project on the CD, or you can create the scene from scratch.

To create the scene from scratch, place the mouse cursor into the Project Hierarchy. Right-click or press the Create button and select Folder (see Figure 3.2). Name the

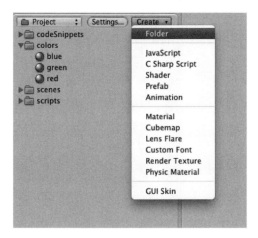

Figure 3.2
Create a folder.

folder "Colors" by highlighting it and then clicking it once again or by pressing Enter/Return with it highlighted. This is where you store basic colored materials.

Now highlight the Colors folder and right-click it and then on Create or click on the Create button in the top portion of the Project Hierarchy menu again. This time select Material (see Figure 3.3). Materials are what give 3D objects additional visual qualities beyond their shape, such as color, texture, and shininess.

Now you should see a shiny circle icon with the words New Material under the Colors folder. Additionally, you should see a blank New Material (Material) in the Inspector on the far right (see Figure 3.4). Press the Enter button while New Material is highlighted in the Project Hierarchy, and you can rename it Blue (see Figure 3.5). Alternatively, you can single-click on the words New Material to rename it as well. When renaming something in the Project Hierarchy, the name of the selected asset will be highlighted in light blue.

With the material renamed Blue, click on the Main Color icon in the upper-right corner of the Inspector. This will open the Colors Color Selection tool. Choose the third icon directly under the menu title Colors. This option allows you to pick discrete colors from a list. Choose the color blue (see Figure 3.6).

Now repeat this process to create red and green colors (see Figure 3.7). You should now have three separate materials to begin assigning to the objects you will be creating.

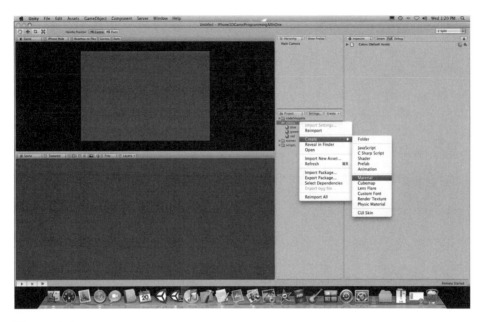

Figure 3.3
Create a material.

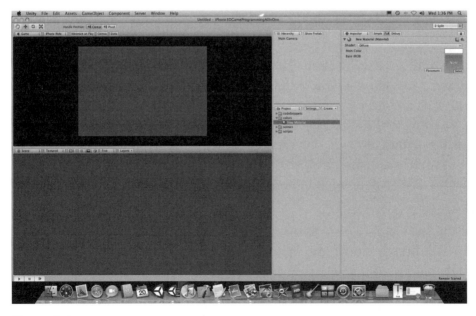

Figure 3.4
Highlight New Material.

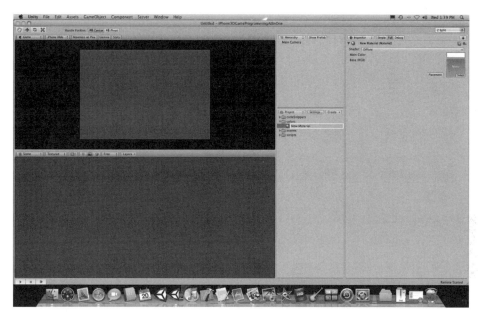

Figure 3.5
Click or press Enter on New Material to rename it.

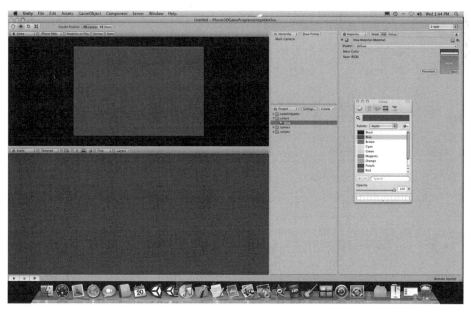

Figure 3.6
Use a main color of blue with a typical diffuse shader.

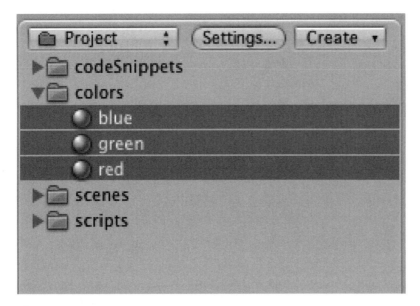

Figure 3.7
Create red and green, too.

It is now time to begin creating a scene. Select GameObject > Create Other > Plane from the main Unity menu (see Figure 3.8).

This operation creates the ground for our first scene (see Figure 3.9). It looks awfully bland, doesn't it?

To remedy the situation, highlight and drag the green material from the Colors folder into the Scene view and on top of the plane you just created (see Figure 3.10). Before letting go of the mouse button, you should see the plane highlight with a slight white outline. After releasing the left mouse button, the plane should turn green, as shown in Figure 3.11.

Note

You may notice that your Unity Editor looks slightly different from the screenshots in the book. This is because the Unity Editor is configurable (see Figure 3.12). I prefer my Game view to be in the upper-left corner and my Scene view in the bottom-left corner. You can select which view each of these windows displays with the drop-down menu in the upper-left corner of each window view. The editor's displays can also be configured under Window > Layouts from the main menu.

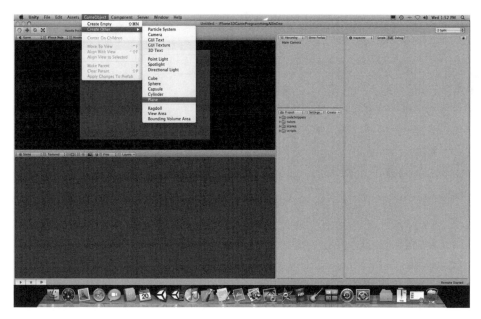

Figure 3.8
Create a flat plane game object.

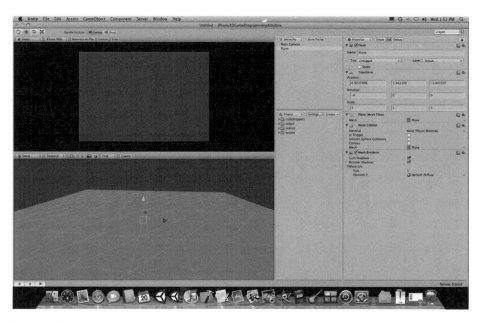

Figure 3.9
Plain Jane plane.

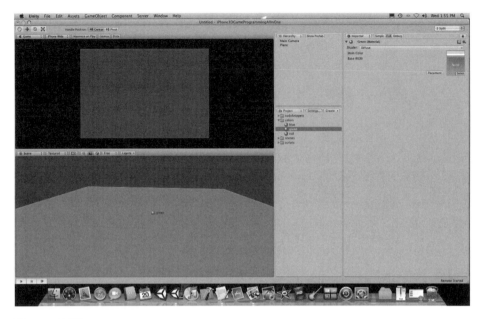

Figure 3.10
Drag and drop green material onto the plane.

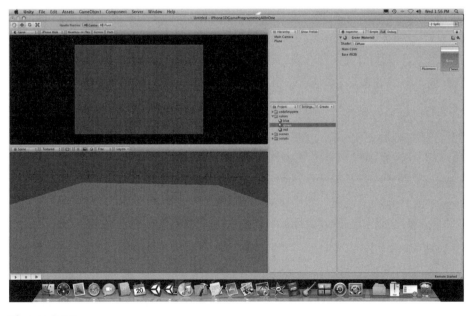

Figure 3.11
The grass really is greener.

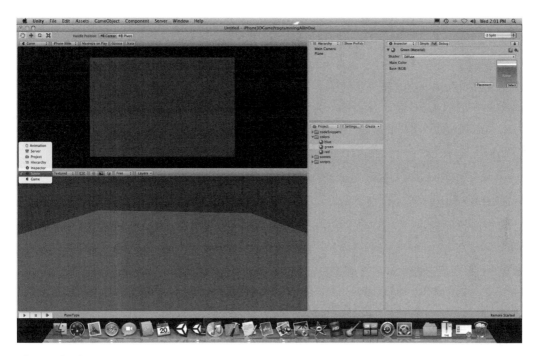

Figure 3.12
Reconfigure Editor Viewports.

You've created and colored your first game object. Now what? It looks lonely, so let's give it a friend. Choose GameObject > Create Other > Cube from the main menu, as shown in Figure 3.13.

You should see a cube intersecting your plane in the Scene view (see Figure 3.14).

Again, it looks awfully bland, doesn't it? Drag either the Red or Blue material from your Colors folder in the Project Hierarchy onto your new cube (see Figure 3.15).

Now we come full circle back to the basic Scene view controls. With game objects in your scene, you can now bear witness to relative motion when you turn, drag, or change the zoom of your camera. Take the time to revisit the camera controls as they relate to the Scene view.

Now it's time to manipulate these objects via the Scene view and the Inspector. When designing a scene, it's OK to use the quick but imprecise gizmo tool present in the Scene view to get a rough idea for the layout of your scene or level.

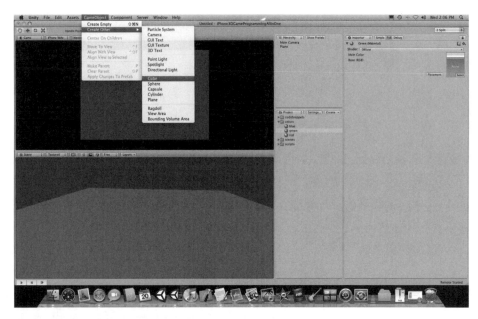

Figure 3.13
Create a Cube game object.

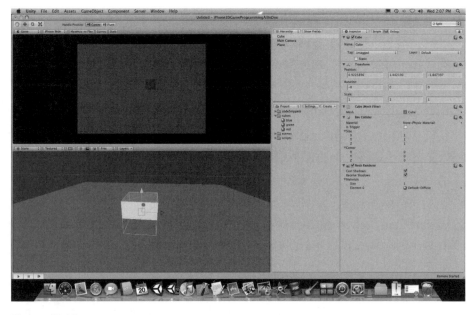

Figure 3.14
The cube runs through the plane.

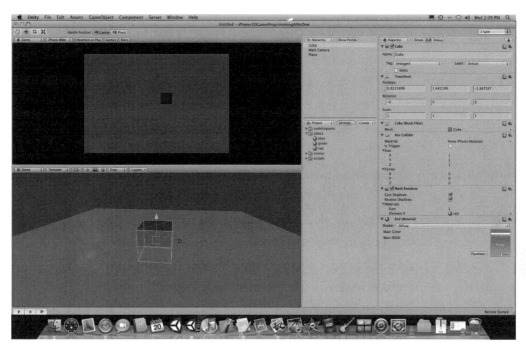

Figure 3.15
Take the red pill or the blue pill?

After getting a rough layout, though, it's critical to use the Inspector to place your game objects precisely.

In our current scene, the newly colored cube is intersecting the green plane. This is called *clipping,* and it tends to be very noticeable in games, not to mention ugly. To fix this, we'll first drag the cube by highlighting the green arrowhead on the 3-axis gizmo, just like the obligatory triple axis image we showed in Chapter 1 (see Figure 3.16). When you click on the arrowhead, it will change color to yellow, letting you know that it has been selected (see Figure 3.17).

With the mouse cursor still on the arrowhead, hold the left mouse button and drag the cube up until there is no green between the wireframe outline of the cube and the red base of the cube (see Figures 3.18 and 3.19).

By moving the cube up above the plane, we have eliminated our clipping problem. However, the scene is still laid out roughly. To align things with precision, we need to use the Inspector. With the cube still highlighted, change all three Position values in the Inspector to 0.0. This means that the X, Y, and Z positions of the cube will be directly on top of the origin (see Figure 3.20).

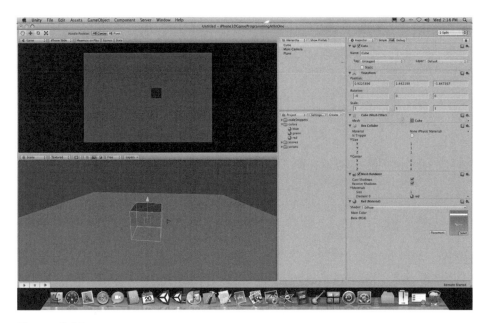

Figure 3.16
Green (Y-axis) arrowhead.

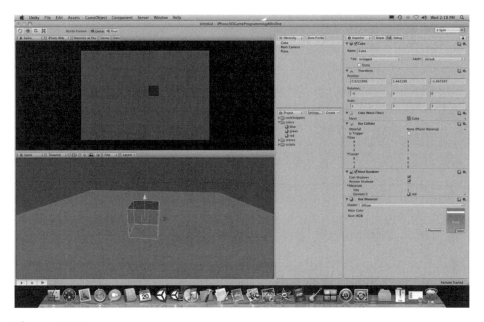

Figure 3.17
Yellow (still Y-axis) highlighted arrowhead.

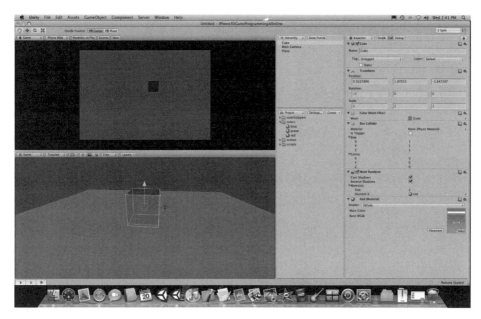

Figure 3.18
The cube is raised, but not enough; note the wireframe line beneath the cube.

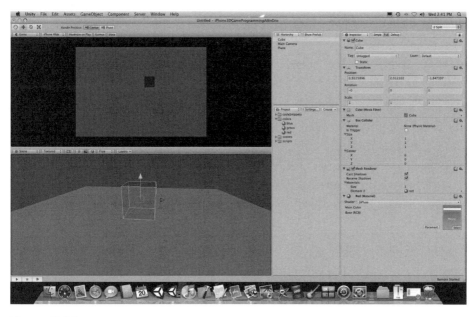

Figure 3.19
Now there is no cube wireframe overlapping the plane.

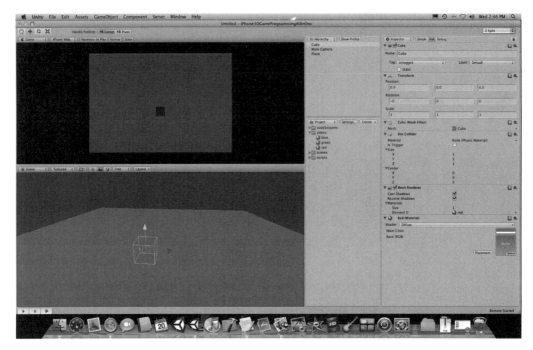

Figure 3.20
Place the cube precisely at (0, 0, 0), the origin.

After you reposition the cube, you might notice that our scene has degraded. Fear not! It is now time to reposition the plane to the origin's position as well. Select the plane either in the Scene view or the Scene Hierarchy and change its three Position values to 0.0 (see Figure 3.21).

Again, the cube is intersecting the plane. Repeat the process where we lifted the cube by its 3-axis gizmo and then placed it precisely via the Position fields in the Inspector. After using the gizmo, my cube is at position (0.0, 0.5093241, 0.0). It's apparent from this position that the exact place the cube should lay is (0.0, 0.5, 0.0). Make this change with the Inspector for a precisely arranged scene, as shown in Figure 3.22.

As you can tell, the process of creating truly fantastic scenes or levels can be tedious. However, the workflow will eventually become second nature to you. In truth, creating a scene like this will take just a matter of seconds for you once you become accustomed to the tools.

Now that you have a fundamental understanding of how Unity functions, it's time to dissect the Unity UI (user interface) in a detailed fashion. As you already

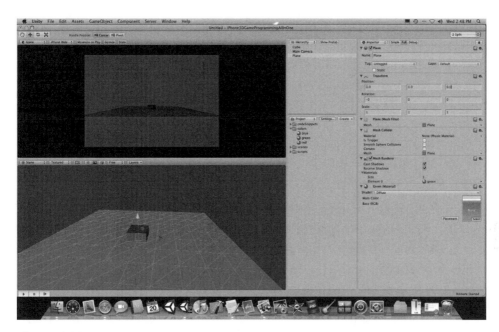

Figure 3.21
Place the plane precisely.

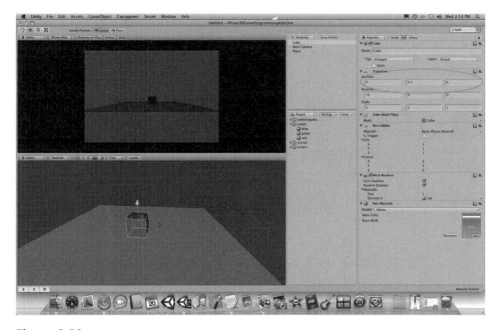

Figure 3.22
Precise placement of the red cube.

know, the UI contains four primary windows: the Scene view, Game view, Scene Hierarchy, and Project Hierarchy. These windows are always visible unless you choose to view one of them in two or more of the windows simultaneously or choose to display the minority Server and Animation windows. Beyond the four main windows, there's the Inspector, which yields detailed information on a selected game object or project asset. In addition, there's a main menu, and there's a Control Selection menu that allows you to lock in on certain camera functions in the upper-left corner of Unity.

Delving a little deeper, you'll notice that each window also contains a submenu that allows you to micromanage that window. Each window type (Animation, Server, Project Hierarchy, Inspector, Scene, and Game) has different submenu options. The primary window types are the Project, Hierarchy, Scene, and Game windows. Before dissecting the Unity widows, we'll first look at each piece of the main menu running across the top of the program.

Main Menu

Unity's main menu runs across the top of the program and contains these options:

- File
- Edit
- Assets
- GameObject
- Component
- Server
- Window
- Help

It's from this menu that the bulk of Unity's functionality stems.

File

The File menu is pretty self-explanatory for any avid computer user. This menu allows you to create a new project or a new scene within the current project, open an existing project, open an existing scene, save projects, save scenes, and build a project.

Building a project is the most complex part of this menu. There are two build options: Build Settings and Build & Run. Build Settings is used to add scenes to the project, choose a Build target (in our case the only option is iPhone), optimize file size, and then either Build or Build & Run. Build is used to create an Xcode project that you intend to modify (see Figure 3.23). For example, if you want to replace the icon that will appear on the iPhone, you'll want to build the project and then open the Xcode project Unity creates and replace the icon. If you want to do a rapid fire test just to see how your game works on the iPhone, you can choose Build & Run, which will automatically build the Xcode project, open it, and deploy the game to your iPhone for release testing (as long as your iPhone or iPod Touch is plugged into your Mac).

Edit

The Edit menu (see Figure 3.24) is more complex than the File menu. Typical options include Cut, Copy, Paste, and Select All. These options allow functionality similar to what you might find in a word processor or your Web browser. The biggest difference is that instead of copying and pasting text, you'll be copying and pasting game objects or project assets. In line with Cut, Copy, and Paste are Duplicate and Delete. These options are pretty self-explanatory and allow you to either instantly copy and paste the currently selected object or completely delete the currently selected object.

The first of the unique options is Frame Selected. This option will move the Scene view camera so that the currently selected object appears directly in the center of the Scene view. This can be very useful when working in a complex scene where you might lose your place with an accidental flick of the mouse.

Next is the trio: Play, Pause, and Step. These allow you to play your game within the editor, pause it at a certain spot, or even step through your game frame by frame. These options are very useful for debugging, and they are also mirrored in the bottom left corner of the Unity Editor.

Beyond the Play, Pause, and Step options is another segregated trio of Special Characters: Load Selection and Save Selection (see Figure 3.25). Load Selection and Save Selection are pretty self-explanatory and essentially allow you to copy

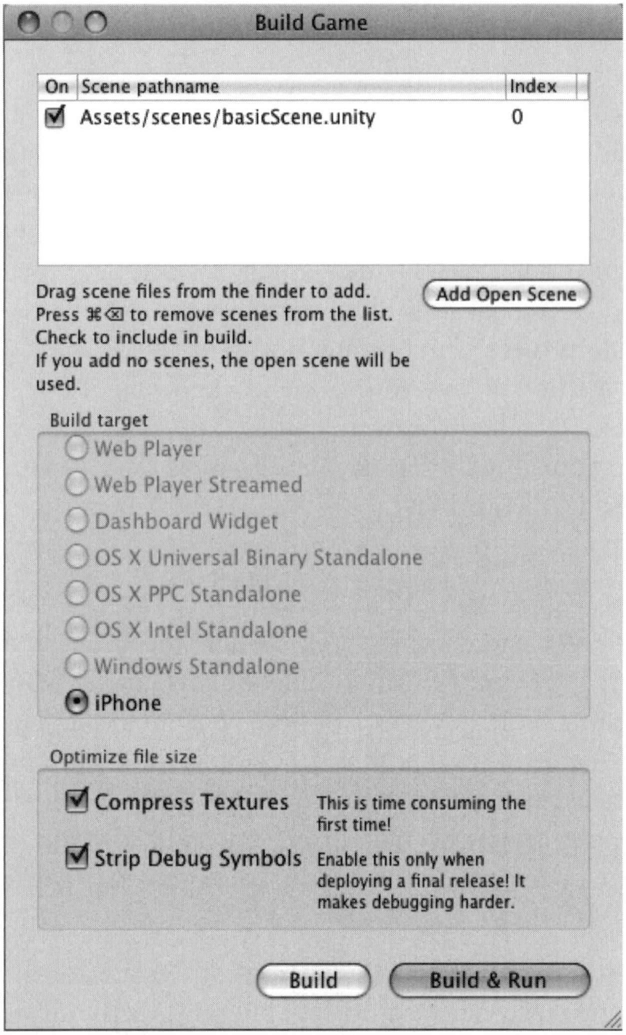

Figure 3.23
Build settings.

and paste various selections of information. For example, if you want to high-light all the houses in a scene and move them and then highlight all the trees in order to adjust them also, you could select the houses and choose Save Selection and then do the same for the trees. Then, with Load Selection, you could switch back and forth, selecting between all the trees and all the houses. Special Char-acters allows you to access a large number of symbols and languages to organize your project. You can use the special characters if you want to label something in

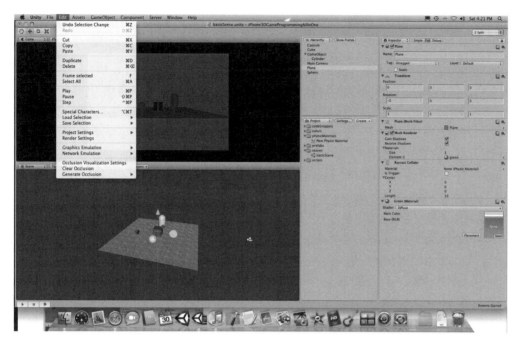

Figure 3.24
Edit menu.

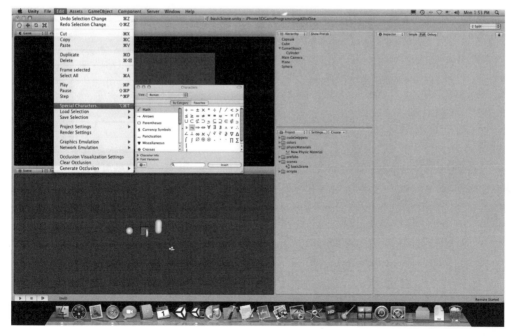

Figure 3.25
Special Characters.

another language or use a specific naming template to maintain a complex but comprehensible project.

Project Settings and Render Settings are the next two options on the Edit menu, and they are very important (see Figure 3.26). The Project Settings option opens up a submenu that contains Input, Tags, Audio, Time, Player, Physics, Quality, and Network options. These options are used to control your game on a macro level.

The Input option opens the Input Manager within the Inspector view (see Figure 3.27). This particular aspect of the Unity Editor isn't useful for iPhone development as of this writing. The current Input Manager was created for Unity iPhone's big brother and is configured for joystick, gamepad, keyboard, and mouse input.

Tags are used to identify and potentially add specialized functionality to a game object. The Tag Manager is where you create these tags, as shown in Figure 3.28. The default tags are Default, TransparentFX, Ignore Raycast, and Water. You can create custom tags to identify specialized game objects, depending on your project.

Figure 3.26
Project Settings.

Figure 3.27
Input Manager.

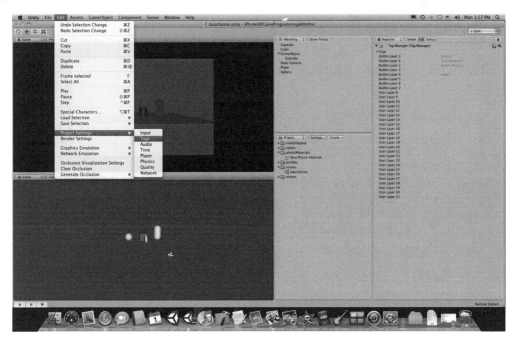

Figure 3.28
Tags Manager.

The Audio Manager is next in the Project Settings submenu and contains just three options: Volume, Speed of Sound, and Doppler Factor (see Figure 3.29). These settings help define the 3D sound profile of your game. The default settings work fairly well, but you might want to experiment with these settings, depending on the sound needs of your project.

Time is the fourth option under the Project Settings submenu, and it's ultra important. The Time Manager allows you to control how often the `FixedUpdate()` script function is called (see Figure 3.30). There are certain algorithms that you want to occur at fixed intervals, and they are not based on the raw speed of the CPU or the GPU. Physics is one aspect of your game that you'll want to execute at fixed intervals. The default setting for Fixed Timestamp is 0.02 seconds. This means that `FixedUpdate ()` will be called every 2/100 of a second, or 50 times per second. Increasing the value decreases the number of times per second `FixedUpdate ()` will be called. For example, if you want to run fixed logic at 30 times per second, you would use a Fixed Timestamp of 0.033; if you want to drop down to 15 times per second, you would use 0.066 as your Fixed Timestamp. The formula to calculate your fixed logic rate is 1/Fixed

Figure 3.29
Audio Manager.

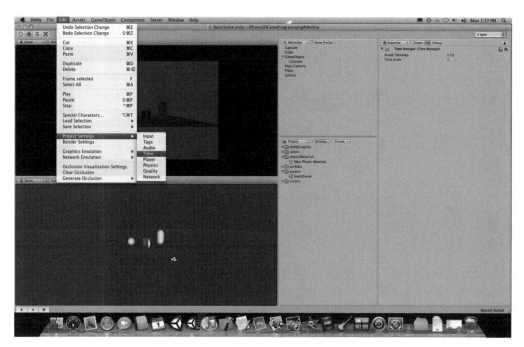

Figure 3.30
Time Manager.

Timestamp. The Time Scale option is used to control the speed at which time progresses. A setting of 1 indicates real time. You can lower this value to simulate bullet time or speed it up to create a fast-forward effect.

The Player Project Settings submenu is where the bulk of important iPhone settings reside (see Figure 3.31). After selecting Edit > Project Settings > Player from the main menu, you will notice a complex Inspector menu. This menu contains the following options:

- iPhone Bundle Identifier

- iPhone Stripping Level

- iPhone Script Call Optimization

- Default Screen Width

- Default Screen Height

- Display Resolution Dialog

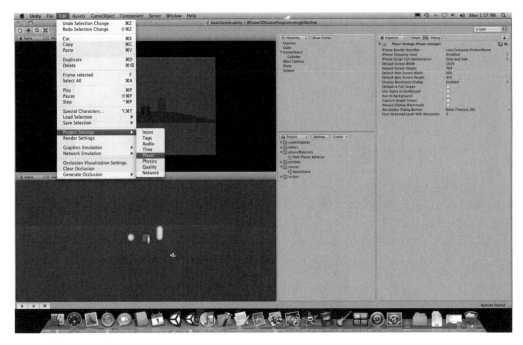

Figure 3.31
Player settings.

- Default Is Full Screen

- Use Alpha in Dashboard

- Run in Background

- Capture Single Screen

- Always Display Watermark

- Resolution Dialog Banner

- First Streamed Level with Resources

Again, many of these options are left over from the desktop version of Unity, but some are critically important for iPhone development.

The first mega-important aspect of the Player Project Settings menu is the iPhone Bundle Identifier. This is a unique tag that is assigned to your iPhone game and is used in a special code signing process controlled by Apple to keep applications unique and up to date. The typical format for this bundle is com.Company.ProductName, as you will notice from the default Unity settings. We'll cover the specifics of the code signing process in more depth later.

The next important option on the Player Settings menu is the iPhone Stripping Level. This option helps with file size reduction. There will be a disparity between the advanced version of Unity and the indie version when it comes to this option, as it is exclusive to the advanced version.

Finally, the iPhone Script Call Optimization option enables you to improve the performance of your game. The trade-off is that no data for crashes or exceptions is provided. Typically, you'll want to use Fast but no Exceptions when you release the final build of your game, but stick to the Slow and Safe option when debugging.

The rest of the options under the Player Settings menu aren't particularly important to us as iPhone developers, which brings us to the next option under the main menu's Edit > Project Settings, which is Physics. The Physics Manager enables us to control our project's physics on a global level (see Figure 3.32). This menu allows us to adjust things such as Gravity, the default Physic Material for

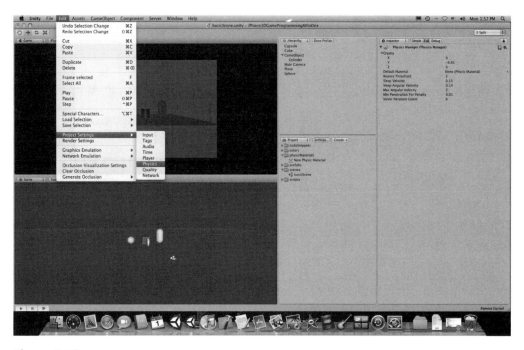

Figure 3.32
Physics Manager.

all collisions, Bounce Threshold, Sleep Velocity, Sleep Angular Velocity, Max Angular Velocity, Min Penetration for Penalty, and Solver Iteration Count.

Gravity controls the amount of gravity affecting rigid bodies in Unity's physics engine. This option not only allows you to adjust the magnitude of gravity but the direction as well. The default up-and-down axis in Unity is the Y-axis, so gravity is applied at −9.8 units per second squared along that axis. You could change the −9.8 if you were working, for example, with a scale other than 1 Unity unit = 1 meter or if you wanted moon gravity instead of Earth gravity. You could also change the direction of gravity if, for example, you wanted your main character to traverse small planetoids, which has become quite popular since a little plumber dressed in red did it in 2007.

Beyond Gravity, there's a Default Material option. This option allows you to set the physical properties of all collisions that don't have a custom physic material involved. All objects that have None specified in their Physics Material field will use this global physic material.

Next up is the Bounce Threshold setting. When two objects collide, they will not bounce away from each other if their velocities are below this number after the collision. It's a good idea to set this number fairly low to reduce physics jitters, which plague many games.

Sleep Velocity is the next option you can tweak. When an object's linear velocity gets low enough, it's good to bring it to rest and save the physics engine some processing cycles.

If the value is too low, objects will appear to be on ice, and if it's too high, it'll be like Velcro. Sleep Angular Velocity is very similar, but it applies to the rotational motion of an object.

Max Angular Velocity controls the maximum "spin speed" of a rigid body. This option enables you to avoid numerical instability when dealing with high-speed spinning objects. This is very useful in intentionally controlling the max speed of wheels on a car, for example.

Min Penetration for Penalty and Solver Iteration Count cuts right to the heart of the physics engine. The Penetration option determines how far two objects can "overlap" before the physics solver pushes them away from each other. The greater the value, the more your objects will overlap, but as a bonus you'll see less physics jitter in your simulation. The Solver Iteration Count controls the overall accuracy of the physics engine. The higher the iteration count, the more accurate the simulation will be, but at the cost of precious CPU cycles.

The last two options under the Edit > Project Settings submenu are Quality and Network. The Quality option is another leftover from the original Unity Editor (see Figure 3.33). The Network Manager allows you to control the network's send rate, as well as the level of detail to which the debugger reports network errors (see Figure 3.34). Send rate is the number of times per second data is sent over the network. Debug Level can be set to Off, Informational, or Full. When the Debug Level is set to Off, only errors will be printed. The Informational setting allows significant network events to be printed. Finally, Full showcases all network events.

With the Project Settings menus all wrapped up, it's time to move on to the next option within the Edit submenu—Render Settings (see Figure 3.35). This menu is fairly self-explanatory and enables you to control global visual aspects on a scene-by-scene basis. The options you can control via this menu are:

- Fog
- Fog Color
- Fog Density
- Ambient Light
- Skybox Material
- Halo Strength
- Flare Strength
- Halo Texture
- Spot Cookie

Some of these options are useless on the iPhone. For example, Spot Cookie is a lighting feature that basically attaches a shaped or colored lens effect to the light (kind of like the Bat Signal) that simply hasn't been enabled as of this writing. The fog options are self-explanatory, and you can instantly see their effects in the editor as you adjust them.

Ambient Light controls the overall amount of global light in a scene. If you are using a scene with many baked-in lights or dynamic lights, you may want to have

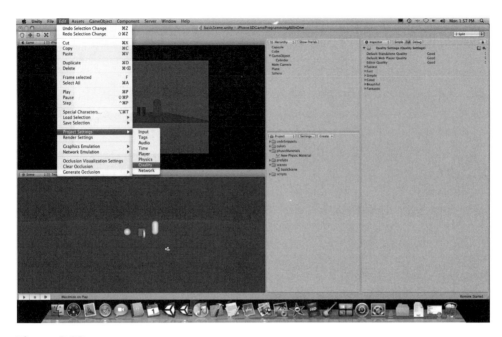

Figure 3.33
Quality settings.

Figure 3.34
Network settings.

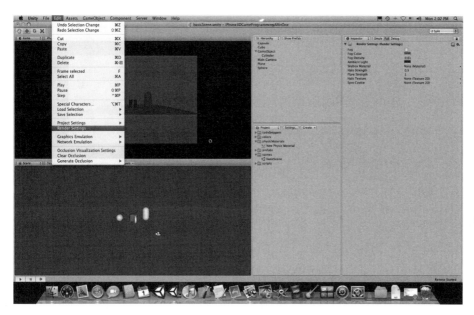

Figure 3.35
Render settings.

no ambient light (black). If you are creating a very colorful cartoon-type game, you may want to have full bright ambient light (white).

The Skybox Material option controls the default material that will be rendered behind traditional scenery when no skybox has been attached to the camera. Traditionally, a skybox is a six-sided figure that is positioned relative to the camera and drawn behind all other scenery. A typical example of a skybox is the unreachable mountains and clouds drawn behind standard 3D interactive geometry to give the illusion of a larger world. Regular skyboxes can be some-what expensive on the iPhone, where draw calls come at a premium. Using this option allows you to have a decent background image with only a single draw call.

The next three options have to do with Unity lights:

- Halo Strength

- Flare Strength

- Halo Texture

Halo Strength controls the size of all light halo images relative to their range. Flare Strength controls the intensity of flares within a scene. Finally, Halo Texture allows you to load a custom texture for the glow of lights in a scene. Lights in Unity change the appearance of textures and polygons in their path, but the lights themselves are invisible. Adding a Halo Texture allows them to be seen.

Down another notch within the Edit submenu is a Graphics emulation expanding list (see Figure 3.36). This is a useful option for debugging your scene data accurately. For our purposes, the iPhone setting will do. By enabling the Stats button in the Game view and running your game, you can compare No Emulation to iPhone emulation. iPhone emulation will show a reduction in draw calls, as well as a reduction in overall quality. For example, you could use per-pixel lighting and even spotlight cookies, but they won't show up if iPhone emulation is enabled. This is a very useful option not only to debug your game's performance properly but also to show you what graphics options actually work with the iPhone hardware. Tread cautiously, though; there are some graphical effects that can only be tested properly on actual iPhone hardware. Finally, it should be noted that the frame rate of your game in the editor will always be much higher than it is on an actual device. Enabling iPhone emulation does not emulate the speed of the iPhone's CPU/GPU.

Figure 3.36
Graphics emulation.

The last options within the Edit menu have to do with occlusion. The iPhone isn't the most powerful piece of hardware, and every little trick helps. *Occlusion* is a process that hides objects automatically if they cannot be seen by the camera (see Figure 3.37). When a camera is pushed directly up in front of a wall, the rest of the scene doesn't have to be rendered, because the wall is "occluding" the rest of the scene. You may notice a huge jump in the frame rate of many games when you're looking in the corner of a room, as opposed to looking over the whole room. This is the result of occlusion. Occlusion is a fairly advanced subject, and as such we'll discuss it and the options later in the book.

Assets

The next submenu within Unity's main menu is the Assets menu (see Figure 3.38). Clicking on Assets under the main menu reveals a list of options dedicated to importing, exporting, and creating new assets to fill your Project view. The most important aspect of this menu is the Create submenu, which yields these options:

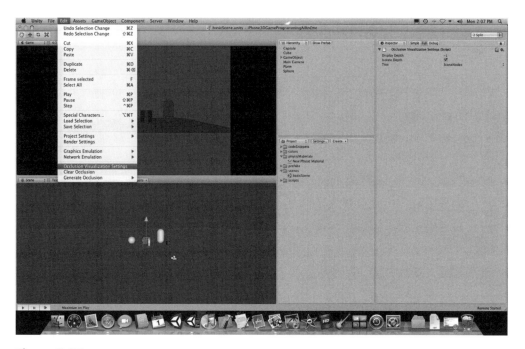

Figure 3.37
Occlusion visualization settings.

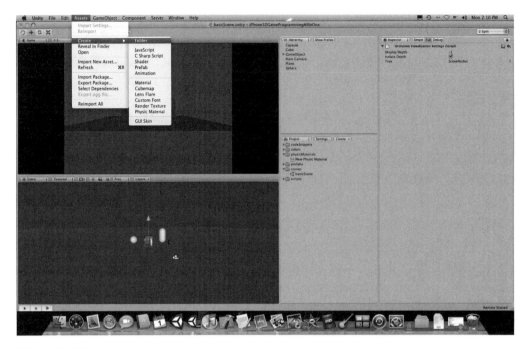

Figure 3.38
Assets menu.

- Folder

- JavaScript

- C Sharp Script

- Shader

- Prefab

- Animation

- Material

- Cubemap

- Lens Flare

- Custom Font

- Render Texture

- Physic Material

- GUI Skin

Beyond the Create functionality, this menu enables you to import new assets from elsewhere on your hard drive via Import New Asset. There's a tagalong Refresh option just below the Import New Asset option that refreshes your Project view to reflect any newly imported assets. The next group of options within the Asset menu enables you to import and export packages. Packages are groups of Unity assets that you might want to pass back and forth between Unity projects. You can select a group of assets from your Project view and export them as a package. Conversely, you could take that package and import it into a new Unity project that might benefit from your previous work.

GameObject

The GameObject menu within Unity's main menu allows us to add new content to our Scene and Hierarchy views (see Figure 3.39). This is where scene creation begins.

Figure 3.39
GameObject menu.

The first two options under this menu are Create Empty and Create Other. Create Empty will drop a GameObject containing only a Transform component into our scene. The Create Other option enables us to add the following:

- Particle System

- Camera

- GUI Text

- GUI Texture

- 3D Text

- Point Light

- Spotlight

- Directional Light

- Cube

- Sphere

- Capsule

- Cylinder

- Plane

- Ragdoll

- View Area

- Bounding Volume Area

These GameObjects represent the primitives or native asset creation functions that Unity has built in. Creating an "empty" game object is the most primitive asset creation function Unity has. The Create Other option will create a slightly more complex GameObject, but the real meat of Unity's complexity comes from components.

Component

The Component menu is one of the most important drop-down menus within Unity's main menu (see Figure 3.40). This menu is where game objects, whether imported or created via Unity's primitive functions, gain complexity and enable your game to come to life. We cannot talk about components without also looking at the Inspector view, which is one of Unity's primary default windows.

Inspector

When examining the Component menu, it's impossible to get a decent understanding of what components really do without also looking at their effects within the Inspector (see Figure 3.41). When adding an asset or a game object to your project, you can see them in your Project and Hierarchy view, respectively. When adding components to your project, you can view and edit the components in the Inspector.

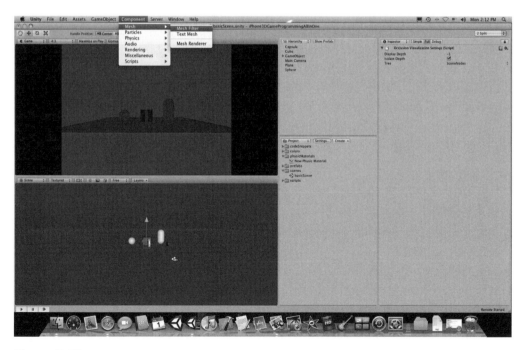

Figure 3.40
Component menu.

Figure 3.41
The bare-bones Inspector.

As you saw earlier, the Inspector is used to micromanage game objects in a scene. The Inspector is used to precisely control positions, rotations, colors, textures, sounds, and components in general. Components are a very important aspect of Unity development. They are the building blocks of complex Unity game objects. In Unity's main menu, there is a drop-down Component menu. Within the menu are these options:

- Mesh

- Particles

- Physics

- Audio

- Rendering

- Miscellaneous

- Scripts

For example, if you want to create a wheel for a car, it might include a physics-based component to handle rolling collisions, a particle-based component for smoke when it loses traction, and, of course, a mesh-based component for the visual representation that the player sees. By stacking the correct components together, you are able to create convincingly realistic game objects to bring your game's world to life. There are a variety of different Inspector UI arrangements, depending on the component being edited.

Transform Component Inspector Menu

The Transform Component menu is one of the most frequently used menus in Unity. We used it before to place our game objects precisely, and now we'll cover it in detail. The transform of a game object consists of three vector fields: the Position, Rotation, and Scale of the game object. Experiment with these fields to see how each of these values affects the visual representation of your game objects.

Mesh Component Inspector Menu

Viewing the Mesh component of a game object only gives us a visual representation of that object. Each visual object in a Unity scene contains a Mesh Filter. Select the small Cube object created earlier to sit atop our green ground plane. The Inspector should contain the following submenus:

- Cube

- GameObject

- Transform

- Cube (Mesh Filter)

- Box Collider

- Mesh Renderer

- Red or Blue (Material)

This cube contains two Mesh components: the Cube (Mesh Filter) and the Mesh Renderer (see Figure 3.42). If you select Component > Mesh from the main menu, you'll see that there are only three types of Mesh components: Mesh Filter, Text Mesh, and Mesh Renderer. As it relates to our cube, we are interested

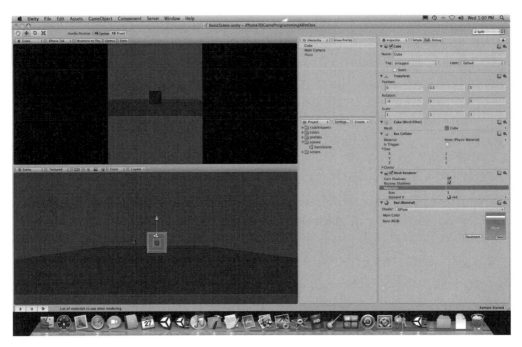

Figure 3.42
The Materials array within the Mesh Renderer component, all inside the Inspector.

only in the Mesh Filter and the Mesh Renderer. The Mesh Filter describes what sort of mesh to render, in this case, a simple cube. The Mesh Renderer contains several options. The first option is the checkbox directly to the left of the words Mesh Renderer. This is a Boolean flag that allows us to hide or show the mesh. There are two other options, Cast Shadows and Receive Shadows, which would allow this object to perform these operations if they were supported by Unity iPhone, but they are not. As it stands right now, they are leftovers from the desktop version of Unity.

Finally, there's a Material hierarchy, which can be expanded. This enables us to control the number of materials accessible by the Mesh Renderer and specifically assign each one. In this particular instance, we have a size of 1 because only one material is assigned to the cube, and it's either red or blue, depending on your choice. To add more detail in the future, we may want to expand the number of materials in the Materials array to two or more. For example, we might have a mesh with multiple parts, such as a human character model, which may have one material for hair and another for clothes.

Collider Component Inspector Menu

Colliders are used to give a sense of physical presence to game objects (see Figure 3.43). Without any sort of collider component, game objects would just pass right through each other.

While you might be able to create some neat visual effects with mesh components and various transforms, you're not going to have much interaction unless your game objects can effect change on each other—colliders help do this. There are several collider types available:

- Box

- Sphere

- Capsule

- Mesh

- Wheel

- Raycast

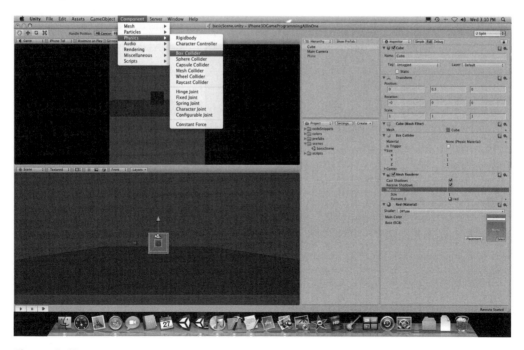

Figure 3.43
Adding a Physics Box Collider.

These are available within the main menu under Component > Physics. Each of these collider types produces a different menu to customize in the Inspector.

Box Collider Inspector Menu

The box collider is the first type and debatably the primary collider you'll be working with. Scene geometry often is represented by box colliders for efficiency, while dynamic or moving objects use sphere colliders. It's important to substitute a simpler collision method whenever possible to get the highest level of performance from your game. Collision is calculated per geometrical face or simply by using a distance check with sphere collisions, so the greater the number of faces in a collider, the more complex it is to compute collisions. A box collider is a very simple geometrical collider in the grand scheme of things because it has only six sides, and yet a box shape can fit a wide range of complex visual geometry.

The Box Collider Inspector menu enables you to adjust the material (a physic material, not the same as we discussed before with colors), a Trigger flag, a Size Vector3 represented as a hierarchy, and a Center Vector3, also represented as a hierarchy, as shown in Figure 3.44.

The Size and Center fields should be pretty self-explanatory. These let you move the collision bounds around your object and change its size so you can get it to line up just right. If you were to try and represent a car, for example, with a box collider, then you'd want the bottom of the box collider to line up with the bottom of the car's wheels, the top of the box collider to line up with the car's roof, and so on. By placing the box at the appropriate central location relative to the car and adjusting its width, height, and depth correctly, the box collider can approximate the shape of the car with a fair degree of accuracy (see Figure 3.45).

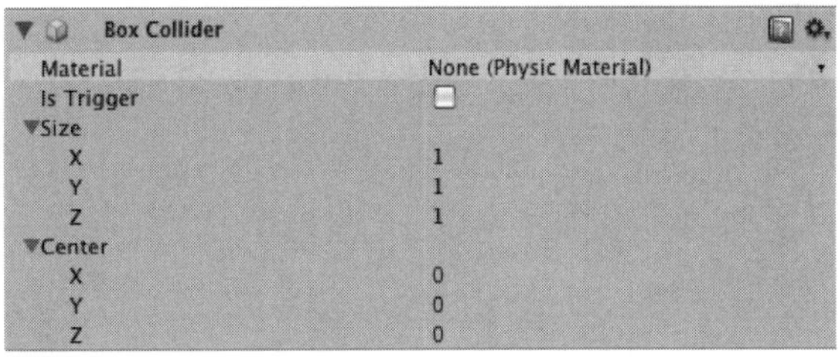

Figure 3.44
Box Collider Inspector menu.

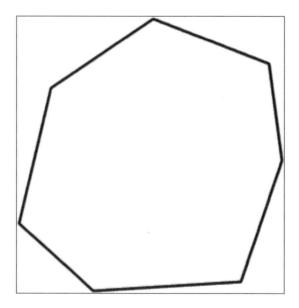

Figure 3.45
The collision box approximates the shape.

The Material aspect of any collider is a bit trickier. Since colliders in Unity are a subcomponent of the physics engine, it's expected that the collisions can have fairly detailed behaviors, especially because Unity employs NVIDIA PhysX technology. PhysX is a complete physics engine that allows game objects to be pushed, pulled, and bounced around as if they were in the real world. To demonstrate, look at the complete iPhone3DGameProgrammingAllInOne project on the CD or just follow along. Create a new folder in your Project view called physicMaterials (see Figure 3.46). Then highlight the folder and click Create > Physic Material (see Figure 3.47).

You should now see a new asset in your Project view called New Physic Material. You can leave the name for now. Looking over at the Inspector view, you can see a host of options dealing with physical properties for the material. This functionality allows you to turn certain objects into ice or concrete, depending on how you want your dynamic game objects to react to it.

For example, if you want the main character to slip and slide when he walks on a collider using this physic material, then setting the Friction low and calling it Ice would do the trick. Depending on your game, different values will be set, but in

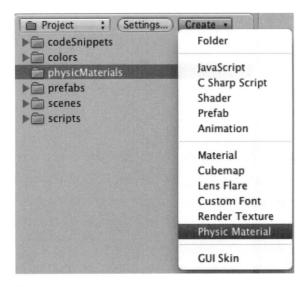

Figure 3.46
Creating a physic material.

general, things that are slick have less friction, and things that are rough have greater friction.

The final option that can be adjusted under the box collider is the Is Trigger flag. If this Boolean flag is checked, the game object containing this component won't collide with rigid bodies (the term for a physics-enabled object that can bounce around in your game). Rather, this object will trigger script callbacks `OnTriggerEnter()`, `OnTriggerExit()`, and `OnTriggerStay()` when a rigid body intersects the box collider's boundaries. This is useful for creating objects such as health recharging stations and the like, which you might want to affect change on your player character without affecting change on its physical movement or transform.

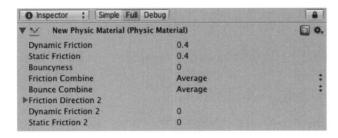

Figure 3.47
New Physic Material settings.

Sphere Collider Inspector Menu

The sphere collider is conceptually the simplest type of collider imaginable. If any object comes within a certain distance from its center, a collision occurs. To demonstrate the sphere collider, it's time to add a bit more detail to our scene. First, click in the bottom portion of the Hierarchy view to deselect any game objects. If you create a new object while another object is selected, the new object will be parented to the selected object, which means that if you move the parent, your new object will also move, similar to when your eyes move when your head moves. In this instance, you simply want to add a new separate object to your scene. From the main menu, select GameObject > Create Other > Sphere.

You should now see a sphere game object in your scene, probably intersecting the cube we created earlier. Remedy this by using the Inspector to adjust the Position field of the Transform component to (−2, 0.5, 0). Now that we have a sphere in our scene, we also have easy access to a sphere collider. You'll notice that the options under the Sphere Collider Inspector menu are very similar to the box collider's menu. The only difference is that the Vector3 representing Size has now been replaced with a single floating-point value called *Radius*. The radius of a sphere is the distance from the center of the sphere to its outer boundary. As we discussed earlier, a sphere is conceptually the simplest collider; if something gets within a distance less than or equal to the radius of the sphere, a collision has occurred. Obviously, we can use the properties we talked about with regard to the box collider to accomplish similar things with a sphere. Of course, a ball of ice isn't the most distinctively spherical property. It might be best to create a rubber-like material for the sphere or maybe a billiard ball–like material. Then again, perhaps we just want the sphere to act like a trigger. In that case, we could forget the physics material all together. The choice is yours.

Capsule Collider Inspector Menu

Sometimes, you need a shape other than a box or a sphere for a game object. A good example is when you want to create a convincing ragdoll. Game developers and game players alike adore the ragdoll; something about watching a body bounce and eventually slouch to the ground in a strangely deformed pose is just so satisfying. Of course, to create those satisfying contortions, you have to use a collision shape that approximates the fit of joints into one another. Boxes have jagged corners that begin intersecting at joints, causing jittery physics and spheres that just don't come anywhere close to approximating a limb. This is where capsule colliders come in. Capsules are elongated shapes similar to a rectangle, but they have smooth poles or ends like a sphere. This means they can approximate the elongated shape of an arm, for example, as well as the joint, which allows the arm to rotate smoothly within the shoulder socket.

I didn't mean to get you all giddy for ragdolls just yet. Throwing them about with your finger like an almighty god will come soon enough. For now, let's just add a capsule to our scene so we can examine its properties. Select GameObject > Create Other > Capsule from the main menu. Once again, the newly formed shape will probably be intersecting the cube, so adjust it with the Inspector so you get something that looks like Figure 3.48. You might notice that, due to the elongated nature of the capsule, you'll need to position it along the Y-axis at 1 instead of 0.5 for it to be resting directly on top of the ground plane.

Finally, you have your Capsule Collider Inspector menu to toy with. This menu employs many of the same options you saw before with the box collider and the sphere collider, but it adds two new fields, which you haven't seen yet. The first

Figure 3.48
Place the capsule at 1 along the Y-axis.

new field is Height, and the second is Direction. What this means for your default capsule collider is that the capsule itself is actually 2 units tall along the Y-axis and has a radius of 0.5, like the sphere you created before. If you change Direction to X-Axis, you'll see something like Figure 3.49.

Notice how the green wireframe image is now running perpendicular to the Capsule Mesh Renderer? This showcases the clear distinction between the visuals a player will see and the physics being simulated in the game world.

Now let's see what happens when we change Height from 2 to 3. You'll notice that the green wireframe became wider relative to the main camera's perspective, not taller. In this instance, Height is a poor description, and the more general term Length should probably be substituted, since what these two options really do is allow us to control the direction and magnitude or length of the capsule collider. For now set the Direction field back to Y-Axis and the Height field back to 2 (see Figure 3.50).

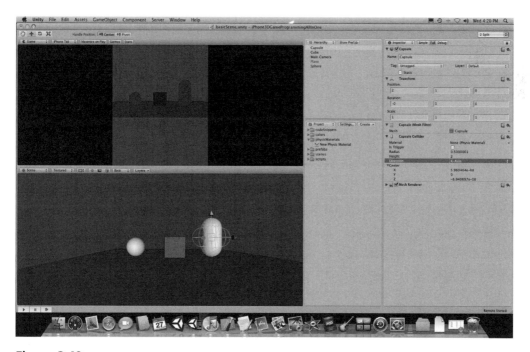

Figure 3.49
Capsule collider direction set to X-axis.

Figure 3.50
Elongated capsule collider.

Note
───
You may have noticed numbers like 5.960464e-08 in the Center X-Axis field in the previous screenshots. For non–math wizards, what this means is 5.960464 × 10 raised to the −8 power. This is short scientific notation and essentially means to take 5.960464 and move the decimal place eight places to the left. The number you get is very close to 0. If you don't like those messy numbers in your Inspector window, change them to 0.
───

Mesh Collider Inspector Menu

The mesh collider is the most process-intensive type of collider you can use. Sometimes, it's necessary to use a mesh collider for certain strange shapes, but usually you want to avoid them. If you do end up using a mesh collider, it's recommended that it be for a low-polygon object; since the object's polygons will be used to determine collision status, the fewer polygons to calculate with the better. For now, let's take the simplest collision type thus far and delete it. Select the Sphere shape in the Scene view. Now right-click or Control+left-click on the Sphere Collider component and choose Remove Component.

You'll notice that the simple green wireframe lines representing the sphere collider in the Scene view are now gone. What you're left with is a blue wireframe representing the sphere mesh itself, which is quite complex (see Figure 3.51). However, at this point it's not so bad because rendering such complexity isn't too challenging for the GPU contained in the iPhone.

Now it's time to add a mesh collider to the sphere game object. Choose Component > Physics > Mesh Collider from the main menu while the sphere is still selected.

Now you can see the Mesh Collider Inspector menu. There are two similar options in Material and Is Trigger, but there are three new options also available. These new choices are the Smooth Sphere Collisions flag, the Convex flag, and the Mesh selector.

The Smooth Sphere Collisions flag enables smoothing of the mesh's normals (vectors pointing directly away from or perpendicular to the polygon faces of a mesh). This is useful if you are using a low-polygon ball as a mesh collider and

Figure 3.51
The blue wireframe of the sphere's mesh renderer.

you still want it to roll smoothly along the surface it's traversing. Essentially, the jagged edges of the low-polygon surface will be removed.

The Convex flag allows this mesh collider to also collide with other mesh colliders. Typically, mesh colliders are very dynamic and may be concave in shape, meaning that the collider may have faces, which form a dip inward toward the center of the shape at some point. Concave collisions are extremely expensive to calculate, so normally Unity only allows convex shapes to collide with concave mesh colliders (see Figure 3.52). With the Convex flag set to true, Unity will create a convex approximation of the mesh collider that is limited to 255 triangles. Many times Unity creates a great approximation, which saves on processing power, but it's important to check on the shapes that it creates because sometimes they are not suitable to the application.

The final new option in the Mesh Collider Inspector menu is the Mesh Selector. This allows you to select any type of mesh contained within your project as the basis for the mesh collider. This is useful when you want to create your own approximation mesh in a 3D modeling app and then import it to Unity.

Now that you have an understanding of the mesh collider, go ahead and remove the Mesh Collider component from the Sphere game object and add a sphere collider back to it.

Wheel Collider Inspector Menu

The wheel collider is a specialized case created almost exclusively for wheeled vehicles, although there are many other purposes. To get a decent understanding of the wheel collider, let's start by adding a new shape to `basicScene.unity`.

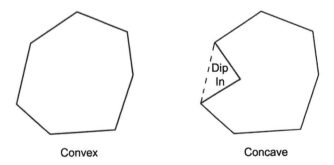

Figure 3.52
The difference between convex and concave shapes.

To add the new shape to our scene, choose GameObject > Create Other > Cylinder from the main menu.

Use the Inspector to place the newly formed cylinder at position $(0, 0.5, -2)$ and then set Rotation to $(0, 0, 90)$. In addition, set Scale to $(1, 0.1, 1)$. What you see should look like Figure 3.53.

What's the problem with this picture? You may have noticed the simple green wireframe surrounding the cylinder. It looks like a sphere, but technically it's just a shortened capsule collider. Go ahead and remove the Capsule Collider component from the cylinder. Now select Component > Physics > Wheel Collider (see Figure 3.54).

Now you can see the Wheel Collider Inspector menu, and it looks almost entirely different from any of the other menus we've seen before. The Radius field is something we're familiar with from the sphere collider. Set Radius to 5, and you should see something like Figure 3.55.

Hmmm… Something's not quite right here, is it? The cylinder and its wheel collider are running perpendicular to each other. In a case like this, the visuals

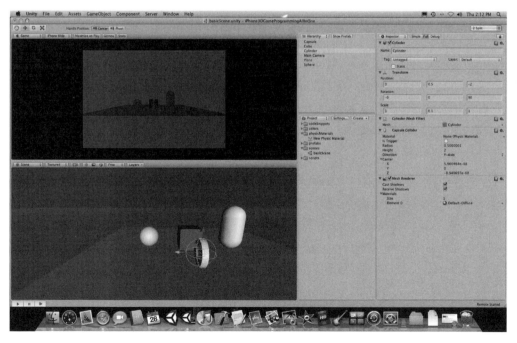

Figure 3.53
The new cylinder.

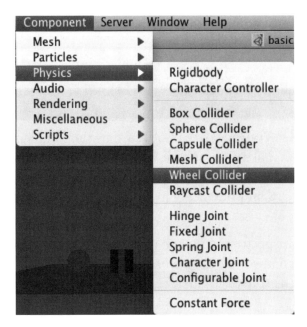

Figure 3.54
Add a Wheel Collider component.

and the physics that would be computed behind the scenes have no correlation. Now is a good time to learn the benefits of parenting. Remove the wheel collider from the cylinder and deselect it. Now choose GameObject > Create Empty from the main menu.

A new game object called GameObject containing only a Transform should appear in your scene. In the Hierarchy view, drag Cylinder onto GameObject (see Figure 3.56).

Now there should be a hierarchy whereby Cylinder is contained within GameObject, as shown in Figure 3.57.

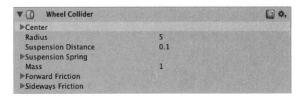

Figure 3.55
Wheel Collider Inspector menu.

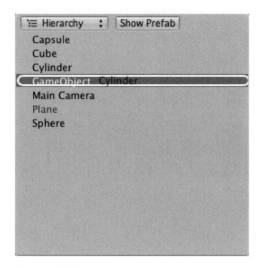

Figure 3.56
Drag the cylinder onto the new game object.

Now set Cylinder's Position field to (0, 0, 0) in the Inspector. Afterward, set GameObject's Position field to (0, 0.5, −2). Now highlight GameObject from the Hierarchy view and then select Component > Physics > Wheel Collider from the main menu (see Figure 3.58).

Once you've added the wheel collider, you should see a very simple green wireframe circle around the cylinder, which is also aligned properly. What happened

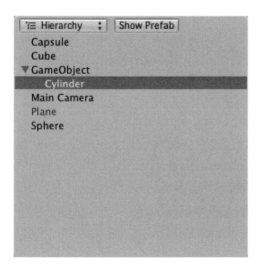

Figure 3.57
Cylinder is contained within GameObject.

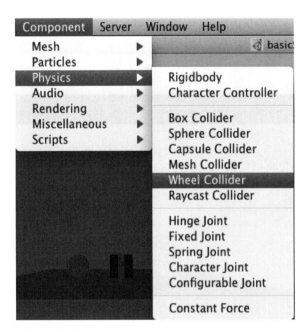

Figure 3.58
Adding a Wheel Collider component.

here is that Unity's default cylinder primitive is more akin to a cup than a wheel. Its Y-axis represents the top and bottom, as opposed to a typical wheel, which would have two flat sides across its local X-axis. By mounting Cylinder to the empty GameObject, we were able to rotate it to look more like a wheel than a cup without affecting the wheel collider, since the wheel collider was parented to GameObject and not Cylinder. The default rotation for any game object is also the default rotation for a wheel collider. However, Unity's default rotation for a cylinder isn't perfectly suited for the visual representation of a wheel.

The Wheel Collider menu itself contains two fields, which we have seen before: Center and Radius. The biggest difference is that the Radius field represents only two dimensions, as opposed to the 3D radius check of a sphere collider. Now would be a good time to set the Radius field to 0.5 so that it tightly fits the circumference of the cylinder (see Figure 3.59).

Beyond the Center and Radius fields, the Wheel Collider Inspector menu contains these fields:

- Suspension Distance
- Suspension Spring

Figure 3.59
Make the wheel collider fit around the cylinder's curved surface.

- Mass

- Forward Friction

- Sideways Friction

Suspension Distance is the maximum distance the wheel is allowed to extend locally. Suspension Spring is what brings the wheel back to its resting position. Mass is fairly self-explanatory and in layman's terms it controls how much the wheel weighs. Forward Friction controls what is essentially the rolling friction of the wheel as it is moving along its standard alignment. Sideways Friction is the amount of friction incurred when the wheel is drifting perpendicular to its alignment.

The wheel collider, much like the capsule collider, is intended for advanced purposes. If you want to create a realistic vehicular simulation, the wheel collider is a good bet. If you are creating simpler gameplay, then one of the other choices would probably suit your game better.

Raycast Collider Inspector Menu

The last collider type is the raycast collider (see Figure 3.60). These are specifically intended to intersect rays cast from one point to another to see if something is in the way. Essentially, raycast colliders test for intersection from the indicated center for a certain length or distance along the negative Y-axis. You could use raycasts for modeling non-wheeled vehicles such as boats or hovercraft. Raycast colliders are very useful in conjunction with spring-loaded physic materials.

To access the Raycast Collider Inspector menu (see Figure 3.61), select Plane in the Hierarchy view and remove its mesh collider; then select Component > Physics > Raycast Collider from the main menu.

The menu itself contains many options we've seen before. The biggest difference is the Length option, which controls the length of the raycast relative to the object's local space. For example, if you were modeling a hovercraft and you wanted it to kick up particles and apply lift within five feet of the terrain it's traversing, you could give it a raycast collider and set Length to 5. You might still attach a mesh or box collider for collisions with walls or other vehicles, but you would want to use the specialized raycast collider to apply lift off of the terrain.

For the Plane object, a raycast collider doesn't make much sense, but it's useful to see the effect the Length field has. Set Length to 10, and you should see something like Figure 3.62. When you're done, remove the raycast collider and add a mesh collider back to the Plane game object.

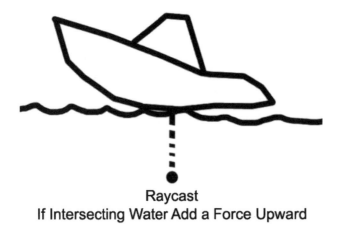

Raycast
If Intersecting Water Add a Force Upward

Figure 3.60
Basic concept of a raycast collider.

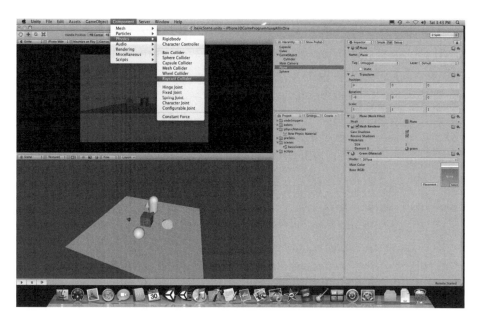

Figure 3.61
Adding a Raycast Collider component.

Figure 3.62
Viewing the length of the raycast collider as it extends below the plane.

Additional Menu Options

We've covered the most important aspects of Unity's main menu. There are only three options left: Server, Window, and Help.

Server allows you to access Unity Asset Server, but that is a separate program sold by Unity Technologies and is beyond the scope of this book. Help is self-explanatory. This leaves us with the Window option. This option controls the main windows you see in the Unity Editor.

The first important aspect of this drop-down menu is the Layouts expansion menu. This menu grants access to a variety of different ways to view the Unity Editor. The default setting is 2 Split. Throughout the majority of this book, this is the layout we'll be working with. You can arrange windows in various ways within this configuration. For example, I prefer my Game view to be in the upper-left window and my Scene view to be in the lower-left window instead of vice versa. You can adjust the layout to suit your project's needs.

The rest of this menu enables you to bring up certain windows. Each window has its own submenu to help you further organize your project. Let's have a look at those submenus now.

Scene View Submenu

The Scene View window allows you to view your editable scene in a variety of ways. Beginning from the left side of the submenu, the first drop-down menu allows you to view the editable scene in Textured, Wireframe, Tex/Wire, or Occlusion mode.

Textured mode shows the editable scene mostly as you would expect to see it in a game (see Figure 3.63).

Wireframe mode (Figure 3.64) displays the lines that connect each vertex of the 3D scene together.

Obviously, Tex/Wire (Figure 3.65) displays both.

Finally, the Occlusion view displays a special optimized view of the scene if you are using Occlusion. Occlusion is a process whereby certain parts of our game world won't be drawn in order to increase performance. We will cover occlusion, which is a more advanced topic, later on, during the production of our game.

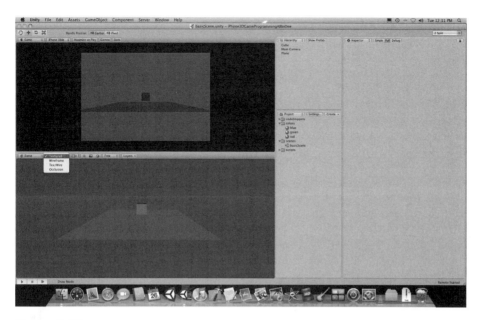

Figure 3.63
Textured view.

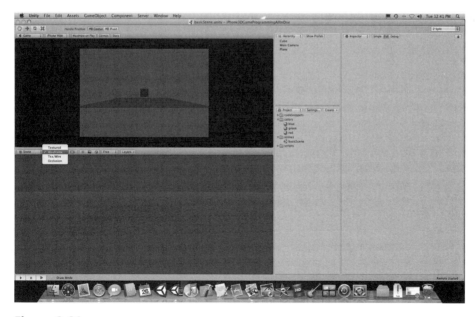

Figure 3.64
Wireframe view.

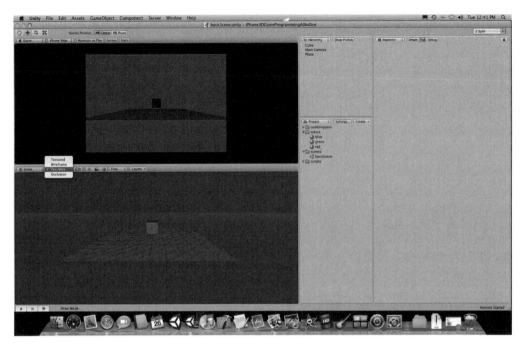

Figure 3.65
Textured and Wireframe views combined.

The next submenu control option is the Render Mode switch. The two options are RGB and Alpha mode. As we outlined before, RGB stands for Red, Green, and Blue color. For all intents and purposes, this is the full-color view of your scene. The Alpha option is a bit more complex. *Alpha blending* is a process that helps create transparency in the scenes. Typically, alpha blending occurs as a scale between white (no transparency) and black (invisible). This process is used when you create graphics such as 2D characters. For example, when a character image is created, you want to see only the body of the character onscreen when playing the game. But all images are stored in rectangular shapes on a computer and contain empty space around the character's form. By creating a special channel called an *alpha channel,* you can eliminate the parts of the rectangular image you don't want displayed, leaving only the character you want to see onscreen.

The same sort of process can be used on a 3D scene for many reasons. The principle remains the same; there may be some objects you want to display at full opacity and some you want to hide completely. There might be other objects such as glass or water, for example, that you want to have just a touch of transparency. These objects will appear gray in the Alpha view. To take advantage of this property in Unity, you must do something similar to what we outlined in the previous character example. You need a base RGB/Alpha image. We'll cover the process of creating an alpha-blended image in more detail later.

Beyond the RGB/Alpha View Selector is a group of three toggle buttons that affect the Scene view. The first of the three is the Lighting switch. By toggling the switch on and off, either you get default scene lighting or you see the effects of the lights actually placed in the scene manually. The second switch toggles the scene effects such as the placement grid, graphical user interface objects, and skyboxes. The final switch is the Orthographic Mode Control. Flipping this switch disables perspective (enables Orthographic Mode) from the Scene view camera. This is useful for placing objects precisely in two dimensions.

The next submenu option under the Scene View window is the View Direction Selector. There are seven choices within this drop-down selection tool:

- Front

- Back

- Top

- Bottom

- Left

- Right

- Free

Free mode is the default setting and lets you travel around the scene, observing it from multiple perspectives. The other options show you the scene as if it was contained within a cube and you were looking in from each face. The other options are very useful when combined with the Orthographic functionality of the last switch we discussed. By selecting the Top view from the Direction drop-down menu along with the Orthographic camera mode, for example, you can place objects precisely along the X- and Z-axes without worrying about perspective altering the operation.

The last submenu option under the Scene View window is the Layers option. Layers are very useful for controlling certain aspects of a complex scene. By default, you see four items checked under the Layers drop-down menu:

- Default

- TransparentFX

- Ignore Raycast

- Water

Each of these titles describes unique scene object functionality. Among the most useful of the default layers is the Ignore Raycast layer.

A raycast is essentially a line or a vector that begins at one point in 3D space and ends at another. The point of a raycast is to find objects that might intersect this line. For example, you might want to make a target reticule turn red if you were aiming at an enemy. The raycast will emit from the center of the game's main camera and extend out as far as possible with every object in the scene being checked for intersection. If an enemy is intersected, it would turn the reticule red. As you can imagine, this is a fairly intense operation for the iPhone's CPU. As such, you'll always want to limit the number of objects being checked for raycast collisions, as well as the complexity of those objects. A good countermeasure for too many objects or objects that are too complex is to first limit the number of objects within the scene that can be checked for raycast intersection, and second to create less-complex shells that might not represent what the player actually sees but approximates what the player sees enough to make the gameplay coincide with the visuals.

Let's say you have a bad-guy character that consists of 500 polygons. This level of detail is acceptable from a rendering (what the player sees) standpoint, but it's quite a lot for the CPU to check against with a raycast. The solution is to maintain the character for visual purposes but to create a far less-detailed approximation of the bad guy, which is invisible to the player but visible to the CPU for raycast purposes. It's possible that the 500-polygon bad guy could be represented for targeting purposes by 10–20 polygons, which is far quicker to check against than 500 polygons.

This goes back to the basics we talked about earlier, and it's tied directly into the Unity UI. Scenes can become complex really quickly when you begin applying the tricks of the trade to gain performance. As your scenes become more complex, it's important to employ Unity tools like the Scene View Layer selector to keep things manageable.

Game View Submenu

The Game View window allows you to see what your game will look like on the iPhone, and it is really useful in conjunction with Unity Remote, a program we'll dissect in detail later on.

The first drop-down menu within the Game View submenu is the Aspect menu (see Figure 3.66). This menu allows you to select an appropriate aspect ratio

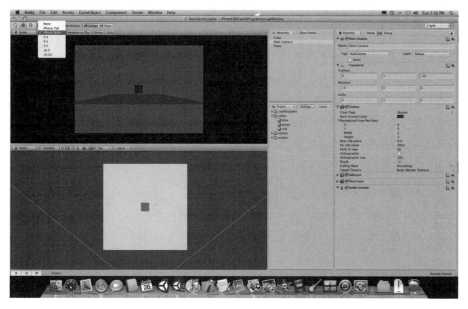

Figure 3.66
Game View Aspect menu.

from a variety of choices (iPhone Tall, iPhone Wide, 5:4, 4:3, 3:2, 16:9, 16:10). For the purposes of this book, we'll be concentrating on iPhone Tall and iPhone Wide, which allow us to view the game within the confines of the resolution of the iPhone screen itself.

The next option is a toggle button to Maximize on Play (see Figure 3.67). This corresponds to the Play option of the Unity Editor, where you can test your game directly within the editor via the Play, Pause, and Step buttons in the lower-left corner of the editor. When Play is clicked to test, Unity will display only the Game view in the center of the screen, as opposed to leaving it integrated with the editor.

Next up is the Gizmos toggle button. Gizmos within the Game view are very similar to the triple axis gizmo in the Scene view, only they are defined within script code in a custom fashion for debugging purposes.

The final toggle button in the Game View window's submenu is the Stats button (see Figure 3.68). This is a hugely important tool for debugging and maximizing

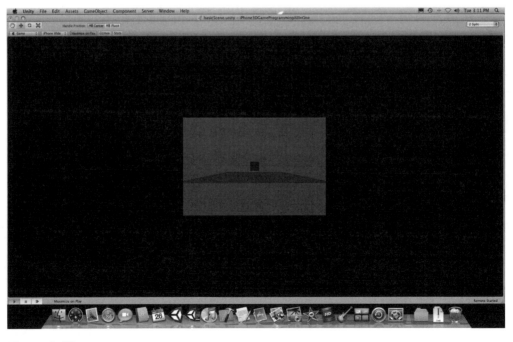

Figure 3.67
Maximized on Play.

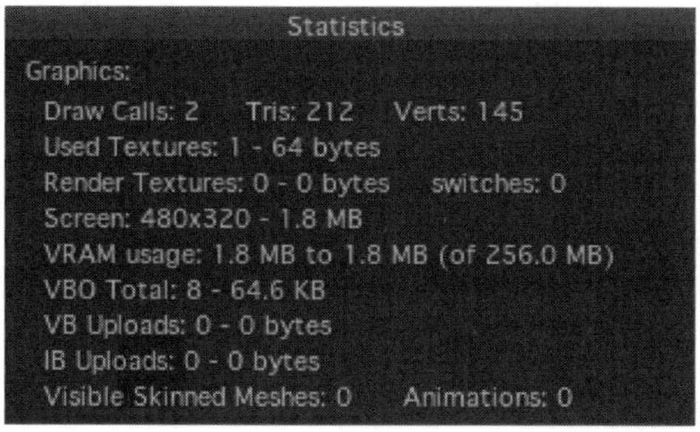

Figure 3.68
Stats window.

performance in Unity. By toggling this on, you enable Unity to report back to you about the graphics resources being used, such as the number of draw calls, polygons, and vertices onscreen.

Hierarchy View Submenu

The Hierarchy view is used to manage objects contained within a Unity scene file. Something very important to the hierarchical presentation is a concept known as *parenting*. Unity organizes objects together based on parent/child relationships, and this is represented by the arrow to the left of an object if the object contains any children. By clicking on the arrow, you can gain access to children and even children of children. This nesting allows for manageable complexity within your Unity scenes.

There's only one toggle button to speak of in the Hierarchy view. That button is the Show Prefab switch. This switch enables a visual reference to the coordinating object in the Project view.

Note

To see how prefabs work, we can create a ground plane prefab right now. Select Create > Folder in the Project view and name it Prefabs (see Figure 3.69). Then highlight the new Prefabs folder and select Create > Prefab. Rename the object New Prefab to groundPlaneGreen. Once you've renamed the new prefab, drag the Plane object from the Hierarchy view down onto the newly named groundPlaneGreen prefab. The square-shaped icon to the left of groundPlaneGreen should now be a blue color instead of the empty white color it was previously.

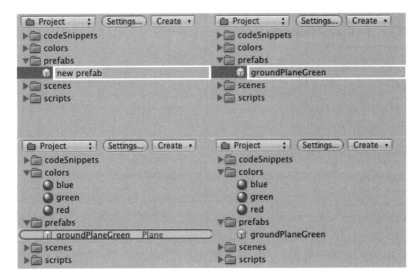

Figure 3.69
Creating a prefab.

Project View Submenu

In the previous section, we accessed some of the Project view's submenu functionality via the Create button or by right-clicking inside the Project view. This functionality is what allows us to manage the raw assets (folders, code, 3D models, textures, scenes, prefabs, and so on) of our project. There is one other button in the Project View submenu, the Settings button.

This button will activate the Import Settings window for certain types of assets. Depending on the asset type, different options will be displayed. To recount, the Project view and its submenu are used to manage a project's raw assets and their import settings.

The Import Settings option in Unity is actually a bit of a miracle in terms of project workflow. It's not uncommon, for example, to test several resolutions for a texture. Traditionally, you would have to open up an image-editing application such as Photoshop, change the size of a texture, and then resave it. With Import Settings you can simply import a texture into Unity at a chosen resolution. Thus, it's best to begin with a high-resolution image and then, depending on memory usage and visual quality, choose a more appropriate resolution when importing into Unity via Import Settings.

The Import Settings menu changes according to the type of asset you are importing (see Figure 3.70–3.72). When importing audio files, you'll see different options than if you were importing a texture file or a 3D model file.

The Audio Import Settings menu is pretty basic. The only options it yields are these:

- Audio Format
- Channels
- Compression Quality
- Decompress on Load

Audio Format lets you choose between Uncompressed (.wav), Ogg Vorbis, and Apple (.mp3, .m4a, and .caf) formats. The Channels option allows you to use the file default or force either mono or stereo sound. Vorbis Audio Compression Quality is pretty self-explanatory: It allows you to compress a file more to reduce

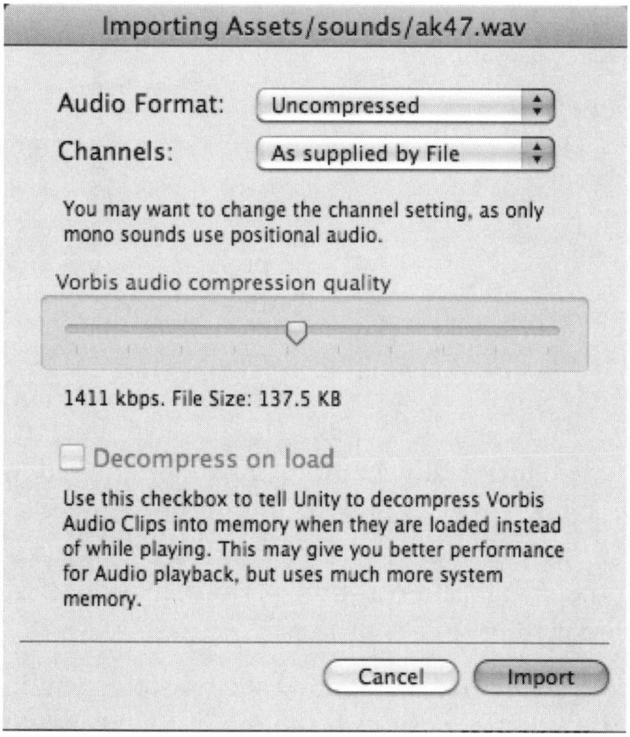

Figure 3.70
Audio Import settings.

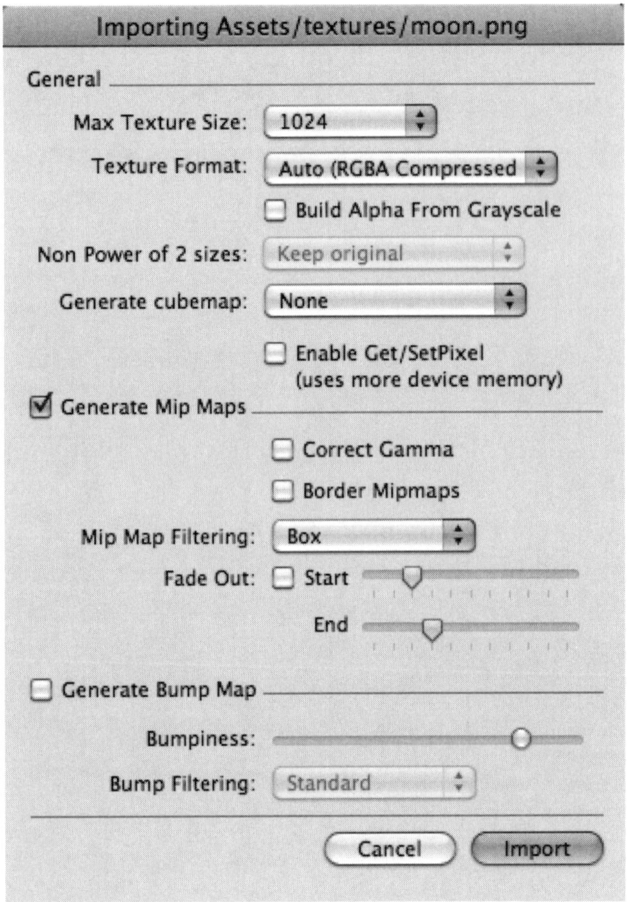

Figure 3.71
Texture Import settings.

the final file size of your game but you lose quality in the process. The last option is the Decompress on Load checkbox. Unity has the ability to decompress an audio stream as it's playing, but this comes at a performance cost. If you decompress the audio at loading time, you'll gain real-time performance benefits. The flipside is that you'll use more memory in the process.

The Texture Import Settings menu is a bit more complex. The first option within the menu is the Max Texture Size selector. Although the menu allows you to select up to 4,096 pixels, the largest texture the iPhone hardware can handle is 1024 × 1024 or what can be called a *1K texture*.

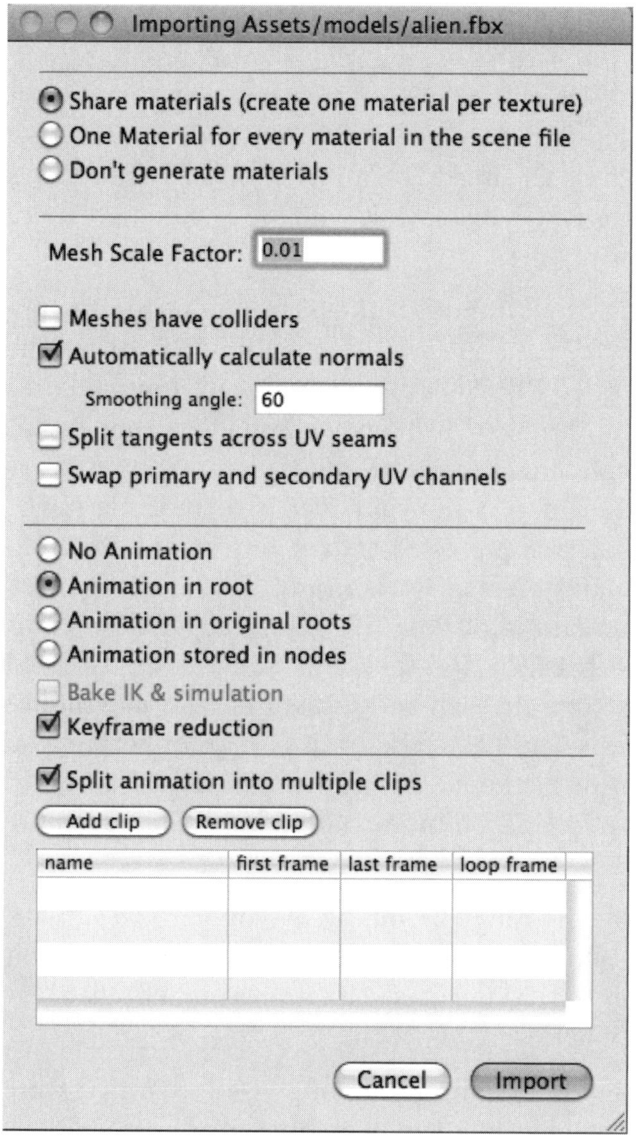

Figure 3.72
3D Model Import settings.

Because the iPhone's screen is so small, the use of 1K textures isn't often necessary unless you're creating something called a *texture atlas,* which is used to texture a group of objects. In these instances, an object receives only a small portion of a 1K texture. This could be the equivalent of using a single 32-square pixel to a 256-square pixel texture for a single object. The advantage of using a 1K texture for multiple objects is the save on draw calls. The iPhone hardware cannot handle many draw calls, which are created by referencing individual materials. Each time, the GPU has to draw a new object onscreen or use a new material, even if it's on an object that's already been drawn once, a draw call is used. It is typical to have one material per texture, although you could have more than one material using the same texture.

The next option within the Texture Import Settings menu is the Texture Format option. This option can be used to specify a number of formats. The default format is RGBA Compressed PRVTC 4-bits. This default format works great with the iPhone hardware's memory bandwidth limitations, but it also creates grainy images. In general, this format works well for 3D geometry textures, but if you are using 2D imagery for your menus or in-game HUD, you'll most likely want to use an uncompressed texture format like RGB 16-bit, RGB 24-bit, or RGBA 16- and 32-bit. By switching from a compressed format to an uncompressed format, you'll lose the grainy appearance compression causes. The difference between 16-, 24-, and 32-bit uncompressed textures is a bit different. When dealing with 16-bit textures, you may notice some graininess, which manifests itself as stark breaks in color where you might expect a smooth gradient or blending. Textures of 24- and 32-bit don't exhibit the same color wash effect as 16-bit textures, but they use more memory bandwidth.

The primary difference between using 24-bit RGB and 32-bit RGBA uncompressed textures is the allowance of an alpha channel in the 32-bit RGBA format. If you need very clear textures with transparency, then the 32-bit RGBA format is your only option.

The next option within this dialog is the Non Power of 2 Sizes option. Texture compression can be used only on Power of 2 textures (for example, a 256 × 128 texture). If you are attempting to use another size (for example, 514 × 257), then the Power of 2 Sizes option will be available (see Figure 3.73).

This option lets you scale a texture to the nearest, largest, or smallest Power of 2 values automatically. If you are using Non Power of 2 textures for your menus or HUD, it's fine (even preferable), as long as you aren't using texture compression. A good example is your game's splash screen or menu backdrop image. The iPhone's screen runs a resolution of 480 × 320. This resolution isn't

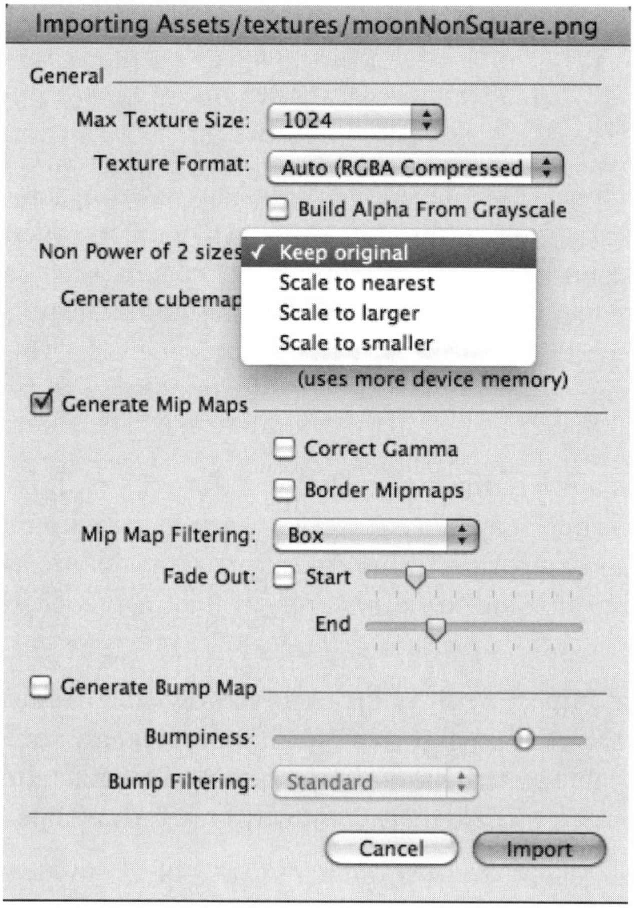

Figure 3.73
Power of 2 Texture Import setting.

composed of Power of 2 sizes. It's plausible that you'll create a 480 × 320 image to represent your splash screen or menu backdrop. Again, this is fine as long as you don't plan on using texture compression on it. If you do plan on using texture compression (there are numerous reasons you might want to), then the best course of action is to create a texture larger than screen size (a 512 × 512 works great) and then paste your 480 × 320 image at the center of the larger image, allowing the screen to clip the remainder away.

The next option available from the Texture Import Settings dialog is the Generate Cube Map option, which allows you to generate cube maps from several different generation methods: Spheremap, Cylindrical, SimpleSpheremap, and

NiceSpheremap. Cube maps are generally used to create reflective surfaces and are typically created by rendering the relative views from an object's center. Cube maps can be used to create effects such as the Predator's cloaking ability or the liquid metal look of mercury.

Beyond cube map generation, Unity also offers a Generate Mip Maps option. *Mip maps* are smaller versions of a base texture, which the engine uses when rendering tiny objects that have no need for a full-resolution texture, such as when an object is being rendered so far away from the camera that its texture occupies less pixel space onscreen than it does in memory. In some cases you may want to avoid mip map generation if you want the texture always to be rendered with a completely crisp look.

The mip map generator also has a few settings: BoxFilter and KaiserFilter. Box-Filter is a very simple method of mip map generation. The map levels become smoother as they shrink. The Kaiser algorithm is used to sharpen the texture as it shrinks. You can use the Kaiser method to regain some of the image's crisp appeal while still using mip maps.

The final option in the Texture Import Settings dialog is the Generate Bump Map option. With this option enabled, the color channels of the texture are used and converted into a format capable of real-time bumpmapping. This adds the appearance of additional 3D geometry where there is actually only texture data.

The last type of Import Settings dialog controls the parameters of 3D models imported into Unity. The first portion of the dialog allows you to select whether you want to share materials, create one material for every material in the scene file, or not generate materials. Generally, the first option is preferable because it will save on draw calls. However, in some instances, you may need to change this. If, for example, you were using the same texture for two distinct materials (perhaps one should have a matte finish and one should be shiny), then you would need to generate two materials that both use the same texture. In the special case that you want to generate custom materials for a model within Unity, you can import a 3D model without generating materials.

Beyond the material generation options, there's a Mesh Scale Factor, which is used to change the size of the mesh upon import in case you model at a different scale than Unity's default of 1 meter = 1 unit in the virtual world. Also, you have four checkboxes that allow you to add colliders on import automatically,

automatically calculate the normals of the polygons within the mesh, split tangents across UV seams, and swap primary and secondary UV channels. If you check the Generate Colliders option, then every mesh within your model will be assigned Mesh Collider components. The Calculate Normals option has a sub-option that allows you to set the smoothing angle. The smoothing angle determines how sharp an edge has to be to be considered a hard edge. Normal map tangents are also split according to the smoothing angle. The Split Tangents option is useful if you have bad bumpmap lighting by the seams of a mesh. This is typically a problem only on characters. The final checkbox allows you to swap UVs, and this is useful for things like lightmapped models, where perhaps the blending isn't functioning properly due to the lightmap and diffuse channel being swapped.

The next few options within the 3D Model Import Settings dialog are used for animation generation. Obviously, selecting Don't Import will import your 3D model with no animation.

The next possibility is to import animation from the original roots. This means that the animations are stored in the root objects from the animation package that exported the file. Those root objects may be different from the root objects in Unity. The Store in Nodes option is useful when animations are stored within each individual object that is animated. This is useful for complex animation setups that require micro-management via scripting.

The final option for animation generation is the Store in Root option. This is the default setting and probably the most common. This is used when all animation information is stored within the transform of the 3D model and is processed throughout a hierarchy of child transforms.

There are two checkboxes below the animation generation radio buttons, which also deal with animation. The first is the Bake IK & Simulation. This option is great when using IK or simulation within an art package. Unity can then convert to FK when the model is imported.

The second checkbox is for keyframe reduction. This option is very useful for saving memory and increasing the performance of your apps.

The final component of the 3D Model Import Settings dialog is the Split Animation into Multiple Clips option. This tool enables you to select frames of animation from within the model and label them to be called from scripts. This allows animations such as run or jump to be called when certain actions are performed. The 3D model file may have 400 frames of animation, and frames 1–50 may be the run frames, while 300–325 might be the jump frames. With this option you can control precisely what frames are associated with what actions within the game.

Conclusion

That wraps it up for Unity's GUI and editor settings. Hopefully, you have a solid understanding of the general workflow Unity provides, and the editor doesn't feel alien to you upon opening the program. If you're still intimidated by the complexity of the editor, don't worry. Once we begin creating our example game, you'll become extremely familiar with the editor, and by the end of your first project, using Unity will be second nature to you.

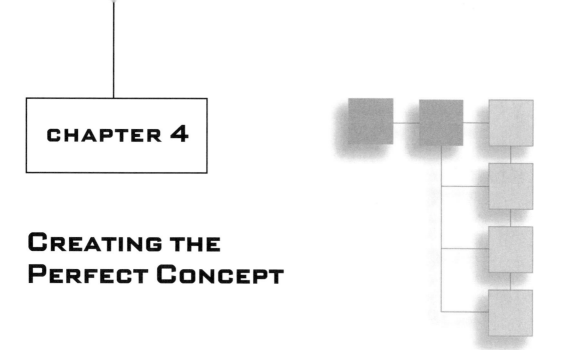

CHAPTER 4

CREATING THE PERFECT CONCEPT

In today's market, it's hard to get noticed, no matter what you're creating. It's even more difficult when you're creating iPhone games. The number of games on the App Store is astounding, and thousands more are being released weekly. However, though it may be difficult, it's far from impossible to create a hit on the iPhone.

Before we analyze the iPhone market specifically, it's important to cover the general concept of disruptive technology, which is a technology that diverges from the flow of current technology in a new direction that wasn't readily apparent to most people before the inception of that technology. Apple and Nintendo both used disruptive technology in this past hardware generation to advance beyond their competitors.

Sony was the leading competitor during the previous video game console generation (see Figure 4.1). The PlayStation 2 was the quickest-selling console, to the tune of 100 million units sold. During the same generation, Microsoft released the first Xbox console, which targeted a very similar market as the PS2, namely hardcore gamers. Nintendo created the GameCube, which was actually very similar to the other consoles. All three competitors pushed graphics technology and the number of buttons that could possibly fit on a controller to their limits.

The so-called next-generation console war kicked off in 2005 with the release of Microsoft's Xbox 360 console (see Figure 4.2). Microsoft's strategy by-and-large

Figure 4.1
Sony: Little disruption, more polygons, and more buttons.

had not changed. The controller maintained the same number of buttons, and the hardware was capable of pushing more polygons. Sony followed suit with a more powerful version of the PlayStation. Nintendo chose to implement a new console based on disruptive technology. The Wii is what they called it, and instead of pushing more polygons, the system simply let players interact with the onscreen polygons via a new, never-before-seen controller. Once people got their hands on the Wii, it was quite clear that Nintendo's new technology was the way of the future. Instead of more polygons and more buttons, Nintendo focused on fewer polygons and buttons and more ease of use. This disruptive concept pushed Nintendo from the back of the console race into the lead position (see Figure 4.3).

In general, disruptive technology is anything that goes against the flow of current popular belief. Many times, developers create clone games, technology, or

Figure 4.2
Microsoft: Somewhat disruptive due to indie game support and early social networking features.

Figure 4.3
Nintendo: Great disruption—we had never played games at home this way.

marketing concepts in an attempt to grab a piece of someone else's pie. This is typically a fairly safe way to conduct business. By "borrowing" a successful concept, you skip the hard work of creating and testing a new concept. However, you reduce the chance of creating a runaway success like the Wii. The way I like to look at it is that creating good disruptive technology is almost like a paradox, because you're attempting to create something that no one has ever seen, but once they have their hands on it, they wonder how they ever lived without it. Let that sink in for a few minutes before continuing!

Apple also created disruptive technology when it unleashed the iPhone (see Figure 4.4). There were so many things about the device that were risky, and yet once users got their hands on it they could not live without it. While other cell phone providers were adding more buttons with full QWERTY keyboards and more moving parts with slide-out screens, Apple reduced the number of buttons, moving parts, and complexity in general.

However, it wasn't the hardware alone that disrupted the mainstream. It was Apple's decision to release a fantastic SDK and a nearly completely free economy in the App Store that disrupted the status quo (see Figure 4.5). Before the iPhone, developers either were forced to pay exorbitant fees to come under the wing of a large platform holder like Sony, Nintendo, or Microsoft or they went it alone or with a publisher on the desktop. Developing for desktop computers presents a plethora of challenges that the locked platforms don't face. On one

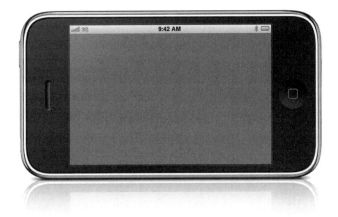

Figure 4.4
Apple: Great disruption—we never had portable computers this powerful before.

Figure 4.5
App Store: Monumental disruption—for the first time, we had full-feature on-demand games anywhere everyday.

hand, developers were allowed creative freedom with tough technological challenges, and on the other, developers were at the whim of the marketing team. Although the technological challenges were reduced, the price of entry was greatly increased. Before the iPhone, no developer was allowed the luxury of freedom, inexpensive development tools, and a locked (or nearly so) hardware platform with a dedicated marketing machine built in.

A few years ago I was talking to my wife's sister (an Apple retail store Creative at the time). I told her I had a gut feeling that Apple was going to do something crazy in the game space. I didn't know about the iPhone yet, but I just had this feeling that they were up to something. As crazy as it sounds, this was before I was a real Mac user. I did have one Mac that I used for ports, but by-and-large I was a PC developer eyeing Xbox Live Arcade (also fairly disruptive at the time but merely a ripple in comparison to the iPhone App Store).

When the iPhone was revealed, I knew what would be coming next, or at least I knew what I wanted to see next—that sweet SDK! It took Apple about a year to finally open up the iPhone to developers. I remember the first time I began really downloading apps; I was on a road trip back from Hilton Head, SC. My wife and I were passengers, and I was bored out of my mind. I opened up the App Store and was entertained until my iPhone's battery died. Immediately after that trip, I began my pursuit of App development.

The pursuit of my own small disruptive technology began modestly. I attempted to upgrade my Mac Mini port machine. I purchased a fresh copy of OS X Leopard and installed it. As soon as that was installed, I moved on to the iPhone SDK, but much to my dismay I found that not only did it require Leopard, it also required an Intel-based Mac to do any real work. Yes, there were hacks available to get the SDK installed and the simulator running on the old Power PC systems, but the code signing process to actually move the examples from my old Mac to my iPhone just wouldn't work. Perhaps at this point someone has figured out how to move past that little hiccup, but I highly recommend investing the money to purchase new hardware. Once I made that step, I was running my own games on my iPhone almost instantly. It was completely worth cleaning out my bank account!

Out with the Old, in with the New

Of course, iPhone development in 2008 was quite a bit different than it is now. Back then, almost anything would fly, and 3D really knocked people's socks off. The example used to market this book would have retired me if it had been released during the summer of 2008, but as with all new video game technology, gamers are happy with the technology at first, but by the middle of the hardware life cycle the puppy love has worn off and people want to see some real meat. Such is the cycle of video game hardware and software; initially, it is the hardware that is disruptive, but in due time it becomes the game developer's job to be disruptive via innovative and well-executed software.

The first and most important action to take when being disruptive is to identify what mainstream encompasses. The next step is to weigh your chances of success, either by going with the flow or by following through with your disruption. It's entirely possible that you may want to skip the hardship of innovating. This is all part of choosing the perfect concept. While it would be fantastic to create the next *Tetris*, it might be better to just create another *Tetris* (if you know what I mean).

At this point your first decision is to be, or not to be, disruptive. First, are you already a fairly seasoned game developer? If you've made some games in the past, then you may have what it takes to disrupt and disrupt well. If the answer is no, then you'll probably want to emulate a pre-existing gameplay mechanic and simply sprinkle some of your own creativity on top. Of course, even first-time developers can be disruptive.

How soon do you want to begin making a living from game development? If you create a disruptive title, your probability of success is lower. Even if you make a great game, chances are that people will skip over it for something more familiar unless you've already got a solid track record.

To demonstrate this point, I'll use my own games as examples. *Skyline Blade* is a 3D helicopter sim and the first title I created that really made a dent in the market. This game isn't too disruptive, and in fact, I created it after seeing *X-Plane Helicopter* and *Hellfire* (the only other 3D helicopter games for the iPhone at the time). *X-Plane Helicopter* had the physics, and *Hellfire* had the gameplay and explosions. I thought I could mix the two together for a better game. This worked for the most part, with the exception of my disruption to the genre, a special iPhone control scheme, which worked fantastic except for the fact that most people didn't comprehend it. In this instance, I created a mainstream game with a disruptive control style, and most people didn't get the controls (see Figure 4.6). In the end, I wiped away my initial control structure in favor of a simplified system, which in my opinion took away from the experience. Of course, my opinion doesn't count for much if most people can't get control of the game. The new style allowed people to gain access to the rest of the gameplay, which also had innovations that its competitors did not have. Either way, *Skyline Blade* was a mainstream-style game carved for a certain niche with little to disrupt the mainstream (see Figure 4.7). Unfortunately, the primary disruption also blew up in my face because, unlike the iPhone or Wii, it did not simplify most user's lives.

Figure 4.6
Skyline Blade, original disruptive controls.

Figure 4.7
Skyline Blade, mainstream controls; everyone understood analog and trackball.

This brings us to an important lesson: If you're going to disrupt the mainstream, you have to do it by rising above the mainstream like a magic carpet and showing your users a whole new world. If you simply rebel against the mainstream, your players will notice, and they will punish you for it. Back in the NES days, most games used the A button to jump and the B button to attack (see Figure 4.8). Every now and then you'd get that rebellious game that would switch this order, and it really just sucked for the players. These games were not innovative—they were just instigators. It should be noted that I did end up creating a third control scheme for *Skyline Blade* in an attempt to merge the intricacy of the first scheme with the easy comprehension level of the second scheme.

Creating Complex iPhone Experiences

As it turns out, the iPhone can host complex gameplay experiences, but other developers, such as Firemint, implemented this better by simply removing control from the player. Their excellent *Real Racing* plays great, just about as good as

Figure 4.8
NES controller.

Gran Turismo or *Forza Motorsport* on the big consoles. The great thing is that they accomplished this by removing the need to touch the input device to control each action. Instead, they give players the same level of control by removing direct input to the throttle and also reducing the need to use breaks. The player can still control these things, but it becomes a matter of not doing something instead of pressing yet another button. For example, players don't touch the screen to accelerate. Tilting the device primarily controls the game, but players can still accelerate and brake. As it turns out, *Real Racing* is an excellent example of a non-disruptive game using a few subtle but still disruptive features to stand out (see Figure 4.9).

For an example of a truly disruptive title, I think nothing stands out more than Firemint's other title, *Flight Control* (see Figure 4.10). In this case, not only did Firemint take advantage of the iPhone touch screen hardware but they also took advantage of the most basic aspect of the iPhone, the fact that it's a mobile device. *Flight Control* was so simple that you could easily play it on the go when you had a minute of downtime. Furthermore it was light on assets, which allowed it to be downloaded anytime, bypassing the 10MB limit many face on the cellular networks.

Perhaps the most telling clue to *Flight Control*'s disruptive force was the whole slew of line drawing games that followed. There are now dozens of games on the App Store than involve drawing the path of the object you want to control. This

Figure 4.9
Real Racing.

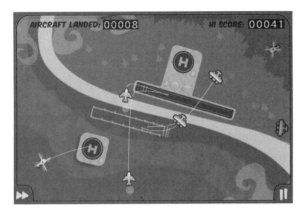

Figure 4.10
Flight Control.

method of control differentiates the iPhone hardware from any other gaming platform and, in fact, started a whole new genre of games. Similar to how Microsoft and Sony followed in Nintendo's disruptive motion control footsteps with Project Natal and PlayStation Move, other game companies began following in Firemint's.

Keeping all of the above in mind, it's plain to see that for every successful disruptive title created there are at least 10 clones with various spins on the original. Typically, the clones are also successful. A crossroads is before you. Will you choose the beaten path or the undisturbed wilderness?

What Will We Create?

To help promote this book, I thought it would be a good idea to create a game on the App Store and pose the question to you:

"Want to learn how to make this?"

For this purpose, I felt that creating a title within an established genre was logical. After all, this book has a target audience, and that target audience already associates itself with several game genres. My purpose in this instance wasn't to create the next big game but instead to show people how to make their own.

Exactly what genre should I choose? After speaking with my editor, we identified the primary audience for this book as the 20-something male. This is the same target audience that the big console makers generally target. One look at the Xbox 360 game library would probably give me a reasonable clue as to what games those guys play. Then again, we might be looking for a more refined crowd of 20-something guys. Not every guy that's tagged an elite in Halo is going to be interested in learning how that's done scientifically. The Xbox 360 library contains a lot of first-person shooter titles, although in recent years it's diversified, thanks to Live Arcade. Still, I would hesitate to create an iPhone FPS because, quite frankly, there are a ton of examples out there already. Even if that's what the majority of our target audience is playing, I don't think we'd bring much new to the table that they can't find elsewhere.

So, an FPS is off the table. What other genres are popular with this crowd? The first genre that comes to mind is racing. Racing is huge with this crowd, not only in the game space but in real life as well. Then again, is Vin Diesel's real-life wannabe alter ego going to be programming games? My initial response would be no, but then again Vin Diesel did become a game developer, so anything's possible. As it pertains to the content, there aren't quite as many racing examples out there as there are FPS examples, but there are still quite a few. In fact, the primary examples included with many game engines are racing and FPS sample projects. We may not want to be disruptive in the game space, but for the purposes of this book, it would be intelligent to be somewhat disruptive in the learning space.

One idea that struck me was to create a *Flight Control* clone and teach people how this newly distinguished genre's mechanics work. This could work for certain. My only immediate concern was the scope of the title; it might not warrant a complete programming guide. Additionally, although we would create the title as a 2D-in-3D game, it's not really 3D. Of course, we could extend the genre a bit to bring it into the 3D space. This idea is certainly valid, but let's see what else we could do.

Last year when I chose to create *Skyline Blade*, there wasn't much in the 3D helicopter sim space. I could tell that it was a hot spot by the success of the only other two titles at the time, so I jumped on it. Most 3D flight simulators on the iPhone do well, and there aren't a slew of them. Also, 3D flight games are popular with the early 20-something crowd, especially if they also offer the ability to blow stuff up. Finally, there really aren't too many examples of 3D flight games. However, the one example I can think of has probably powered more flight games than any other example in the history of examples. Unity itself came with a very simple flight example. There are at least three moderately successful titles already out on the App Store that ripped the code straight from this example and created whole new games around it.

Since you're reading this book, chances are you're going to look at Unity's flight example. It could be redundant for me also to create a flight example. Of course, I have to weigh the possible redundancy against the chances of this app getting noticed. As it stands right now, a 3D flight game stands a greater chance of being noticed than anything that looks remotely two-dimensional. Additionally, I have to admit that although there's a thing or two to learn from the default Unity flight example, those mechanics could be a lot better, and I would have to say that the games that utilized them suffered from the limitations of the example. Perhaps we'll see some better flight simulators on the platform if I take it one step further.

So there it is, my choice for the perfect concept to sell this book is a 3D flying game. To sum up, I made this choice because it's not a disruptive new genre, it's popular with our target audience, it's completely 3D, and I think I can one-up the current Unity example, bringing something new to the table for everyone involved.

The Devil's in the Details

Although we've picked the genre for our perfect concept, we still have a long way to go before our perfect concept is created. Even with the genre of your game in hand, you still need to decide how it will look, how will it play, will it be single player or multiplayer, will it be quite realistic, or will it take a more light-hearted approach? These are questions that a simple genre choice just won't answer.

For this book, we need to target a fairly diverse set of needs. On one hand, we need to make sure our game is edgy enough not to get lost in the shuffle, but on the other hand, it needs to be friendly enough to be viewed as useful to parents who might be purchasing this book for their children or to learn alongside them. In general, when it comes to education, something too violent or edgy is viewed as detrimental. Of course, there are educational studies released almost weekly arguing either that violence in video games is bad or that it actually doesn't matter. Depending on who performs the study, different results occur. For the purpose of this book and the concept I will use to sell it, I want to create something I think hooks a broad range of people from technical families to core gamers who want to know more about their favorite pastime.

So now we've chosen a genre (3D flight sim) and identified that we need a broad reaching theme for it. The resulting game won't be super hardcore, but it won't be a mainstream 2D casual game, either. Furthermore, this game isn't planned to be disruptive in the game space (although it might be considered slightly disruptive in the tech book space), so we'll want to find a pre-existing game to "borrow" our mechanics from. Over the past five years, nothing has expanded the gaming market like Nintendo's Wii, and in general, picking any single one of their first-party titles to base your mechanics on would be a wise if non-disruptive decision. During the summer of 2009, Nintendo released *Wii Sports Resort*, which was one of my favorite titles of the year. If you played this game, then you know that it contained dozens of mechanics, but you probably already know which one I'm thinking of using as a stencil for this book's project. The game mode I enjoyed most and believe would make an intriguing game to play on the iPhone and learn from is *Wii Sports Resort's Aqua Biplane Island Tour*. A concept based on this general premise has merit for players of all ages and backgrounds.

So the concept we'll be bringing to the iPhone is an aqua biplane island touring 3D flight sim. This concept involves cartoon-style flying, shooting, and exploration. Players of all ages and disciplines should be able to enjoy playing it and more than likely will find something to learn from it whether it be targeting, flight mechanics, touch-and-tilt programming, or level design. Finally, this is a non-disruptive concept with a running example already available to us to analyze. Therefore, we can identify its strengths, weaknesses, and features, which may or may not be transferable to the iPhone platform.

iPhone Tailored

At this point, we've identified the genre of our perfect concept, as well as choosing to take a non-disruptive path by basing our game mechanics on a pre-existing title. Now we have a pretty good idea of what this game will entail from an art and programming perspective. The next step involves transforming that perspective to fit the iPhone platform. We need to leverage the unique but tiny touch screen interface, tilt, and always-networked (or almost always) capabilities of the iPhone. Also, we have to consider the digital distribution system of the App Store and the 20MB limit for 3G users. We'll want to create a fun and satisfying flight experience that uses the touch, tilt, and built-in social networking features the iPhone provides and make sure that it has the smallest memory footprint possible. Something to note is that it's impossible to create a Unity executable under 10MB without the Pro version. If you are working with the indie version of Unity, then it is much more challenging to create a game under 20MB. For users really looking to leverage the full potential of the iPhone from both technical and business standpoints, I highly recommend Unity Pro.

The first thing to consider for our perfect concept is the general control scheme. The way in which people control the gameplay is really the principle element of a good game. People will forgo almost all other elements of a game if they can have fun simply controlling the onscreen action. For our 3D flight example, we need to simulate a few elements. First, we need to control the pitch, yaw, and roll of an aircraft. Next, we need to have some control over the throttle, viewpoints, weapons, and additional action features of the aircraft. The iPhone has no hardware buttons so all of this functionality must fit within the confines of the touch screen and accelerometer capabilities of the device.

Obviously, the preferred method to control the pitch, yaw, and roll (or attitude angles) of the aircraft is the accelerometer. This is just a natural control method for aircraft control, and it has been used in countless other titles as well as Nintendo's lighthearted sim. There are a few technical aspects of using the accelerometer on the iPhone. First, there's a question of accuracy. Nintendo's biplane game used the Wii Motion Plus accessory, which included 1:1 tracking via gyroscopes. The iPhone only has an accelerometer, which doesn't provide full 1:1 tracking along all three axes of rotation. We may have to either cut some functionality or find some clever solutions to retain all of the functionality of *Wii Sports Resorts's* flight model. Beyond general accuracy, we will also have to cover the basic concept of calibration. The iPhone's accelerometer can measure acceleration in three dimensions. This could be used for all manner of motion-based gestures, but if the iPhone is just sitting still, then the only acceleration acting on the device is the acceleration of gravity. If you sit an iPhone on a flat surface with its back cover facing down, then the accelerometer will record an acceleration of (0, 0, −1). This indicates that the device is experiencing an acceleration of 1G backwards or in the direction of its backcover. If you look at the device in a portrait orientation, then the X-axis runs horizontal and the Y-axis runs vertical. You can check out the included `accelerometerBasic.js` script to see a readout in Unity's debug log.

Calibrating the accelerometer is a bit tricky and what it involves is allowing the user to hold their device at some other angle and still have the device record an acceleration (at least relative to our game) of (0, 0, −1). In reality, the device is going to always record the true acceleration of gravity on the device if the device is sitting still, but we need to adjust our own internal values to take that acceleration and interpret it to mean something different, depending on what angle the user wants to consider "flat."

Of course, calibration of the accelerometer won't be our only technical challenge while creating a 3D flying game for the iPhone. We'll also have to create code to interpolate between the raw vector the accelerometer is spitting out and the angle we would like our aircraft to be rotated. If we created a flight game where our aircraft were to be aligned directly to the vector recorded by the accelerometer, we'd have a very *herky jerky* experience.

With the basic challenges of accelerometer controls outlined, we move on to the touch screen. The first thing to keep in mind is that the iPhone only provides a few inches of screen real estate. The last thing you want to do is clog the player's view with all manner of virtual buttons. Simultaneously, virtual buttons do make it easier for players to figure your game out. It's important to devise a clever way to communicate the touch screen hotspots to your players and also keep the screen clear of clutter so they can enjoy the 3D world you've worked hard to craft.

Luckily, we've chosen a pretty simple concept for our flight example. The controls are limited to a speed boost, camera changes, cutting the engines, and shooting. These actions could be represented by small onscreen buttons, or the screen could be divided into easily accessible quadrants with minimalist markers in each corner to help players remember which quadrant is associated with which action. In my experience, the onscreen icons are more accessible, although they do restrict the viewport. In general, it's better to create an accessible experience above all else.

Now, we've settled on our genre, a blueprint for our general mechanics, a rough control scheme for our target platform, and we've identified some of the challenges that will be involved with developing this game. With any game project, there will be unforeseen challenges, but obviously the more thought you put into the project before actually developing it, the fewer unforeseen challenges will arise. At this point, we'll begin plotting our perceived course through the development of this title. We'll identify all of our perceived challenges with regard to specific aspects of the game and then create early solutions, which will help us make the most efficient use of our development time. Often, we can make exponential use of our time by aligning certain forces or actions together. We'll see if that's possible on this project.

The path to creating and releasing a game on the App Store will begin with a breakdown of the iPhone's hardware. This will be the first challenge to overcome while developing this game. No game mechanics, art, or sales tool can be implemented unless the hardware allows for it. The hardware is our ground floor, so we'll begin there by identifying every strength and weakness in the foundation we plan to build on top of.

Once the hardware has been dissected, we will be well aware of what sort of art assets we can implement, as well as what sort of game mechanics we can implement. You may have the greatest idea in the world, but if it's too ambitious, then your execution will fail. Knowing the limits of the hardware will help you craft a game that pushes the boundaries without eclipsing them. Creating a well-rounded game that fits the system is what creates the most fun gameplay experiences.

With the hardware dissected, we'll move on to creating concept art for our flight game. The style of the game shouldn't stray too far from our inspiration in this particular case. We will generate cartoon-style art for this project. The art won't be cell shaded but more of a colorful exaggerated reality. With some games, you can use completely abstract art (for example, puzzle games), while other games require very realistic art with stringent proportion, detail, and lighting standards. Our title lands somewhere in the middle, which gives us a bit of leeway but not as much as a more abstract title. We still need to create an airplane, an island, buildings, trees, and perhaps some people with big heads. Since our style is exaggerated, we don't need perfect proportions or lighting, but our game assets need to be identifiable.

Our concept art process will consist of creating some paper sketches, collecting reference material, and finally creating some prototype pieces that can actually be imported into Unity for experimentation. When creating a game, the concept art is often what sparks the rest of the project. Without some good visual concepts, it's hard to get excited about a video game, which, as the name implies, is one part visual.

Once our concept art is complete, we'll move onto game mechanics. The initial stage of the game-programming pipeline is called *prototyping*. During this phase, we'll sketch out some rough ideas with fully functional code and see what best suits the game, the platform, and our artistic vision. During this phase of development, we'll experience a lot of trial and error and run into some algorithmic challenges, but it won't be anything we can't overcome and hopefully, we'll also experience some serendipitous moments where new ideas emerge from our trials. Sure, we've started off with a nicely scoped concept in mind, but it's possible that we'll experience some epiphany along the way, which will, in fact, change the direction of the project and make it something we did not intend from the outset but will indeed be a change for the better. It doesn't always happen, but when it does it's actually a nice feeling.

It may seem that creating concept art and the initial algorithms for our game prototype is a lot of thankless work, but nothing solidifies this feeling like having people play-test your title for the first time. Many times when developing a game, you have a certain view of how the game should flow, and you program it according to that view. Of course, other people have their own views on things. Don't get discouraged when people attempt to change the flow of your stream; instead, use them and their actions as just another tool in the development process. When your programming debugger sends you an error message, do you argue with the compiler? Of course not! The same behavior and thought process should be applied to feedback. If someone doesn't understand a part of your prototype, make note of it as if it were a bug (in many cases it may actually be one) and then revise your concept to fix whatever stumbling block the player experienced. There's a lot to be taken away from the play-testing process, but it's quite possibly the most important part of developing a game. You can have all the great graphics and gee-whiz features in the world, but if people don't understand what's going on, it's all for nothing. Your play-testers are more important than your compiler, and if you start getting discouraged with feedback, just start to think of it as a compiler, which must run with no errors before you release your game.

Once you've got your prototype art assets in the engine, knocked out a few algorithms, and tested them out on some people, it'll be time to start iterating. Every step you've taken so far must be taken again, but in some better fashion. The best games in the world are often developed from the ground-up twice. We won't be taking that extreme route, but we will be looking at our prototype code and assets for cracks or chinks in the armor and identifying ways to fix them. We'll also do another play-testing round with new players to see if we've avoided some of the pitfalls our first trial included. Iteration is a concept many people talk about with regard to game development, but few people really identify the proper way to go about iterating. We're going to cover it in detail for the concept we're creating in this book.

The next challenge you'll face while on your journey to App Store glory will be creating the production art. By this point, you've prototyped your game, tested it, and you know that it's fun. Of course, to create a hit, that's not enough. If you want people to notice your game, you need the production values to go along with the fun. Creating really great production art usually requires a dedicated artist or the purchase of high-quality assets. Some individuals are lucky enough to have fantastic artistic ability and the ability to program. I consider myself be a reasonable artist, but I would never expect anyone to say my artwork is good. At the very least, you need what I would consider sellable production art if you want to create a game all on your own. The iPhone makes it easier because your art only needs to be detailed enough to look good on a three-inch screen.

When dealing with your production art, it's important to remember that the "bells and whistles" are just as important as proportions and color theory when it comes to games. Menus need to animate and chime in reaction to user input. Images must fade and transition smoothly between scenes, and text displays must be interesting to look at, even if they're just telling you how to play the game. These tiny details signal to players the difference between a complete product and something that falls somewhere between conception and completion.

During the production art phase, you will also revise all art assets to optimize their memory footprints and make sure there aren't any jagged edges, Z-order issues, or even collision tolerance problems. At this stage, the code and art must be massaged together to create a harmonious user experience that goes above and beyond the typical game.

After you've got your production art in place and things seem as if they are as optimized and as pretty as they could possibly be, you'll realize they aren't. Many developers say that 90% of the game is in the last 10% of the work. This, to me, is the loose-ends stage. Many times while developing a game, you'll realize that a certain score multiplier isn't balanced, a certain art asset still isn't right, or that some piece of code is causing a crash one in 1,000 times the game is played. When you reach this stage, you'll be dealing with the nitty-gritty aspects of game development, and it's your attention to detail during this late stage of the game that will make players love what you've done.

The final challenge you'll face before your perfect concept launches as a complete game is the packaging. During the packaging stage, you'll have to create the perfect icon, splash screen, game description, and price for your game. It is widely agreed that a game's icon alone can have a huge impact on App Store sales. Typically, you'll have to create many revisions of the icon and game description before you hit the nail on the head. Packaging is really the final stage before actually unleashing your title, and make no mistake, it's just as important as tying up the loose ends or creating a great base concept. If your title isn't packaged right, people won't care about it.

Name That Game

Now that we've logically analyzed what type of concept we should produce and plotted a road map that covers all the points we'll need to connect to get there, we're going to go right back to the top. One of my favorite moments is when I come up with the title of a game. In a way, we've saved one of the best parts of creating the perfect concept for last. By now you probably have a really solid idea of how your game will look, what controls it will use, and what goals the players will complete for fun. However, do you know what you're going to call it?

The name of your title is very important. You can get wildly creative with it, or you can choose a name that perfectly describes the game people will play. For an example, let's jump back to the Wii and the iPhone. Both of these technologies are disruptive, but only in function. By name, the iPhone is a very generic option that tells you exactly what you're getting. The name Wii, on the other hand, is pretty creative, and most people probably don't remember what it means, even after Nintendo held endless press conferences covering it.

On a game-specific level, you might create a game called *Silent Wolf* that is about a spy. That name is fairly creative. You might decide, though, that instead of being creative, you just want to call it *Spy*. One title provokes the imagination, and the other provokes a dictionary definition. Many popular titles on the App Store have unimaginative names. Keeping in mind the mobile nature of the platform, it's sometimes better to be more direct with your title's name because people don't necessarily have much time to go picking and prodding through full game descriptions. A title like *Silent Wolf* could be about a spy, or it could be about a wolf that can't howl. The only way a potential customer will know is by reading your game description, and by that time, you may have lost him if he wants to play a game where he shoots people and he wants to get into it quickly while he's on the Metro coming home from work.

Now let's come full circle to our example game, which is a 3D cartoon-style aqua biplane game that draws inspiration from Nintendo's *Wii Sports Resort*. Obviously *3D Cartoon Aqua Biplane* would be a terrible name. It's good to be direct, but too direct a title loses any sense of fun or soul. Instead, we might go with something like *Tropic Island Tour* or *Air Tour*. Of course, there's a statistic stating that alliterations are quicker to read and remember. Keeping that in mind, we may want to stick with something like *Real Resort*. Obviously, this game will be anything but real, so that alliteration makes zero sense. Also, this title has nothing to do with flight. A good title might then be *Tropical Tailspin*. This gives us an idea of the game's environment and what we'll be doing within it. As a bonus, this title also contains the alliteration that will help people read and remember it more quickly and easily.

Now we've got a fairly catchy title that suits our game, but is it the best title we could possibly muster? To elaborate, there are certain advantages even beyond alliteration or gameplay cues, especially on the App Store. The new release list of the App Store appends new titles daily, and those titles are sorted alphabetically. From a marketing standpoint, it is advantageous to be at the top of that list by using a title that begins with "A" if you can. A good solid name like *Aerial Antics* would probably work quite well. Unfortunately, that name belongs to one of my earlier games already, and I'm not doing a sequel to it right now, so we can't use that one. Other options are wholly possible, though. Perhaps *Aerial Adventure* or *Aerial Acapulco* would work. Of course, there's usually a point at which you have to admit that one title is just better than another even if it's not the most efficient name from a marketing standpoint. Back when I created *Aerial Antics,* I came up with the name because the cockamamie story I came up with was based on an aerial circus. I didn't choose it because it started with "A." I chose it because it just sounded right and suited the story I made up.

After this short brainstorming session, I think we have to admit to ourselves that *Tropical Tailspin* is a pretty cool name. It might not begin with "A," but that's OK! This name contains alliteration, it's fairly direct, and yet simultaneously there's a nice creative ring to it.

Creating a name for your game can be quite a challenge. I've seen people spend months trying to craft the perfect name. It's not uncommon to see people posting screenshots and descriptions of their titles on forums asking people what they should call it. I don't recall ever having this problem, but it does happen. My advice is to create your name before your game. To me, the initial concept of a game is like a direction vector in physics. The name of your game is like the notation of that vector—it organizes it into something comprehensible. When I think or read the title *Tropical Tailspin*, I can see the whole game appear within my mind. The title is a jumping-off point that leads all the way to a finished product. Whenever you look at or speak the name of your game, it should instantly invoke memories of the finished product in your mind.

Conclusion

Now I think we've finally covered all the bases behind the conception of a concept. As it stands now, you have a rough mental outline of the game you're creating. With this outline set, it is time to begin crafting some tangible assets, beginning with concept art. We'll now begin walking the long road toward a finished game in the App Store. Good luck!

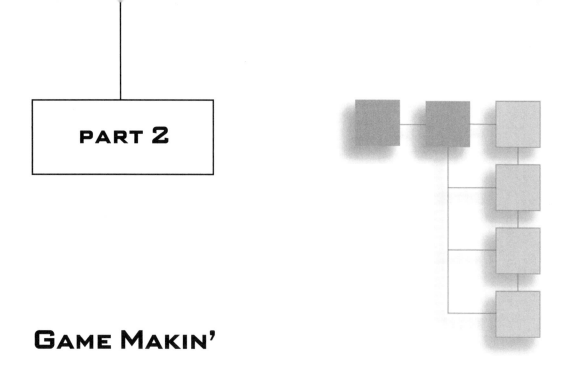

PART 2

GAME MAKIN'

Making a game is a long, complex process. There's no sure-fire way to create a hit, but there are certain steps you can take to have the best shot possible. In this part of the book, we'll cover all the techniques you need to have a shot at making the next big hit. We'll begin with the basic algorithms necessary to take advantage of the iPhone hardware, including accelerometer control and calibration, as well as touch, multi-touch, and gestures. Next, we'll cover the creation of concept art from the collection of reference materials to creating mock-ups with your favorite 2D image editor to creating basic 3D scenes to demonstrate gameplay concepts. The remainder of this section will cover prototyping, play-testing, iterating, production art, tying up loose ends, and finally packaging your title for sale on the App Store.

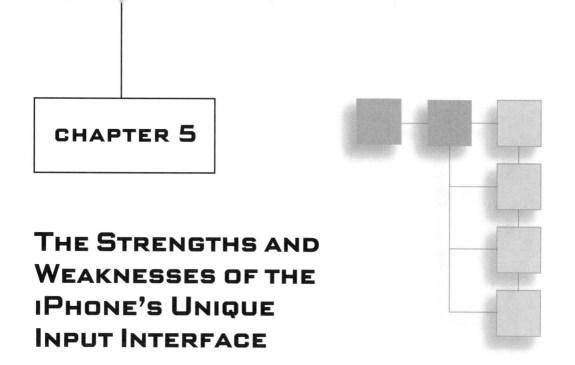

CHAPTER 5

THE STRENGTHS AND WEAKNESSES OF THE iPHONE'S UNIQUE INPUT INTERFACE

The iPhone hardware is different from all other gaming platforms that predate it. To make solid games for the platform, you need to understand the device's unique strengths, as well as its weaknesses. Only then will you be able to fully capitalize on the platform and deliver a great game. Since creating a game is a process that builds upon layers of knowledge, it's hugely important to get the foundation correct. The very foundation of any good game is the user interface. The iPhone hardware has a very unique interface that players will interact with, primarily through touch and secondarily through tilt via the accelerometer. This chapter will describe the best algorithms and design principles to use when designing your game.

Out with the Old, Input with the New

Before we dig into some actual iPhone input code samples, let's discuss some of the differences between a new disruptive interface like the iPhone's and some of the previous portable gaming systems to figure out what makes the iPhone more or less effective as a game machine.

When the iPhone first arrived on the gaming scene, it was scorned for having imprecise touch input. The iPhone's accelerometer tilt-based input wasn't considered much better unless it was used to simulate a steering wheel or for rolling a marble. Even today, many people refuse to play games on an iPhone because the lack of hardware buttons can create a disjointed gameplay experience, which requires players to always look at their fingers in relation to the screen.

Prior to the iPhone's existence, the mobile games market was dominated by Sony and even more so by Nintendo. Sony's PSP was the first mobile gaming device to offer living room–quality experiences that could fit in your pocket. Meanwhile, Nintendo's DS (and all of its subsequent updates) had another goal: to create innovative gameplay experiences that only a portable could provide using two screens, touch screen technology, and a microphone. At the time of those consoles' release it was widely believed that Sony would finally trump Nintendo in the handheld space.

History has since told a different story. As we know today, mobile players don't necessarily want to bring their living rooms with them wherever they go. In fact, the DS proved that people were more interested in shorter, simpler games while on the go. The DS also proved that people weren't afraid to try new input methods like touch screen games, although in the DS system's case many people were thankful that regular old input methods like the D-pad and standard face buttons were also included.

Enter the iPhone. This new revolutionary device brings the sleek style and media capabilities of the PSP with it, along with the cool new input methods that the DS pioneered. The big problem, of course, is that it lost all the hardware buttons that DS players know and love. The first iPhone games were, by traditional gaming standards, pathetic. It wasn't until six months after the App Store launched that the first few decent iPhone games began appearing. Titles like *Rolando* and *Hero of Sparta* really upped the ante and gave people a glimpse of what might be possible on the iPhone.

All was not well, though. Player reaction to even the best iPhone games of late 2008 was still mediocre, citing the PSP and DS as "real" gaming systems. Over the course of 2009, developers worked hard, pushing the envelope until finally, somewhere between *Modern Combat* and *Grand Theft Auto: Chinatown Wars,* the tide started to turn.

I mention those two games for two very specific reasons. *Modern Combat* was the first iPhone FPS with great controls. *Grand Theft Auto: Chinatown Wars* also has to be mentioned because it was ported over to the iPhone after getting slaughtered at retail on both the DS and PSP. The iPhone port managed to maintain the game's playability even without hardware buttons, and it held the top-grossing sales position for a long time. Many of the reviews for *Chinatown Wars* cite it as the superior version of the game because the iPhone manages to take the best of the DS and PSP and consolidate it into one console.

Currently, the input considerations of the iPhone are of minimal concern. While it is clear that the lack of hardware buttons impedes gameplay to a degree, it is also clear that good game design can overcome this shortcoming. When designing an iPhone game, it's important to take cues from games like *Real Racing* and remove or invert the need to hold a finger down to cause a recurring action. It's just as important to lay out a game's HUD or GUI properly so that the game view isn't obstructed.

As an example, let's compare ngmoco's *Eliminate Pro* to Gameloft's *Modern Combat*. *Eliminate* doesn't have any onscreen GUI objects, maximizing the screen real estate for the player's view. Of course, *Modern Combat* doesn't require the player's fingers to be near the center of the screen ever. *Eliminate's* HUD does require the player's fingers to sometimes occlude the center of the screen but on the upside it doesn't display many GUI objects, so typically it's only your fingers getting in the way of the action. *Modern Combat's* input tracking keeps the player's fingers farther from the center of the screen but leaves the screen quite cluttered with GUI objects. The goal of any good iPhone input system should be to increase the player's field of view while also making it clear as to what the screen's hotspots are. Furthermore, players should not have to look at their fingers to figure out where they need to move them.

Unity Remote

Now that you have a general understanding of the iPhone's input interface, it's time to begin using it. Before we begin analyzing and interacting with the iPhone's unique input system, we need to get a handle on Unity Remote. This program is a necessary companion for the Unity iPhone development environment. What Unity Remote does is allow you to control your Unity game view as if it were an iPhone itself. Traditional iPhone development uses the iPhone Simulator, which is useful for testing basic compatibility but doesn't support tilt-based interactions; actually, it's completely useless for our purposes because it doesn't work with Unity-based apps. For these reasons, Unity Technologies created Unity Remote to allow developers to debug their apps without even having to launch Xcode.

After installing Unity iPhone, you can navigate to the folder where it was installed, and you'll find another folder titled Unity Remote. This folder contains an Xcode project, which you can build and deploy to your iPhone or iPod Touch. After successfully building and installing the program on your development device, you can boot it up and as long as your device is on the same Wi-Fi network as the development machine running Unity iPhone, you should see it pop up (see Figure 5.1). If you're running more than one computer with Unity, you'll be able to select which computer you want to connect to. The basic

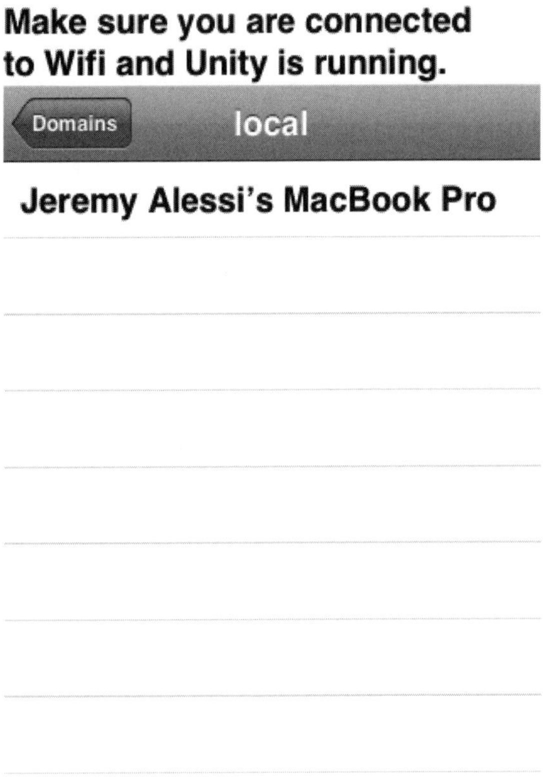

Make sure you are connected to Wifi and Unity is running.

◀ Domains   local

Jeremy Alessi's MacBook Pro

Figure 5.1
Unity Remote screen.

premise of Unity Remote is to connect over Wi-Fi in order to control your game when you press the Play button in Unity.

Touch and Tilt Input

The first interaction any user has with an iPhone is the large round button with the rounded square image on it at the bottom of the device when held in portrait mode. That's where the traditional electronics interaction pretty much ends. After you press the iPhone's only face button, the screen lights up, and you are then prompted with a slider widget hooked to the message Slide to Unlock. This is where the iPhone's dominant input interaction begins.

Apple invested heavily in great touch technology while developing the iPhone. In fact, they invested so heavily in the touch mentality that they appended the word "Touch" onto the title of their previous flagship portable device, the iPod. Besides the obvious marketing hype, there's a lot beneath the surface from an engineering standpoint. The iPhone's touch technology is worlds better than anything else on the market. The touch screen included on the iPhone and iPod Touch doesn't simply recognize crude touches and swipes. Instead, it features five-finger multi-touch support, high-speed delta tracking, and an array of gesture recognition capabilities to tell when touches begin and end. Unity interacts with the iPhone's input systems via the `iPhoneInput` class. This class gives us access to both accelerometer and multi-touch functionality. If you are a beginner, then a quick explanation of what a class is may be in order.

Classes are collections of functions and variables, which form a greater data structure. Typically, we refer to this concept as object-oriented programming. Once classes are created, they can be instanced so that you have multiple copies of a class that hold different data values. For instance, you might have a car class, which can then be used to create a race car, a sedan, or both simultaneously with the same basic data structure. Unity consists of a large collection of classes, which lets us control our game's environment. With that in mind, let's have a look at the class that lets us manage an iPhone user's input.

iPhoneInput Class

This class has the following variables:

> **accelerationEvents**: This read-only variable returns a list of acceleration measurements that occurred during the previous frame.

touches: This read-only variable yields a list of objects representing the status of all touches that occurred during the last frame.

touchCount: Another read-only variable that returns the number of fingers touching the screen.

multiTouchEnabled: This flag variable tells us whether the system handles multi-touch support.

accelerationEventCount: This tells us how many acceleration measurements took place last frame.

acceleration: This read-only variable reports the last measured linear acceleration in 3D space.

orientation: A read-only variable that reports the current device orientation.

lastLocation: This reports the geographical location last recorded by the device.

The class has these functions:

GetTouch: This function returns a touch object with information about the status of a specific touch. You would use this as GetTouch(0) to get information about one finger touching the screen, or you would use GetTouch(0) through GetTouch(4) to get information about all fingers touching the screen if the touchCount is equal to 5.

GetAccelerationEvent: This function returns a specific acceleration measurement that occurred during the previous frame.

As you can see, there's quite a bit to cover with regard to the iPhone's very specific input system. Overall, the system is very good and with an innovative thought process you can achieve great results even without hardware buttons.

iPhone Input Code Samples

Now let's look at some simple touch code.

```
function OnGUI()
{
    for ( i = 0; i < iPhoneInput.touchCount; i++ )
```

```
    {
        var tPos = iPhoneInput.GetTouch( i ).position;
        var x = tPos.x;
        var y = tPos.y;

        GUI.Label( Rect( x, 320 - y, 300, 20 ), ''Touch#'' + ( i + 1 ) + '' Position ''
        + tPos );
    }
}
```

This code is from the `touchReading.js` script component included in the iPhone 3D Game Programming All in One Unity project on the CD-ROM. This simple component loops from 0 to the number of touches reported by `iPhoneInput.touchCount` and then prints the touch number and the touch's position onscreen.

Beyond simply touching the screen, there are other deeper touch interactions that can be tracked to enhance the interface to your game. Anyone who has used an iPhone knows that touches can be associated not only with positions onscreen but also with velocities and the illusion of momentum being integrated with the general iPhone UI. Even beyond this sort of flicking behavior, the iPhone presents users with the ability to zoom in and out as well as rotate the view and more. All of these functions are extensions on the basic gesture system created by Apple to interface with the touch screen. Not only can the iPhone touch screen track the contact points of five fingers, but it can also track how fast those fingers move across the screen, when a new finger touches the screen, and when a finger leaves the screen. By working with these basic features, we can determine if a user is pinching or stretching with two fingers or perhaps rotating two fingers in a circle. We'll get into a whole series of touch gestures, but first let's cover the basic touch tracking in more detail from our example.

```
private var highSpeed : Vector2;
function OnGUI()
{
    for ( i = 0; i < iPhoneInput.touchCount; i++ )
    {
        var tPos = iPhoneInput.GetTouch( i ).position;
        var x = tPos.x;
        var y = tPos.y;
```

```
    var tSpeed = iPhoneInput.GetTouch( i ).deltaPosition;

    if ( tSpeed.magnitude > highSpeed.magnitude )
      highSpeed = tSpeed;

    GUI.Label( Rect( x, 320 - y, 300, 20 ), ''Touch#'' + ( i + 1 ) + '' Position''
    + tPos );
  }

  GUI.Label( Rect( 0, 0, 200, 20 ), ''Fastest Finger Moved '' + highSpeed.
  magnitude + '' pixels per frame!'' );
}
```

This code from `touchReading2.js` is very similar to the first example, but it contains a private variable called `highSpeed`. This `highSpeed` variable is a Vector2, which is essentially just a variable for storing X, Y coordinates or, in this case, the difference of coordinates between frames. The result of this code is a little game in which you can test the speed of your fingers. The fastest recorded movement will be printed in the upper-left corner of the screen as the number of pixels per frame your finger traveled. This is all very interesting, but now let's have a look at some specific gestures, beginning with `touchPinchStretch.js`, which shows us how to implement a two-finger zoom.

```
private var touchDifference : float;
function OnGUI()
{
  if ( iPhoneInput.touchCount == 2 )
  {
    var touch1 = iPhoneInput.GetTouch( 0 );
    var touch2 = iPhoneInput.GetTouch( 1 );

    var tempTouchDifference = ( touch1.position - touch2.position ).
    magnitude;

    Camera.main.transform.position.z += ( tempTouchDifference -
    touchDifference ) / 100;

    touchDifference = tempTouchDifference;

    for ( i = 0; i < 2; i++ )
```

```
   {
       var x = iPhoneInput.GetTouch( i ).position.x;
       var y = iPhoneInput.GetTouch( i ).position.y;
       GUI.Label( Rect( x, 320 - y, 300, 20 ), ''Touch# '' + ( i + 1 ) );
   }


   }
}
```

This code snippet is from `touchPinchStretch.js`, and what it does is track the relative distance between two touches. Then it moves the main camera along its Z-axis (the in/out axis) according to the relative distance between the two finger contact points from one frame to the next. I placed this code in the `OnGUI()` callback to keep things simple and to display text onscreen where the touches actually occur. Typically, you'll want to place any camera movement code inside the `LateUpdate()` callback to remove any tweening jitters that may occur.

The zoom functionality is one of the most interesting and important gestures for use with the iPhone's touch interface. Of course, the iPhone wouldn't be what it is without its momentum-tracking interface. We hit on this feature with the `touchReading2.js` code snippet above, but we didn't actually apply the speed of the touches to the visuals of the application. Let's have a look at that now.

```
var cameraVelocity : Vector3;
function LateUpdate()
{
   if ( iPhoneInput.touchCount == 1 )
   {
       var touch = iPhoneInput.GetTouch( 0 );
       cameraVelocity.x += touch.deltaPosition.x;
       cameraVelocity.y += touch.deltaPosition.y;
   }
   Camera.main.transform.position += cameraVelocity * Time.deltaTime
   * 0.1;
}
```

This code is a bit cleaner than what we showcased earlier and more appropriate for what you might use in an actual application. The first thing to note is the private variable `cameraVelocity`, which is a Vector3. This is how fast our camera will move in 3D space. For the purpose of this particular code snippet, we modify only the X and Y components of the camera's velocity, but we could just as easily take things into the third dimension by modifying the Z component.

The next interesting thing about this snippet is that we've switched from placing our code in the OnGUI() callback to the LateUpdate() callback. As we discussed previously, proper camera displacement code should be kept inside the LateUpdate() callback at all times to avoid screen jitters. Inside the LateUpdate() callback, we have a conditional that checks to see if iPhoneInput.touchCount is equal to 1. This is indicative of the single finger swipe any iPhone user has grown accustomed to when browsing the Web with Safari, for instance. Inside the conditional, we register the single finger contact by assigning iPhoneInput.GetTouch(0) to the variable touch. The next thing we do is add the X and Y components of touch.deltaPosition to their counterpart components inside cameraVelocity. Note that we cannot simply assign touch.deltaPosition to cameraVelocity because touch.deltaPosition is a Vector2 and cameraVelocity is a Vector3. It's fine to handpick and set the individual components, but there would be a dangling component missing if we tried to assign a Vector3 to the value of a Vector2. Last, but not least, we place the line that actually moves the camera outside of the conditional to make sure we're touching the screen with only one finger. This line simply adds cameraVelocity to the camera's transform position.

You will notice that we multiply the cameraVelocity by Time.deltaTime and then again by 0.1. The first operation by Time.deltaTime is to make sure the movement of the camera is based on the passage of time and not the framerate or processing power of the device. Without this multiplication, the camera would move faster on an iPod Touch 2G than an iPhone 3G, for instance. The second multiplication operation is really just to slow things down. Multiplying by 0.1 allows us to see the reaction to our finger swipes in this scene, which consists of only a camera and a cube. Try changing 0.1 to another number to see what effect this operation has on our finger swipes.

With the touch gestures we've covered thus far, we could create a pretty cool touch interface and even some pretty neat gameplay, but we're not done yet. The next operation we're going to look at is a rotation effect much like Google Earth and the game *Star Defense* (see Figures 5.2 and 5.3) use to allow for different vantage points around planetary geometry.

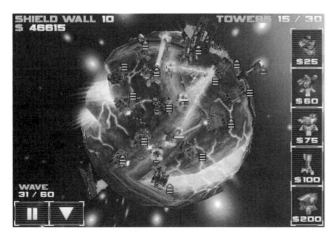

Figure 5.2
Star Defense screen.

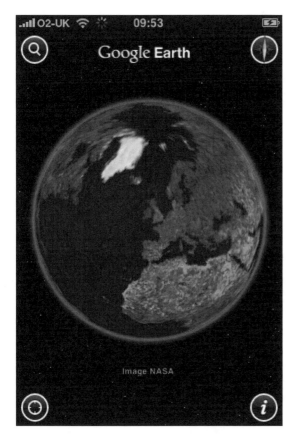

Figure 5.3
Google Earth screen.

```
function LateUpdate ()
{
  if ( iPhoneInput.touchCount == 2 )
  {
    var touch1 = iPhoneInput.GetTouch ( 0 );
    var touch2 = iPhoneInput.GetTouch ( 1 );

    var pos1 = touch1.position;
    var pos2 = touch2.position;

    var angleBetweenTouches = Mathf.Atan2 ( pos1.x - pos2.x, pos1.y - pos2.
    y ) * Mathf.Rad2Deg;

    Camera.main.transform.localEulerAngles.z = angleBetweenTouches;
  }
}
function OnGUI ()
{
  if ( iPhoneInput.touchCount == 2 )
  {
    for ( i = 0; i < 2; i++ )
    {
      var x = iPhoneInput.GetTouch ( i ).position.x;
      var y = iPhoneInput.GetTouch ( i ).position.y;
      GUI.Label ( Rect ( x, 320 - y, 300, 20 ), ''Touch# '' + ( i + 1 ) );
    }
  }
}
```

With this rotation code (contained in touchRotation.js), things are really beginning to get interesting! First of all, we have now started maturing our code snippets to account for the various callbacks employed by Unity to keep things robust. In this sample, our camera transform code is kept inside the LateUpdate() callback, and our print-to-screen GUI labels are kept inside the OnGUI() callback. The next thing to focus on is that this code is quite similar to the zoom code contained in touchPinchStretch.js. The major difference is the line where we assign angleBetweenTouches. This line uses two of the math library's finest capabilities to first acquire an angle between two points in two-dimensional space via the Mathf.Atan2() function. The code then multiplies this value by the constant Mathf.Rad2Deg, so we can get an angle in degrees, which is useful for setting the `localEulerAngles.z` component of the camera's transform.

With the addition of the rotation gesture, we have a handy grab bag of iPhone touch tricks, which we can use to create compelling interactions with the device. As crazy as it may sound, there's so much more we can do. Initially, many people believed the iPhone's lack of hardware buttons was a huge limitation. As we run through these various touch gestures, I think it becomes apparent that with a little imagination, the iPhone's touch screen goes a long way.

Earlier in the book, I mentioned *Flight Control* as a prime example of a disruptive game that really capitalized on the iPhone's unique capabilities. *Flight Control* relied solely on the ability of the iPhone's touch screen to track a finger's contact point over a period of time to create a line or path for tiny 2D virtual aircraft to follow. This sort of gameplay mechanic is a little more complex than any of the gestures we've covered thus far, but by utilizing the beginning, movement, and end of a touch, we can create something very similar with Unity. Let's have a look.

```
private var pointA : Vector2;
private var pointB : Vector2;
private var pointA3D : Vector3;
private var pointB3D : Vector3;
private var line : GameObject;
private var lineRenderer : LineRenderer;
function Update()
{
  if ( iPhoneInput.touchCount == 1 )
  {
    var touch = iPhoneInput.GetTouch( 0 );

    switch( touch.phase )
    {
    case iPhoneTouchPhase.Began:
      pointA = touch.position;
      pointA3D = Camera.main.ScreenToWorldPoint( Vector3( pointA.x,
      pointA.y, Camera.main.nearClipPlane ) );
      break;

    case iPhoneTouchPhase.Moved:
      pointB = touch.position;
```

```
        pointB3D = Camera.main.ScreenToWorldPoint ( Vector3 ( pointB.x,
        pointB.y, Camera.main.nearClipPlane ) );
        break;

     case iPhoneTouchPhase.Ended:
       line = new GameObject ( ''line'' );
       lineRenderer = line.AddComponent ( LineRenderer );
       lineRenderer.SetWidth ( 0.005, 0.005 );
       lineRenderer.SetVertexCount ( 2 );
       lineRenderer.SetPosition ( 0, pointA3D );
       lineRenderer.SetPosition ( 1, pointB3D );
       break;
     }
   }
}
function OnGUI ()
{
  GUI.Label ( Rect ( pointA.x, 320 - pointA.y, 300, 20 ), ''A'' );
  GUI.Label ( Rect ( pointB.x, 320 - pointB.y, 300, 20 ), ''B'' );
}
```

What we have in this code snippet (`touchLineDrawing.js`) is a very simple line-drawing application that uses the iPhone touch screen and the phases of a touch. This code begins with the declaration of six private variables:

- `pointA`

- `pointB`

- `pointA3D, pointB3D`

- `line`

- `lineRenderer1`

The first two variables represent the point of contact that a single finger has with the touch screen in two-dimensional screen space. The next two variables represent these first two points after being transformed into 3D camera space. This is a necessity because Unity does not offer any native 2D graphing functions. Finally, we have the `line` and `lineRenderer` variables. `line` is a simple game object that then plays host to the `lineRenderer` component, which ultimately allows us to draw lines onscreen. Unity uses the `lineRenderer` component to draw lines in 3D space. For our purposes, we want to draw simple 2D lines, so we simply replace the Z component of the Vector3 instantiation call inside `Camera.main.ScreenToWorldPoint()` with `Camera.main.nearClipPlane`, which essentially constrains the simulation to 2D screen space. One thing to note about this code is that we use the `Update()` and `OnGUI()` callbacks because we aren't moving the camera at all. We don't need `LateUpdate()`, but we still need `OnGUI()` to render the A and B onscreen while our contact finger is moving.

Of course, the most important aspect of this code snippet is the use of the `iPhoneTouchPhase` enumeration class. We use a `switch` statement inside the `Update()` callback, which asks which part of the touch we are at now. If the touch has just begun, then let's lay down `pointA` and its 3D counterpart, `pointA3D`. If the touch has moved, then let's update `pointB` and its 3D counterpart, `pointB3D`. Finally, if the touch has lost contact, let's create a new line game object, attach a `lineRenderer` to it, and set the properties, which allow it to be properly rendered onscreen.

In this example, we used only the `Began`, `Moved`, and `Ended` flags. While these are arguably the most important touch phases, it should be noted that Unity also supports the `Stationary` and `Canceled` phases of an iPhone touch screen. The `Stationary` flag is pretty self-explanatory. The `Canceled` flag can happen for numerous reasons, including when a user puts the device up to his face or when a user touches the screen with more than five fingers simultaneously.

The Accelerometer

The accelerometer is one of the most controversial input methods on any platform. The Nintendo Wii was hugely successful and created new experiences based on the use of accelerometer technology. Many would also say that the accelerometer is a gimmick that only allows for rampant spurts of wrist flicking and isn't useful for any meaningful gameplay experiences. The application of accelerometer use on the iPhone is quite different from the Wii because you don't need to keep your eyes focused on the Wiimote while waving it around. The iPhone has hosted a great many racing and flight games very well because subtle movements involving the accelerometer are actually quite rewarding. The recent racing title from True Axis, *Jet Car Stunts* (see Figure 5.4), features some of the most fluid accelerometer controls on the market, and it clearly would not be as enjoyable without them.

Figure 5.4
Jet Car Stunts screen.

As you might notice, not all games feature great accelerometer controls. To make the best use of the accelerometer, you need to use interpolation to smooth out the readings being spit out by the hardware in order to create fluid gameplay. In addition, you need to include a solid calibration option so that the user can hold his/her device at any angle and still enjoy accelerometer-driven gameplay.

For our first example involving the accelerometer, we're going to simply spit out the raw vector reported by the device. This code snippet is contained in `accelerometerReading.js`.

```
function OnGUI()
{
   GUI.Label( Rect( 0, 0, 480, 20 ), '''' + iPhoneInput.acceleration );
}
```

This is a very simple code component that uses only the `OnGUI()` callback to print the value of `iPhoneInput.acceleration` to the screen. You may notice the double quotations and the addition operator. This is a simple way to cast `iPhoneInput.acceleration` (a Vector3) to a string useful for being displayed onscreen.

As you move your iPhone or iPod Touch around, you'll see how the acceleration vector changes according to which side or face of the device is facing the ground. The premise most titles use for accelerometer-driven gameplay is to compare the direction of gravity to the rotation of the device. What you'll notice by running

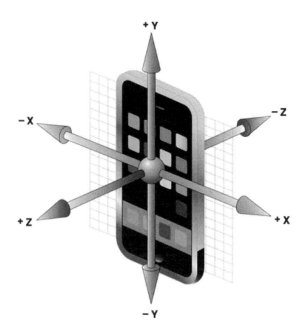

Figure 5.5
iPhone accelerometer axes.

this example is that the device's X-axis runs side-to-side, the Y-axis runs top-to-bottom, and the Z-axis runs front-to-back. These axes apply if you're holding the device straight up in portrait view, with the Home button at the bottom and the screen Off button at the top (see Figure 5.5).

For our next example, we'll build some visual elements onscreen to represent the accelerometer values. If you've seen any of the 1,001-level apps on the App Store, you'll know what to expect. This example won't be a fully featured bubble level, but it will form the basis for such an application.

```
function OnGUI()
{
  GUI.HorizontalSlider(Rect(0, 0, 480, 20), iPhoneInput.acceleration.y,
    -0.5, 0.5);
  GUI.VerticalSlider (Rect(0, 0, 20, 320), iPhoneInput.acceleration.x,
    -0.5, 0.5);
}
```

This code is very similar to our first example. The only difference is that we've replaced the text representation of the Vector3 reported by `iPhoneInput.acceleration` with two sliders representing the X and Y components of the `iPhoneInput.acceleration` vector.

As you will notice by running the app using Unity Remote, the slider widget jumps around quite a bit. If we applied the raw vector as reported by the accelerometer to a game object like an aircraft or a race car, you would see the same sort of jerky movement. This is where interpolation comes in. You will also notice that perhaps one of the sliders isn't centered, even when the device appears to be on a flat surface. This is one use for calibration. Each iPhone and iPod Touch will report slightly different values from the accelerometer. It's up to the user to place the device on a surface they know is flat and calibrate the device when using it for a bubble level–type application. Of course, for gaming purposes we just want users to be able to hold the device in a comfortable position. Now let's have a look at what such an algorithm entails.

```
private var myPitch : float;
private var myYaw : float;
private var offsetPitch : float;
private var offsetYaw : float;
private var calibrationZ : float;
private var graphPitch : float;
private var graphYaw : float;
function OnGUI()
{
  GUI.HorizontalSlider( Rect( 0, 0, 480, 20 ), graphYaw, -0.5, 0.5 );
  GUI.VerticalSlider ( Rect( 0, 0, 20, 320 ), graphPitch, -0.5, 0.5 );

  if ( GUI.Button( Rect( 190, 150, 100, 40 ), ''Calibrate'' ) )
    setCalibration();
}
function Update()
{
  var accel : Vector3 = iPhoneInput.acceleration;

  if ( calibrationZ > 0 )
  {
    myPitch = -Mathf.Atan2( accel.x, accel.z ) * Mathf.Rad2Deg;
    myYaw = -Mathf.Atan2( accel.y, accel.z ) * Mathf.Rad2Deg;
  }
  else
```

```
  {
    myPitch = Mathf.Atan2 ( accel.x, -accel.z ) * Mathf.Rad2Deg;
    myYaw = Mathf.Atan2 ( accel.y, -accel.z ) * Mathf.Rad2Deg;
  }
  graphPitch = ( wrapAngle ( offsetPitch ) - wrapAngle ( myPitch ) ) / 360;
  graphYaw = ( wrapAngle ( offsetYaw ) - wrapAngle ( myYaw ) ) / 360;

}
function setCalibration ()
{
  var accel : Vector3 = iPhoneInput.acceleration;
  calibrationZ = accel.z;

  if ( calibrationZ > 0 )
  {
    offsetPitch = -Mathf.Atan2 ( accel.x, accel.z ) * Mathf.Rad2Deg;
    offsetYaw = -Mathf.Atan2 ( accel.y, accel.z ) * Mathf.Rad2Deg;
  }
  else
  {
    offsetPitch = Mathf.Atan2 ( accel.x, -accel.z ) * Mathf.Rad2Deg;
    offsetYaw = Mathf.Atan2 ( accel.y, -accel.z ) * Mathf.Rad2Deg;
  }
}
function wrapAngle ( angleToWrap : float )
{
  return 180 - angleToWrap;
}
```

This is by far the most complex piece of code we've looked at so far. We're using the two callbacks OnGUI() and Update(), which we are so familiar with, but we've also extended beyond callbacks with a couple of custom functions: setCalibration() and wrapAngle(). The setCalibration() function is where a lot of the action happens; what it boils down to is setting the offset angles for our X and Y axes. wrapAngle() is a utility function that returns the angle we pass to it subtracted from 180. This function allows us to extract 180 degrees of magnitude out of the acceleration vector's components. Heading back to the callbacks, OnGUI() stays pretty much the same except that we're using two special variables, graphPitch and graphYaw, which have been adjusted for the fact that we're working with degrees and not just vector components between −1 and 1. The Update() callback is what produces our graph values; it does so by checking calibrationZ to see if the device is facing up or down. The calibrationZ variable is set inside setCalibration. The point of this is that we need to know whether or not the device was facing up or down when we calibrated it. If we don't account for this factor, then we can extract only 180 degrees from either the X- or Y-axis. Essentially, the way we extract 360 degrees is to use 180 degrees on both sides of the Z-axis.

Quite a few of the early iPhone titles shipped without a calibration option. This led to an early distaste for accelerometer-based games because you had to sit straight up, and usually you had to tilt the device in such a way that you could no longer see the screen. Developers were pretty quick to begin adding calibration measures to their apps, but even today you'll find the occasional title that doesn't include calibration or includes calibration that doesn't work particularly well (for example, by not accounting for a full 360 degrees of rotation). By reading and comprehending this last code snippet, you've just gained a huge advantage over many other iPhone 3D game programmers.

Conclusion

That about does it for the iPhone's unique input considerations. I think it's obvious that the iPhone possesses a very powerful input interface. In the right hands, I'd wager that the iPhone is a more deadly input weapon than any console with typical hardware buttons. As with most game development conundrums, it's the organization of events that constitutes a fulfilling experience, and the iPhone's input solution is no different. If you approach development on the iPhone with an open mind and an active imagination, there's no limit to the type of gameplay experiences you can create.

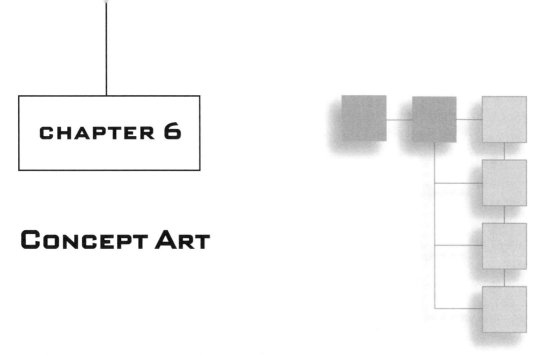

CHAPTER 6

CONCEPT ART

You've come a long way in the quest for iPhone game development greatness. It might seem crazy that we're just now diving into the creative aspects of development, but in reality that's the way it works. Before developing a great game, you need to arm yourself to the teeth with knowledge and insight into the technology, tools, and your target market. We've done quite a bit of that, so now it's time to begin visualizing your game concretely.

Concept art is important for both motivation and logical planning. Sometimes, an idea simply cannot be fleshed out properly without a piece of concept art to support it. In this chapter, we'll be drawing by hand and working with digital tools to create concept art. My primary 2D image tool of choice is an old version of Photoshop (version 5.5), but most of the functionality covered in this book will transfer over to GIMP, PaintShop Pro, or other 2D image editors. Now let's begin creating some concept art to support *Tropical Tailspin.*

Research in Theory

One of the first steps to take when creating concept art is to research prior source material. Years ago, this could be a fairly arduous task. Today, this involves nothing more than a Google image search. At worst, you may have to search more than once before finding the imagery to inspire you.

Something to keep in mind when doing research for your concept art is whether you're researching objects or locales. When searching for objects, it's great to find clip art, schematics, and general photos, which can help you build your own version of whatever it is you are researching. If you are searching for locales, then an image search may not be enough.

I have found Google Earth to be an invaluable tool when doing real-world locale research. A few years ago I was building a re-creation of Liberty Island, where the Statue of Liberty resides in New York. Obviously, image searches were useful for colors and the general feel of the environment, but there were some aspects of the island that couldn't be found in images. The dimensions are one such aspect. Using a combination of Google Earth and Wikipedia actually yielded all the dimensions I needed to model the island and the base the statue rests upon accurately. Wikipedia and Google Earth complement each other quite well in this regard because many of the architectural details about the statue's dimensions are provided, but not every detail is included. For example, the length of the star-shaped points comprising the base was nowhere to be found. Such horizontal data is easily deciphered by using Google Earth.

I remember as a child reading about game developers traveling to real-world locales to research the environments to be re-created in the game space and thinking that must have been among the best parts of the job. These days that's still a practice many developers adhere to, but if you're developing something based on a real-world locale on a budget, Google Image Search, Google Earth, and Wikipedia are your friends, thanks to all those who have traveled the world before us. Still, if you have the means, I recommend actually visiting the sites you're modeling.

If you're not modeling real-world objects or locales, it's still very useful to search for ideas, even if you're creating something completely imaginary. After all, any idea is just the combination of two or more previous concepts being merged.

Something else to keep in mind is that many artists are trained in the creation of 3D as well as 2D artwork, both of which they'll happily post to the Internet. Searching for images and dimensions can help you create your own 3D models to a T, but there's a possibility that someone has already created exactly what you're looking for or something that you can at least examine in full 3D to help conceive your game better. TurboSquid is invaluable for this purpose. Through the TurboSquid Web site, you can find thousands of art resources right at your fingertips. Many of them need a lot of work to be useful in a real-time game, but for concept art, they can really speed up the process.

Up to this point, we've covered the very simple, although incredibly useful, avenues that can help you create concept art necessary to create an entire game. Use all of these resources, but keep in mind that you must create most of the content your game will contain for it to be really original. Some of what you might find online will be royalty free and useable in your final game, but keep in mind that your game is only as original as the resources used to power it. Use prebuilt resources when absolutely necessary, but try to bring your own creative flare into the mix. Nothing's worse than seeing a game thrown together that is composed entirely of prebuilt code and art resources. This happened with several Unity games early in the iPhone development craze. Several developers ripped the art and code directly out of the Unity samples and sold them off as their own. While this may have been perfectly legal, it doesn't bode too well for a developer's reputation to compose a game entirely of off-the-shelf resources. Such a game is more of a mod than an original piece of work.

Owning Your Creative Vision

The next step when creating concept art is to pull out your favorite doodling tool (anything from a pencil and paper to a full-blown modeling app is fine) and begin tinkering to create new content based on a combination of your research and your original game concept. This is where you merge your own thoughts and experiences with newly acquired knowledge collected via the research stage. You may think you can just pop great content out of thin air, but in truth there will be small details that you never would have accounted for without doing your homework. It's imperative that you adjust your vision for these details as early in the content creation process as possible. Some details could actually have long-reaching effects that extend far beyond simple aesthetics and actually bend the rules of your gameplay.

At this point, you may not be too familiar with the various content-creation tools available for your computer. This is fine, and even if you are, sometimes there's nothing better than a scribble pad and a pencil. Even the most advanced digital artists use the good old tools every now and then. You may even find that using traditional methods in conjunction with a digital pipeline yields a more accurate perspective from which to tackle the creative process. As you begin to develop your game, start carrying a scribble pad with you and sketch anything that comes to mind. Draw pictures, gameplay diagrams, or even abstract shapes. This sort of freeform doodling can really help start the creative juices flowing.

As I stated earlier, any idea is just a merger of two or more previous ideas. Extending from that thought, ideas are, in fact, stimuli that create a cause and effect process. Doodling is one easy method to bring these stimuli to the forefront. Each stroke that you take while sketching is possibly a lead onto a great new idea. Most of the time, this won't be true, but every now and again you will reveal something to yourself with these sketches.

One recent iPhone (and Flash) game called *Canabalt* was born out of a sketching process by creator Adam Saltsman. If you check out www.boingboing.net/2009/ 11/11/the-running-man-behi.html, you can see his creative process unfold through his pencil and paper sketches (see Figure 6.1).

Canabalt is an excellent example of how concept art was used effectively to create an incredibly simple yet wholly complete experience. Adam's concept art certainly dictated not only the aesthetics of the game but the gameplay as well.

Often, it's tempting to dive right into the digital creation process, especially if you're proficient with digital image editing tools or 3D modelers. However, there are a number of detrimental processes associated with using a computer's file system to create your concept art. It doesn't let you make mistakes in the same organic fashion as a sketchbook. Personally, I always like to forget my mistakes, but this isn't the best practice. Sometimes what you think is a mistake initially can turn into a serendipitous achievement. When you begin the creative process,

Figure 6.1
Adam Saltsman's *Canabalt.*

no idea should be discarded. Each tiny idea is a building block, and the more building blocks in your arsenal, the higher the probability that one of those blocks will turn out to be a great cornerstone for your project.

To sum up, the best way to take full ownership of your creative vision is to begin the process of creating concept art with only the bare essentials: a canvas and a writing utensil. If you begin with digital tools, then you are playing within the confines of a predetermined system, which isn't as flexible as the simple and elegant paper-and-pencil method. When you begin to sketch your vision, you want to reduce distractions and also have a real paper trail of every step you took during the process. There are no mistakes, only steps along the road of creation. If you take enough steps, you'll arrive successfully at your destination.

Going Digital

Although you can accomplish quite a bit with a pencil and a sketchbook, no one can play your iPhone video game on a sheet of paper. If you're already proficient with digital content creation, you may have been chomping at the bit to get to this point. If you don't have much or any experience with digital content creation tools, such as Photoshop or 3DS Max, you may be a bit intimidated by this step. My advice is: Don't be. Digital content creation is pretty easy. Depending on your artistic abilities, you'll find different levels of success, but it all boils down to a few simple conventions that I'll outline here.

2D Digital Pre-School

The first step in the digital concept art process is typically within the confines of two-dimensional space, using an image-editing tool such as Photoshop, GIMP, or PaintShop Pro. The first rule of 2D digital creation is to start big, but for real-time games you're going to end up small. If your concept art is simply that, then there's no need to panic, but if you plan to include some elements within your real-time game, they will have to be small. You may want to work with images with dimensions as large as 4,096 pixels, but remember that the largest possible 2D images you can have on the iPhone hardware are 1,024 × 1,024 pixels, which are typically used only for texture maps. If you're talking purely 2D, then obviously the largest image you can display visibly onscreen is 480 × 320 pixels. Another rule to keep in mind is that the iPhone hardware has only a certain amount of precious memory bandwidth to work with 2D images/ textures, and in order to use texture compression (which greatly enhances the processing speed of 2D image handling), you have to create power of 2 images/ textures. For example, an image with dimensions of 256 × 64 is acceptable. Obviously, if what you're creating is intended to be used only as concept art and will have no place within your game, then there's nothing to worry about, but it's good to keep in mind the limitations of your game world's host environment. Eventually, your concept art will be ported to work in a real-time world, and you'll want to lose as little as you possibly can from your initial concept. Going back and looking at *Canabalt* is a great example of the concept art making its way into the game world without skipping a beat. By scaling your concept art appropriately to your target platform, you can create a rich aesthetic that translates well into a real-time atmosphere.

Concept art that gets adopted directly into your game is great, but more often than not your concept art becomes part of your collection of marketing tools, your splash screens, and your Web site. It's not every day that a game's aesthetics mate perfectly with its gameplay. Such will be the case with the example project *Tropical Tailspin.* As we discussed earlier, this will be a non-disruptive 3D flight game in the vein of *Wii Sports Resort's* flight mode. The fact that the title is 3D makes it rather impossible to use most of the 2D concept art within the real-time environment. The 2D concept art will be used to depict the general aesthetic, feeling, and perhaps even the color theory we want to employ in the game. Practically speaking, we'll use this concept art to create icons, splash screens, and perhaps in-game menus or dialog screens.

Research in Practice

The first step in creating the digital screens is to pull up some research material. For this purpose, we'll search for tropical locales, pictures of water planes, and perhaps some images of the various air races that take place around the world. The first keywords I searched were "water planes." These keywords turned up a fine image of two water planes on a dock with a palm tree in the foreground. This is essentially the perfect image to describe *Tropical Tailspin* (see Figure 6.2).

Based on this image, there's a lot we could do. First, there are many details on the planes themselves that are pertinent to the design of the game. For example, the front window is fairly small; will we include a cockpit view in the game? From that tiny window, a large portion of the iPhone's screen might be taken up by foreground material. Tiny details like this one are imperative to notice early in the development process.

Figure 6.2
1,000-word description of *Tropical Tailspin.*

Going along with that thought process, let's determine from that picture what sort of gameplay mechanics will be necessary to create a solid experience representative of the subject material. Besides the challenging cockpit view (which is usually a feature that players like to see), you might also notice the flotation devices at the bottom of the plane. This is an obvious feature in a water plane simulation, of course, but a floating mechanic is another challenge we will face when programming the gameplay.

Diving a little deeper, you might also notice the flimsy-looking rods that appear to attach the flotation devices to the main fuselage. Another gameplay element we can already predict based on the appearance of these rods is that the plane could break apart at these locations. One of my favorite things to do as a kid was crash the biplane in *Pilotwings* (an early console flight simulator for the Super Nintendo) over and over again, trying to find all the possible ways in which the aircraft could receive damage. Players like crashing, and this feature would add a lot to the experience as well as to the modeling pipeline and codebase.

There are a few more elements comprising the planes themselves that we'll have to account for in the simulation: the propeller and the flaps. Like the support rods and flotation devices, these should also be breakable, but before they break off, they must be animated. The propeller should spin in the proper direction and be synchronized with the simulated engine speed and the simulated engine sound. The flaps are responsible for changes in the plane's direction or heading—the pitch, yaw, and roll. The flaps must animate dynamically when the player inputs some change of direction.

You're probably asking yourself what the best way is to control the input of the flaps and other aircraft hardware, considering the iPhone's hardware. If it's not obvious already, a picture really is worth a thousand words and then some. Just by analyzing a simple picture, we have already identified several key gameplay elements that will be modeled and simulated, in addition to asking ourselves even deeper questions about player interaction. To develop a game, we must be able to maintain focus. Before we begin to dissect the player's input options, let's identify a few more elements that we'll need to model and simulate in order to create a compelling water plane experience.

Having already identified a number of elements on the planes that will create a great experience, let's move on to the environment. The largest element in the scene is the palm tree. It won't be too much of a challenge to get a 3D palm tree into the environment, but nothing ruins suspension of disbelief as quickly as an in-game element that looks good but doesn't act right. It would ruin the experience if we run the water plane full-bore into a palm tree and the plane blew up but the palm tree lived out the rest of its days unharmed. We need the palm tree to be destructible. There are more subtle elements to a palm tree that we might consider simulating, such as the fronds moving in the breeze, or perhaps coconuts dropping if we buzz close enough to the palm tree. It's the small details like that that can take an experience from mediocre to "Holy cow! I can't believe they added that feature" in the player's eyes.

One thing you may notice from the examination of this single source image is how quickly the workload is adding up. If you've developed a game before, you know what I'm talking about. If you've never developed a game, then the features I've mentioned might seem fairly trivial. If that's the case, you're about to learn a big lesson. Each of the features listed involves hours of modeling and coding time. If you want to create a compelling experience, attention to detail and devotion of the time necessary to execute those details properly are necessary.

The picture also contains water, the sky, a floating dock, and a canopy of sorts. Each of these elements will require similar modeling and programming elements, although not as complex perhaps as the plane and palm tree. Better still, there's room to reuse certain elements from the simulations we mentioned earlier. The floating dock and the flotation devices from the planes will use similar if not the very same code components. One nice thing about Unity is its implementation of object orientation. You can write one script component and then drag and drop it onto as many objects as you like. We may find 100 uses for realistic flotation code and yet be required to write that code only once.

Sometimes You Have to Sketch Before You Can Run

So far, we've taken a single 2D image and dissected it. Now it's time to begin using our imaginations a little. As we mentioned before, there's a hierarchy involved when creating the concept art for any game. First we begin with an idea, then we find research material, next we move on to pencil and paper, and, finally, we end up creating some real digital art, useful either within the game or in conjunction with the sales tools used to market the game. At this point, we're up to the sketching phase involving our old friends—paper and pencil (or pen if you like). Knowing what we know about the future modeling and simulation the game will employ, let's create some imagery to demonstrate what sort of dramatic effects we might see in the game that aren't outwardly visible from the first picture (see Figure 6.3).

Figure 6.3
A tunnel vision.

In Figure 6.3, we see the water plane crashing and losing its flotation devices. By hand drawing this image, we get an innate feel for the physics reactions taking place. If nothing else, drawing a scene like this should serve well as a simple inspiration to re-create the same concept in digital 3D, making sure it's just as cool as you'd imagined.

Drawing an action seen like this is great for getting a feel for the action your game will present, but it doesn't tell us much about the gameplay. One of my favorite hand-drawn activities of all time is cartography, or map making. Even drawing a map for non-gaming purposes can be fun. When applied to game design, cartography can help you predict how the aesthetics of your game will combine with the mechanics in meaningful ways that enhance the overall experience of your product. For example, you may end a challenging segment of gameplay with the player facing the sunrise, which is an aesthetic reward for completing the challenge.

When drawing a top-down 2D map (see Figure 6.4) for your game world, you should think about things like path dynamics, object placement, and even

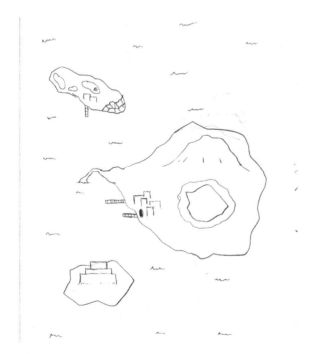

Figure 6.4
Tropical Tailspin's topology.

lighting. *Path dynamics,* how a computer-controlled game object or player moves through a given space, is important in a 3D game, especially in conjunction with object placement and lighting. The first thing you might do is place a sun icon on your 2D top-down map. Keep in mind that all objects facing this light will be bright and easy to see, while objects not directly facing the light will be darker.

The next element we'd probably add is the main island. If you haven't played the flight mode in *Wii Sports Resort,* the basic premise is simple: You fly your plane around an island searching for key landmarks. When you draw the basic shape of the island, you may want to think about the shape of the geography in relation to which objects you might want to light.

Something to keep in mind as well is that we might include several different times of day. Depending on the time of day, you may want certain landmarks or parts of the island to "shine" differently. Perhaps you will have a nighttime setting where a certain building or statue is lit only artificially or only by moonlight. Tackling these types of decisions during the concept art stage of development is helpful, even though it doesn't necessarily mean you're going to stick to your original plans. You have at least asked the right questions and will be prepared and unsurprised when you lay out your map in full 3D.

2D Digital

I recommend starting the concept art process with sketches because they aren't terribly time consuming. When creating sketches, don't be too hard on yourself. Communicate the general point (mainly to support your own thoughts on the project) and move on quickly. If you spend a half-hour on a sketch, that's not bad. A quick digital 2D composition created in Photoshop typically will take two hours or more for a first revision, depending on how proficient you are with the tools and your knowledge of art composition in general. A decent 2D piece of concept art useful for splash screens or marketing materials may take a full day or perhaps two days to create.

Now is the time to create that first piece of 2D digital concept art for *Tropical Tailspin.* More than likely, the first few pieces of concept art you compose will have little to do with your actual game and more to do with inspiring the creation of the rest of the project. Nevertheless, it doesn't hurt to keep the technical limitations of your game in mind when creating this art. Remember *Canabalt,* the previous example? The concept art could easily be mistaken for the art that actually appeared in the game. This is a strategy you may want to employ on your own projects. As it pertains to *Tropical Tailspin,* there are only certain pieces of concept art that will likely be useful in the 3D world. One such use may be a logo that also can be used as a decal on the plane's exterior. The logo, which might be the game's marketing icon, could then be displayed within the 3D game world.

With a few sketches behind us already, it's time to create our first 2D digital image, which will act as a concept for the game's logo. First revisions are never perfect, but they are a stepping stone on the way to a complete and polished game. Logos for iPhone games are often used as the icons as well. Icons come in two sizes: 512 × 512 used in the desktop version of iTunes and 57 × 57, which is displayed on the App Store and on the users' mobile top after they download a game. Another place the logo will show up is on the title screen and perhaps the splash screen for your game in some capacity. Depending on which screen orientation your game is designed for, this means your logo will have to fit and look good in either 480 × 320 (landscape) resolution or 320 × 480 (portrait) resolution. It's a good idea to design something that scales well and fits with all of these resolutions.

When designing a logo, you have to think of what sort of things you want to communicate with it. *Tropical Tailspin* was almost perfectly described with the image we found. The problem is that an icon needs to be more concise. Your game's icon needs to provide a huge amount of information within a very small space. Luckily, pictures usually hold up to the adage of being worth a thousand words.

Keeping in mind that we want scalability for the logo from 512 × 512 down to 57 × 57 pixels, we need to consider a limited color palette to keep the icon crisp and clear. A photograph would not be recognizable at 57 pixels most likely, and many of the colors would conflict and the whole image would look like a blob of mud. Using high-contrast color theory helps create the best app icons. We want to use colors that are able to create separations in content without any artificial borders. Before we get started on *Tropical Tailspin*'s icon, let's research some other app icons and pick them apart (see Figure 6.5).

There's a lot of diversity between these icons at first glance, but I've categorized them by row. The first row contains really elegant icons that get their point across without much detail and are primarily concerned with topics of gameplay.

Figure 6.5
Other icons.

Of these, I think *Sky Burger* is the best; the art is crisp and detailed, and there are even subtle details such as the alpha-blended cloud cover. The best thing about this icon is that it gets the point across and even looks almost like the game itself.

The second icon is for *Sailboat Championship 2009*. This is a very elegant icon that contains only two colors, but it is crisp and communicates the point and feeling of the game without much fanfare. The icon also stands out from the crowd by including a white frame without looking like it's trying too hard to stand out.

The third icon in this row is from the now world-famous *Flight Control. Flight Control* is now itself an icon, and the game's icon is fantastic because it is simple and yet looks like the game, and it also contains an element of hand-drawn simple fun, evident in the black outline around the plane and the tasteful diagonal stripes in the background. These elements all associate with older cartoons that many people think of as being fun.

The final icon in this row is for *Implode!* (the second controlled demolition game for the iPhone). *Implode* is a fantastic game, and its icon could probably be better. The dynamite is clear as well as the hand-drawn explosion, but it doesn't give any idea what we are blowing up. When it comes to blowing things up, does it really matter? Dynamite is planted so that it could lead to the conclusion, along with the title of the game, that this game is about the controlled demolition of buildings. In all fairness, I created *Debris* for the iPhone a year earlier, and I think *Implode* is a better execution all around. It's not easy to fit exploding buildings on a 57 × 57 icon, so you have to use something people will associate with— controlled demolition. I chose to use the detonator itself on a brightly colored background composed of a starburst design that was supposed to be explosive and eye catching. *Implode*'s icon design gets the point across and also gives you an idea of what the game looks like, but of the four icons pictured, I think it's the least effective, although it is still better than 90% of the icons on the App Store.

The second row of icons is character based, which is a very tough segment to represent well via iPhone icons. The first is a terrible icon from the game *Sharp Shooter*. This is what happens when you attempt to scale a photograph down to 57 square pixels: It looks like mud. As far as I can tell, it's probably a guy in camouflage taking aim with a sniper rifle, but it's not clear.

The next icon is from Gameloft's *Blades of Fury*, and it's the face and shoulders of an armored character. Even though this is a render and not a photograph, it's still way too detailed to be compressed into 57 pixels. This is a case where an iconic logo would have probably been a better choice.

The third logo is from the Halo-inspired *NOVA*. While this icon is far better than the other two, it's still not a great example of what can be done. What it gets right is a decent amount of color contrast, which clearly demonstrates a foreground and background. Where it goes wrong is by attempting too much detail in the foreground, which appears to be a helmet and shoulders like *Blades of Fury,* but it's hand drawn and scales down better than the detailed render of the other title.

The final icon in this row is from *Eliminate Pro* by Ngmoco. This is an excellent example of a detailed character-driven icon. The icon is mostly white with only the small details containing any color contrast. Those details are then effectively color coded (for example, the glass face shield is the only blue within the image) to highlight the details and communicate that this is a game about armored figures shooting each other.

The third row of icons consists of all text logo–based icons, which can be an effective way to have the title of your game resonate throughout the iPhone gaming population. The first icon is from *Grand Theft Auto Chinatown Wars*. If this were any other game, it would be a terrible icon, but the *Grand Theft Auto* white text is so prevalent throughout the gaming world that it works. In addition, the red, green, and white color scheme is attractive. Still, any lesser-known game would not do well with this design.

Next up is another popular licensed game based on *Star Wars Trench Run* from the first movie; again, this icon works well because the text is engrained in people's minds. Still, even if this was a new intellectual property, this icon might work. The text is bold enough to make an impression and stand out from the crowd.

The last two icons are both based on new properties that are iPhone exclusive. The first thing you'll notice about both the *Mini Squadron* and *Skies of Glory* icons is how they both appear to be crafted out of metal and use a background starburst effect. These details tell us that these games are solid and explosive. Metal textures are useful for communicating strength or stability, while the starburst is good for communicating explosive action. These two icons are much better than the first two as announcements to the world that something new, exciting, and solid has arrived. Where they fall short is the text that portrays the name of the product. *Mini Squadron* and *Skies of Glory* are both more difficult to read than their big-boy counterparts. If you were going to create a new game and announce the title of that game to the world, it would be best if everyone could read it. To combine the best of both worlds, you might take the legible text from the *Star Wars* icon and combine it with the bursting backdrop of the *Mini Squadron* icon. To do that would showcase a solid experience via the metal texture with the explosive excitement of the starburst, and you would know that the title was clean and neat, so it's legible for the whole world to read.

Last but not least, we have a row of icons that contain both a logo and in-game elements. These are probably the most difficult to pull off on the iPhone because there's just not enough pixel real estate to do this concept justice. The first icon is from *Need for Speed Shift*. The first downfall of this icon is that the *Need for Speed* text is completely unreadable. This icon would fail where the *Grand Theft Auto* and *Star Wars* icons would succeed in communicating this as a licensed product that you already know and love. Luckily, Electronic Arts has enough marketing muscle to overcome this mistake. If you're a smaller developer, perhaps with a known title on another platform but without unlimited marketing resources, this oversight could cost you. There is also a car in this icon, and it is communicated fairly well for a photograph or detailed render due to the strong color contrast of being white on a blue background. The details are filled in with black, much like the *Eliminate Pro* icon, which makes it pretty easy to decipher; there aren't too many colors confusing the issue.

The next icon is from *X-Plane Helicopter*. This icon succeeds in communicating that this is a licensed *X-Plane* title with the giant X and the view of Earth from space that every Laminar Research title showcases. The problem is that this icon has to showcase the helicopter, and because the helicopter is composed of the same colors as the backdrop, there's little color contrast and the image is somewhat lost in the shuffle. Overall, the icon works, but it could be executed better. If you're going to overlay game objects on top of your logo, they should be the same color as the background behind your logo.

The next icon is from *Marble Blast*. This is far and away the best text and game element combination icon among our examples. The text is legible and has the metal texture. Many people may remember *Marble Blast* as Garage Games' flagship title back when that company launched the Torque Game Engine. If not, they will remember it from Xbox Live Arcade, where it sold very well and was chosen by Bill Gates' son as the best game for that particular platform. Overall, *Marble Blast* is a known property. It doesn't have the star power of *Grand Theft Auto* or *Star Wars,* but if someone who knows the game sees the logo, they'll know the game. Simultaneously, if a newcomer sees the title, he will immediately grasp this as a solid product from the bronzed text, which stands out distinctively with plenty of color contrast from the blue background. Finally, the gameplay is communicated very well by the marble rolling across the bottom of the image. This particular game is simple enough to use that sort of visual cue to communicate the action found within the game. Overall, this icon is a candidate for the best icon of all those we've discussed so far.

Last and quite possibly least, we have the icon from *Clue,* which tussled with *Monopoly* for the position of best board game in my mind as a child. *Clue* is a long-standing property that should be instantly recognizable by anyone who's partaken in the gaming world sometime within the last 50 years. The icon at least gets the logo font and color correct. Beyond that, it has too much color contrast. White text on a black background causes eyestrain, and though this icon appears to make an attempt at a metal texture, this isn't translated over to the text itself. A brown or dark blue background would have been better. This icon fails mostly by not featuring the creepy character or mystery that the game presents. Instead, this icon uses two incredibly tiny detailed characters to portray the gameplay. A better solution might have been a simple mansion image (one or two colors) with a lighting bolt over the top and a puddle of blood beneath to suggest the concept of a mystery murder in a huge mansion on a dark and stormy night. Obviously, creating a better solution would take some work, but the point is that you should think about how you can communicate the most information possible within the confines of those 57 square pixels.

Now that we've researched material related to the game, sketched a bit to inspire our imaginations, and researched material specifically related to creating the logo, which will be scalable all the way down to 57 × 57 pixels, it's time to create the first revision of the icon. *Tropical Tailspin* will have the most in common with *Mini Squadron* and *Skies of Glory,* two other newcomers to the market with aviation themes. Where *Tropical Tailspin* deviates is by focusing on exploration of a tropical island paradise instead of blowing other planes to bits. Something I mentioned previously was the use of a metallic texture to insinuate a solid experience. This approach may not work too well for *Tropical Tailspin* because metal is cold, not relaxed, and it just plain doesn't suit the motif we're after with *Tropical Tailspin.* Instead, we can shift to a bold wood texture, perhaps a tiki hut–type look. Wood is another material that can suggest strength and usually presents a feeling of structural integrity.

Tropical Tailspin's logo will be text based in order to announce the title proudly to the world, but the logo will also include some form of imagery to suggest aviation within a tropical environment. Obviously, we could include an image or silhouette of a water plane, but this may be a bit too obtuse and crowd the image when shrunk down to icon size. On the environment front, a seemingly easy call is the use of a palm tree to suggest the tropics. Another useful tactic may be the use of a starburst emanating from a setting yet bright sun in the background.

This is a decent setup because a setting sun with a palm tree silhouette in front of it makes sense visually. If the light is coming from behind the palm tree, it won't be reflecting off the front of it, thus eliminating the need for detail in the tree. I'll take it a step further and suggest that many people have actually experienced such a scene in real life or come across another piece of art that used this technique.

Now the only thing is the aircraft. Will a small aircraft silhouette make sense flying over the tree/island, or will it be too small to comprehend? I think it is worth a shot to experiment with this setup because people are used to seeing aircraft far away up in the sky. Since this isn't uncommon in real life, it should translate to the concept logo.

Before we begin, I want to state that this chapter will assume a general under-standing of 2D image-editing concepts such as text tools, line drawing tools, and layers (the ability to control what gets drawn first to last). If you're not familiar with any of these concepts, you may want to use Google to search "photoshop beginner tutorials" to find out more. You may also find that this chapter pro-vides enough of a base through examples to learn the basics.

Let's begin crafting this icon. I use Photoshop for all of my 2D graphics work, but the techniques applied can be replicated easily with other graphics editors such as GIMP. First, we need to create a blank 512 × 512 image. This is the largest size required for iTunes general-purpose marketing, and practically speaking, if we start out with a larger image, it will be more difficult to scale down in order to ensure consistency throughout all the places this logo might appear.

With the 512 × 512 in place, we will focus on the title text of the logo first; all other imagery will play second fiddle to the title. The first thing we need to think about is the font. There are thousands of free fonts available online, and for our purpose, this is the best place to start. A Google search for "tiki font" brings up a link to fontspace.com and a large array of fonts that suit the purpose. Interest-ingly, there's a font titled LMS Tropical Island Dream that has a palm tree on an island attached to every letter of the alphabet. The font already has the silhouette look I described earlier, but it doesn't look strong or solid. Silhouettes by nature are vague and ghostly. This doesn't rule out silhouettes for background imagery, but it isn't suitable for the title of the game, which needs to be bold and solid. One font I'm unsure about but like the look of is Jungle Rock, which includes solid stone-looking letters surrounded by vegetation.

N o t e

If you're not familiar with the installation of fonts, this is a good link to follow:

www.fonts.com/AboutFonts/Help/InstallingFonts.htm.

Something to keep in mind is that, depending on your 2D graphics editor, you may need to restart the program after installing a new font in order to use it. If this is the case and you already had your editor open, simply restart it, create a blank 512 × 512 image, and use the text tool to select your newly installed font.

After installing the new font and using it within my 512 × 512 image, things are looking a bit grim. The font is decent, but more than likely it's far too detailed to use effectively once it's scaled down. Have a look at Figure 6.6.

This font is unsuitable for the logo because it's not scalable. We now have to go back and examine the other free fonts. Three of them seem useful: Jurassic Park, KR Bamboo, and LMS Tropical Island Dream. Go ahead and install them now all from fonts.com.

Once the fonts are installed, we can get back to the composition of *Tropical Tailspin*'s logo. If you couldn't tell by now, the creative process using digital tools is time consuming because there are so many intricacies involved in getting the programs to adhere to your vision. I've purposely contoured this chapter to the creative process and all its follies to demonstrate what it takes to make a game.

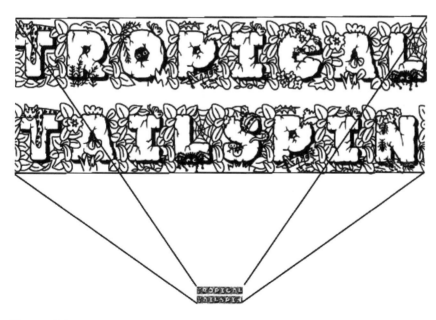

Figure 6.6
Font scaled down from 512 to 57 square pixels.

It's not a cut-and-dried process, and completing a game requires tenacity. Now let's get back to work.

Create a blank 512 × 512 image in your image editor, and then using the Jurassic Park font, type *Tropical Tailspin* with each word on a separate line. You'll want to use the largest font possible so that the text will still be large once it's scaled down. Also, keep in mind that you need a fair margin because Apple processes these images before they appear on the App Store and iTunes. If your margins aren't large enough, you'll have to revise the image. More than likely, you will have to revise your text, but it would be best if any revision in size weren't monumental enough to wreck the whole composition of the image. I used a 260-point size with the Jurassic Park font, and you can see the results in Figure 6.7. The margins around the corners are what we are especially concerned with because that's what Apple's image processing removes. You can expect the process to remove about 5% of the pixels moving diagonally from the outermost corner of the image to the rounded corner, where imagery begins to appear again after processing. On a 57 × 57 icon, the rounded edges of the image after processing are 3 pixels deep.

This looks promising, but at the small resolution, the text loses some of its bang and doesn't represent the solid quality we want to project about the software. At this point, we could cut our losses again and find another font or perhaps do some custom lettering, or we could continue and see if there's any way to salvage

Figure 6.7
260-point font size.

this weak appearance. Creating games is an exercise in experimentation. Each tiny aspect has to be great, and they all need to combine well to form a whole product.

This icon represents the flagship component of the whole game, so it will certainly pay off to work on it as much as possible. The more you examine and learn about this first component, the better prepared you will be to configure other high-quality components into the mix. With that in mind, and also the fact that this is only the first revision, I think we should create one full-fledged logo even if we don't like it much right now. Let's see what we can do to raise the quality, and if we exhaust all possibilities, we can always start over, but this time with a wealth of knowledge gained by completing one task completely.

To begin with, we'll need to delete Tailspin from the text layer and create another layer of text so that we can position the words closer together. Using the Text tool, edit the original text by deleting Tailspin (see Figure 6.8).

Once you've deleted Tailspin from the original text layer, left-click on the image with the Type tool again to create another text layer. Using the same font and

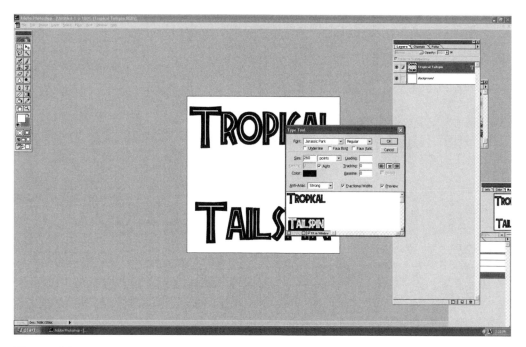

Figure 6.8
Delete Tailspin.

color, type Tailspin into this new layer. With Photoshop it's possible to left-click and drag the text in the image into position while the Type Tool window is open. Position the text as it appears in Figure 6.9.

Now that we have positioned the text prominently and it looks decent, we can begin working from the back to the front of the image using layers. Create a new layer and name it Sunset. In this particular image, the Sunset layer will be the image farthest from the foreground. Make sure this new layer is under all the text layers in your layer hierarchy but still above the Background layer, which is created by default. Once the Sunset layer is in position, use the Gradient tool to paint the layer from blue in the lower-left corner to orange in the upper-right corner. You really don't need to drag the tool very far, only one-fourth of the way into the image from the bottom-left corner (see Figure 6.10).

After Sunset is in place, we can begin adding the island and water plane silhouettes. To create the island silhouette, I'm going to use the Type tool and the LMS Tropical Island Dream font we downloaded. The letter A from this font looks like a vague mountain island. Of course, we'll want to use the color black for this

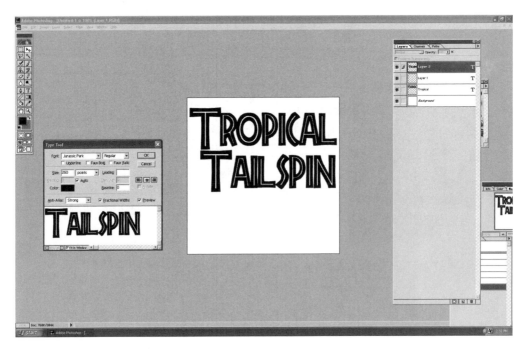

Figure 6.9
New Tailspin text.

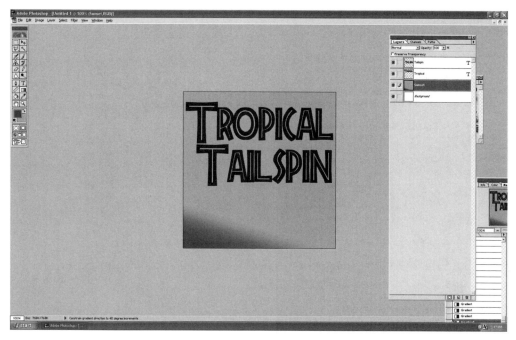

Figure 6.10
Sunset background.

text, and the font size will have to be smaller than the title size of 260 points. I went with a font size of 150 points. Also notice the placement of the island. I've placed it on the cusp of the gradient where it transitions from blue to orange. This is symbolic of the water lapping at the shore of the island.

Next is to somehow get a water plane image into this logo. For concept art, the point, in general, is to conjure up thoughts or imagery alluding to the overall point or plot of the game. As such, we want to get a water plane silhouette image into this logo quickly. A good quick solution is to find an image of a water plane with an image search and then clip the water plane out and remove all color from the image.

What we want to find using a Google image search is a water plane with a single colored background so that it's easily manipulated with the Magic Wand tool. Figure 6.11 is a perfect image for this purpose.

Using the Magic Wand with a Tolerance of 35 and the Contiguous option unchecked, select the background and cut it out. Next, select Inverse and paint it black. You should be left with a stencil of a seaplane, as seen in Figure 6.12.

Figure 6.11
Easy-to-manipulate seaplane image.

Figure 6.12
Seaplane stencil.

Before we can use this image in the logo design, we need to resize it. Currently, the image is 1,400 × 1,050 pixels. We should shrink it to 256 × 192, which is easily done with the Image Size dialog (see Figure 6.13).

With the image size reduced to 256 × 192, use the Magic Wand selection tool again on the plane itself (see Figure 6.14).

With the plane highlighted, press Ctrl+C to copy the stencil and then press Ctrl+V on the logo image to paste the stencil into the primary image. After pasting the image, use the Move tool to position the silhouette to the right of the island (see Figure 6.15).

Figure 6.13
Image Size dialog.

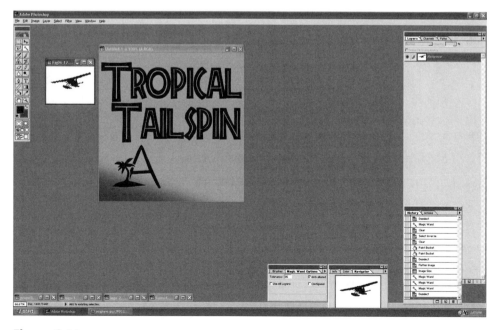

Figure 6.14
Magic Wand the stencil.

Figure 6.15
Paste the stencil or silhouette onto the primary image.

The first logo design is almost complete! The last step is creating the starburst background imagery, which should be placed ahead of the Sunset later but behind the text and silhouettes. The first step toward creating the starburst is to create a new layer called Starburst Outline. This layer will be used only to select where the rays of light emanating from the starburst will be. Still, this layer should be positioned properly in the layer hierarchy above the Sunset layer and below the LMS Tropical Island Dream A text layer (see Figure 6.16).

The next step is to select the Airbrush tool and choose a thin brush. In addition, we will expand the window we're working on by dragging the bottom-right corner of the image down and to the right (see Figure 6.17). This will manifest itself as a gray area surrounding the image but still contained within the logo's window. The reason for doing this is that we want to be able to begin and end lines drawn with the Pen tool at the extreme bounds of the image; otherwise when we paint in the starburst, the Paint Bucket may cover more area than we want.

Moving on, it is now time to choose the Pen tool and begin drawing the boundaries of the starburst highlights. Beginning just to the right of the island,

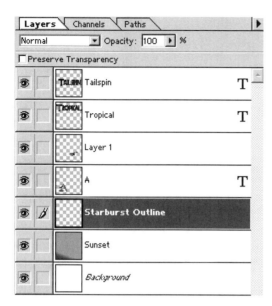

Figure 6.16
Hierarchal position of the outline.

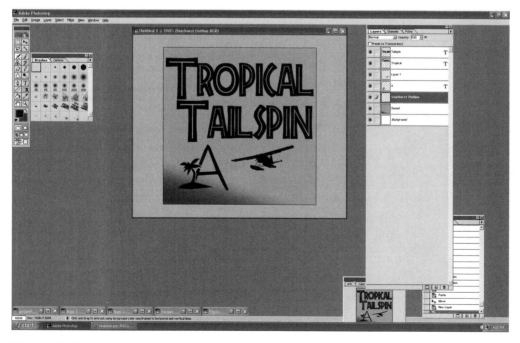

Figure 6.17
Small airbrush and expanded window.

left-click and then drag the mouse up and to the left until the cursor is outside the bounds of the image's upper-left corner (see Figure 6.18).

Now right-click on the start point of the line and choose Stroke Subpath. Right-click on the start point and choose Turn Off Path. Once the path is deactivated, you'll notice a straight black line on the image extending from the island all the way to the upper-left portion of the image, where it ends next to the T in Tropical at the left boundary of the image.

Now repeat this step, starting at the island and extending past the boundaries of the image in a fan pattern four more times. You should get a result similar to Figure 6.19.

Once you have created the four rays leading away from the island, it's time to create a new layer, called Starburst. This new layer can reside in the hierarchy just above the outline. Now we must select portions of the fan created by the four stroked subpaths and then paint that selection yellow on the Starburst layer. First, select the Starburst Outline layer from the layer hierarchy. Next, choose the Magic Wand tool, and this time check the Contiguous option. Now, left-click

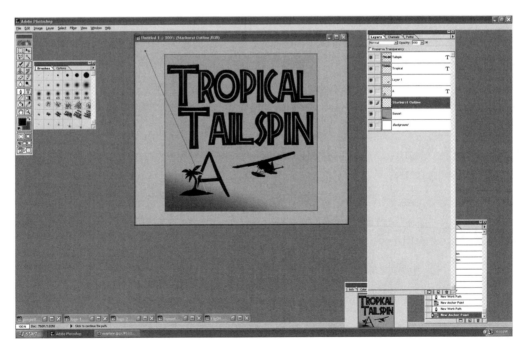

Figure 6.18
Pen tool path.

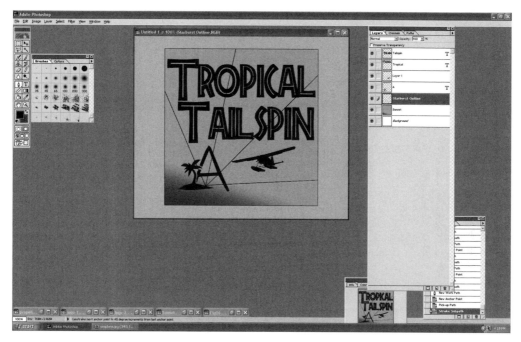

Figure 6.19
Four stroked subpaths.

between the first and second rays. You should see the first part of the fan you created highlighted as seen in Figure 6.20.

With the first fan blade of the starburst outline highlighted, select the Starburst layer. Afterward, choose yellow as the primary color.

Now select the Paint Bucket tool and paint the Starburst layer yellow within the selection (see Figure 6.21).

Repeat this process, but this time use the Magic Wand tool between the third and fourth rays of the Starburst Outline layer (see Figure 6.22). Again, be sure to paint on the Starburst layer and not the Starburst Outline layer.

Now we have the basic logo complete. The image we've created covers all the aspects that we dreamed up earlier, from the starburst to the silhouettes. The question still remains as to whether or not this logo will be used. Look at Figure 6.23 for the product thus far.

Overall, I don't think this logo strikes the point we would like. However, there's a lot of valuable information to take with us on to the next design.

Figure 6.20
First fan blade highlighted.

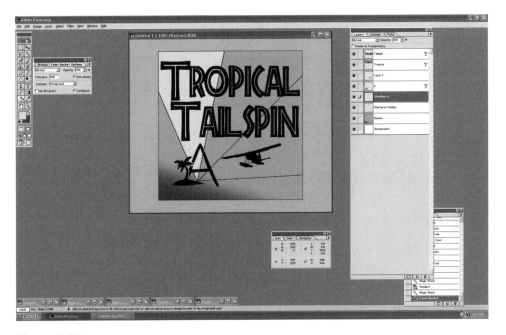

Figure 6.21
Paint the first fan blade yellow.

Figure 6.22
Paint the third fan blade yellow.

Figure 6.23
Sunset logo and silhouettes.

First, the silhouettes and starburst don't work particularly well here because the text loses its strength, the silhouettes are too vague, and the overall effect just isn't very bold. To that end, we may need to rethink the design of this logo. That's not to say this design can't or won't be used but that it's worth pursuing a different design just for the sake of argument.

The initial concept of the logo was sound, but it's just not working here. Instead of conjuring up images of tropical sunsets and silhouettes, we need something bold and strongly defined that still manages to communicate the concept of an island water plane flight simulator. This time, instead of silhouettes, I would like to use the metallic theme we discussed earlier, which clearly indicates stability. What I'm picturing now is a propeller with beveled text stating the game's title *Tropical Tailspin* with each word on a separate blade. The blades will be silver metallic with red tips, and the text should be popping out of the silver metallic area of the blades. This propeller will probably be on the front of the plane, in which case we will have a few other details, but the backdrop should be deep blue water below a cloud-filled light-blue sky. If we have enough space, I'd like to drop an island with a palm tree in there as well. The composition I'm envisioning involves the propeller in the upper-left corner with two or three blades poking down into the scene and the background encompassing the whole image but obviously obscured by the propeller.

Before we get started, Figure 6.24 shows a quick sketch of the composition that I created using Sketchbook Mobile by Autodesk for the iPhone. If you're in a pinch without pencil and paper, this little app can make your life easier. Take note of the seemingly out-of-place curvy line down the center of the image. This is what happens when my wife gets curious about my iPhone.

I don't see too many problems with this design as long as we can strike the proper balance between the strength of the propeller and the subtlety of the background. The next step is to create this in a full desktop image-editing application. Let's go ahead and detail step by step how we will create this logo.

The first step is to make a new 512 × 512 image. We will be working back to front since we have layers to aid the design. The first layer will be the Sky layer. Name your new layer Sky (see Figure 6.25).

Next, select the Paint Bucket tool (see Figure 6.26) or equivalent in your preferred software and paint this layer light blue.

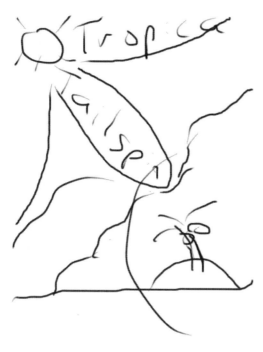

Figure 6.24
Propeller concept composition.

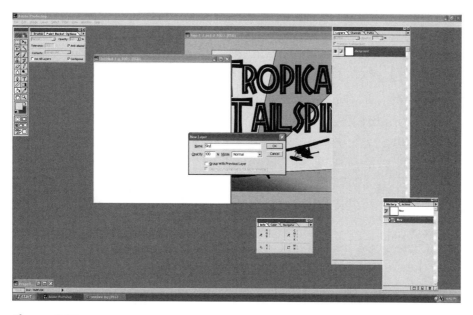

Figure 6.25
Name the layer Sky.

Figure 6.26
Paint Bucket.

You have created the first layer, which is the farthest from the perspective. The next-closest layer will be the Clouds layer. Repeat the layer creation step and this time name the layer Clouds. Before painting anything on this layer, be sure that it is on top of the Sky layer in the layer hierarchy; otherwise, you won't be able to see it (see Figure 6.27).

Next, using the paintbrush/airbrush tool and the color white, paint a puffy mountainous outline with the top leading curve starting at the lower-left and leading to the upper-right corner of the image (see Figure 6.28). Keep in mind that you may want to expand the window again, thereby creating empty space between the window's bounds and the actual canvas by dragging the bottom-right corner of the image window down and to the right.

With the top of the cloud line established, you can now select the Paint Bucket tool and paint the area under this curve (see Figure 6.29).

Next is the Water layer. Creating this layer will be very similar to the Sky layer, but it will encompass just the bottom portion of the image. To make this happen, we will need the Box selection tool. After creating a new layer and naming it

Figure 6.27
Layer hierarchy.

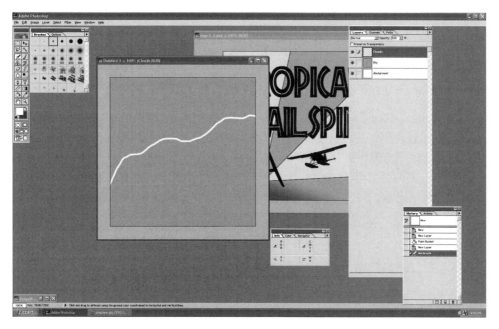

Figure 6.28
Top of the clouds.

Figure 6.29
Paint under the cloud curve.

Water, use the Box selection tool to highlight a good portion of the bottom of the canvas (see Figure 6.30). Once you have made the selection, highlight the Paint Bucket tool, select a darker blue color, and fill in the selected area.

After creating the water, it is time for the island to be placed. Create a new layer called Island, just as you did with the layers. Next, use the Airbrush tool in a similar manner as you did for the clouds, only this time come full circle and connect your end point and your start point. Finally, paint the island using a sandy color (see Figure 6.31).

The last layer, which won't be part of the foreground, is for a palm tree. Create a Tree layer and then, using the Magic Wand tool, highlight the palm tree and island from the first image (see Figure 6.32).

Sometimes, it's better to use a stencil as we did before with the seaplane than to attempt a sloppy drawing with the airbrush. Copy and paste the selection into the new logo. After the tree is pasted, use the Box selection tool to cut away the island part of the Tree layer (see Figures 6.33 and 6.34).

Figure 6.30
Box selection.

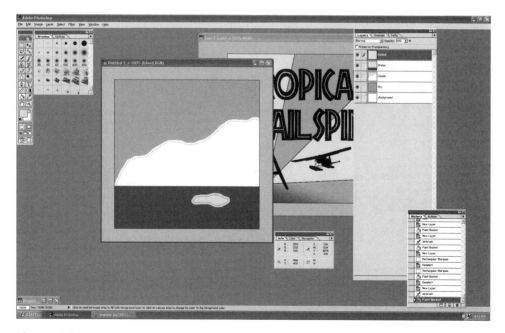

Figure 6.31
The island.

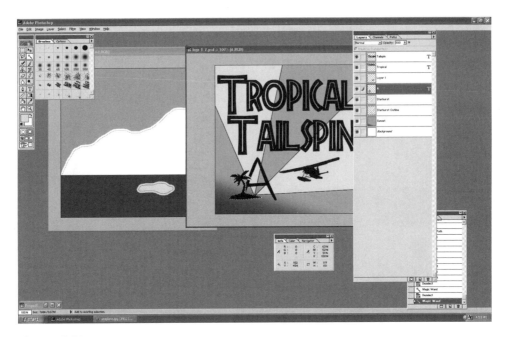

Figure 6.32
Select the old tree.

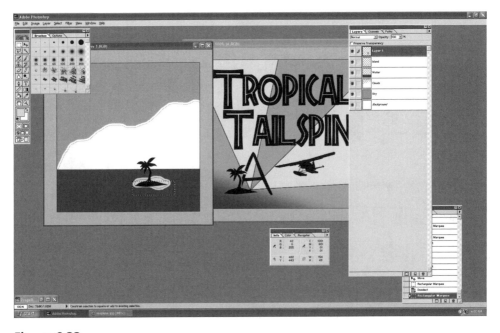

Figure 6.33
Box select.

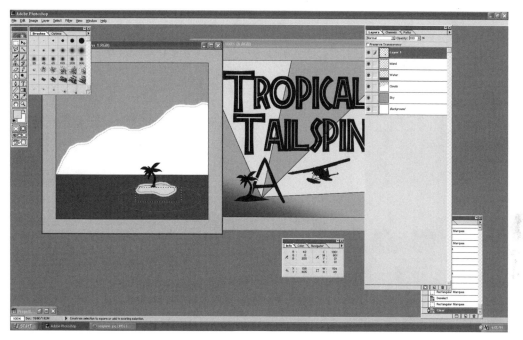

Figure 6.34
Delete.

Now all that's left to do is paint the palms green and the trunk brown. To do this, we'll use the polygon selection (or Lasso) tool, which is like the Box selection tool but more dynamic. With this tool, highlight just the palms as displayed in Figure 6.35. To do this with precision, you may need to zoom in using Ctrl+.

Once the palms are highlighted, cut and paste them to a new layer. Name the new layer—you guessed it—Palms!

After the layer is created and named, move the palms into position with the Move tool (see Figure 6.36). You can gain extra precision with the Move tool by using the arrow keys in Photoshop. Using this option allows movement at the single pixel level.

Once the palms are in position, we'll need to paint them green. Select the Paint Bucket tool, change the primary color to green, and click within the bounds of the palms on the appropriate layer.

Now we can paint the trunk dark brown by selecting the Tree layer and painting within the bounds of the trunk with the Paint Bucket tool.

Figure 6.35
Highlighting the palms.

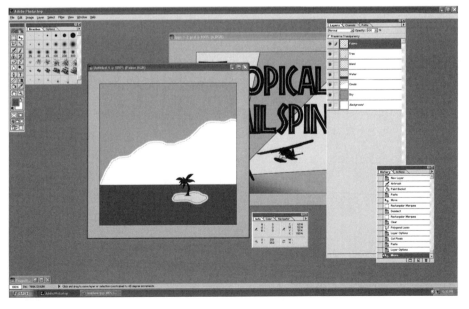

Figure 6.36
Move the palms back.

We have now created all of the background detail, and I have to say that the original logo we created looks a lot more convincing at this point (see Figure 6.37). Of course, the most crucial part of the new logo, the propeller blades, has yet to make an appearance.

To create the propeller blades, we'll need a new stencil. Google image search again provides a great place to find stencils for the concept art. After we've found one that looks decent, we'll bring it into the image editor. Once the image is loaded, we can use the Magic Wand tool with a tolerance of 10 and the Contiguous option unchecked to select the white area around the propeller.

Next, choose Select > Inverse from the menu bar.

Now copy and paste the propeller image into the main image and name the new layer Propeller. This propeller obviously doesn't look right in the context of the simplistic background, so we'll have to simplify the propeller itself. To begin with, we'll again select the blank space around the propeller, this time in the logo image. Then we'll select the inverse so that only the propeller is highlighted. Finally, we'll paint the propeller silver or gray (see Figure 6.38).

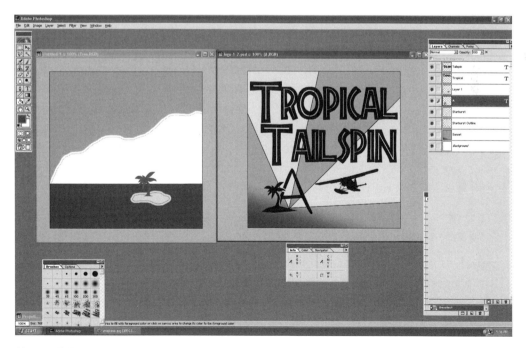

Figure 6.37
Logo comparison.

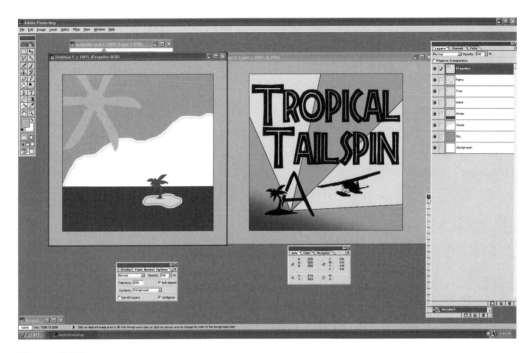

Figure 6.38
Paint the propeller silver.

When the propeller is one color and not photorealistic, it fits the image's un-realistic style much better. There are some problems, though. First, the propeller is not nearly large enough to convey the bold look of the title embossed out of the metallic blades. To fix this, we will use the Scale tool. First, choose the Move tool and then choose Edit > Transform > Scale from the main menu (or the appro-priate equivalent in your 2D image editor). Now drag the bottom-right corner of the Scale box selection to the bottom-right corner of the entire image (see Figures 6.39 and 6.40). Click on the Move tool again and choose Apply Transformation.

Once the propeller is enlarged, move it back to the upper left so that the blades reach down only so far (see Figure 6.41).

The problem with this picture is that, due to the perspective of the base image, the two longest blades aren't aligned properly. To correct this, we'll need to ro-tate this layer. Select Edit > Transform > Rotate from the main menu and rotate the propeller counterclockwise (see Figure 6.42).

When the blades are rotated to a desirable angle, we can again move the propeller with the Move tool to get the best composition (see Figure 6.43).

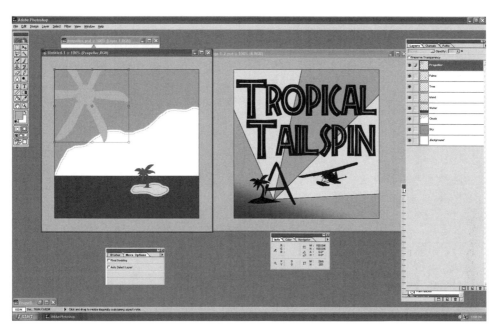

Figure 6.39
Grab the bottom-right corner of the Scale selection.

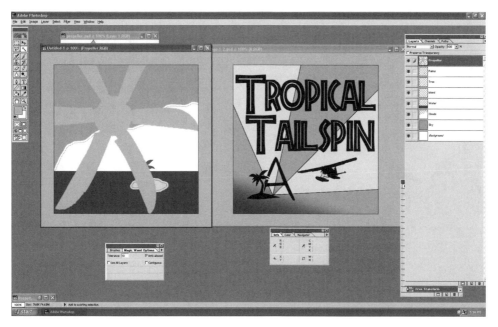

Figure 6.40
Pull it down and apply the transformation.

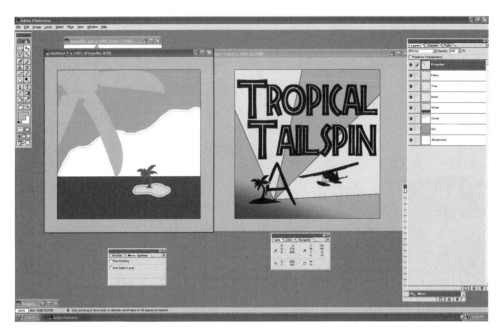

Figure 6.41
Move the propeller up and left.

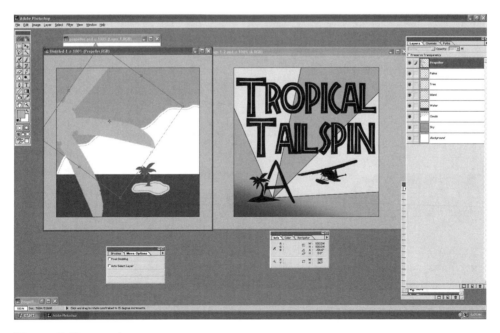

Figure 6.42
Rotate counterclockwise.

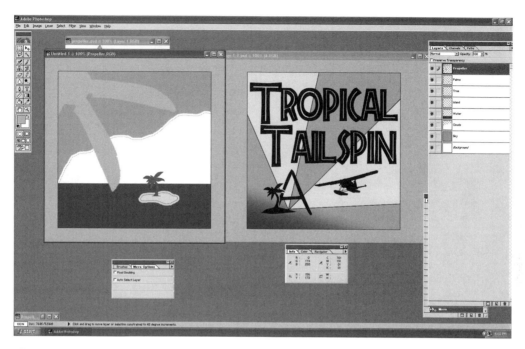

Figure 6.43
Position the propeller again.

Overall, this image is more detailed in terms of steps taken to create it than the previous image, and it still doesn't have the same appeal. In general, it's easy to see that this image is not as elegant in its design as the first one. Typically, the simplest solution is the best, but we cannot stop until we've achieved at least the basic premise of the original plane. In this instance, creating a solid metallic title embossed out of a propeller blade is simply more complex than creating silhouettes in a starburst.

We must now press on and see if we can achieve the look we were after to begin with. The blades have a lot of imperfections that take away from the sharp, bold look we're trying to create. To fix this, we must select the blades or propeller with the Magic Wand tool. Next, choose Select > Modify > Contract from the main menu. Choose 3 pixels for the amount to contract by (see Figure 6.44).

Now, we must smooth out the jagged edges of the selection. Choose Select > Modify > Smooth from the main menu and use a Sample Radius of 8 pixels. Select Inverse and cut away the excess. What we're left with are fairly clean edges (see Figure 6.45).

Figure 6.44
Contract by 3 pixels.

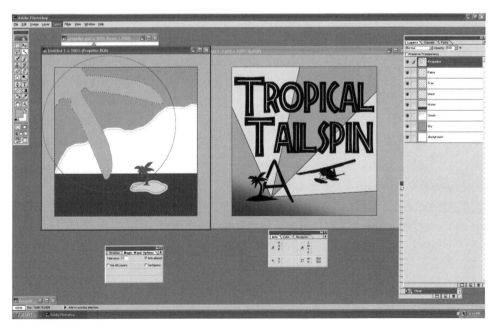

Figure 6.45
Cut away the excess.

The next step is to enhance the propeller so that it looks bold and metallic but not photorealistic. To begin this process, we'll choose Layer > Effects > Bevel and Emboss from the main menu. The default settings for this effect should suffice (see Figure 6.46).

Next choose Filter > Artistic > Plastic Wrap. This is a special filter that applies a texture over the image, creating a plastic wrap or shiny look (see Figure 6.47). There are several ways to accomplish this look, and depending on your image editor, you may have to try a few options.

Beyond the Plastic Wrap filter, we'll further add to the shiny look of the object by applying both Inner Shadow and Outer Glow (see Figure 6.48). Choose Layer > Effects > Outer Glow and set Mode to Normal, Blur to 10, and Intensity to 600. To apply the inner shadow, choose Layer > Effects > Inner Shadow. The default settings should be adequate.

Now that we've given the blades a shiny metallic yet non-photorealistic look, we'll need to start on the details, such as the red tips and the text. Let's apply the red tips to give a better idea of the boundaries that will encapsulate the text.

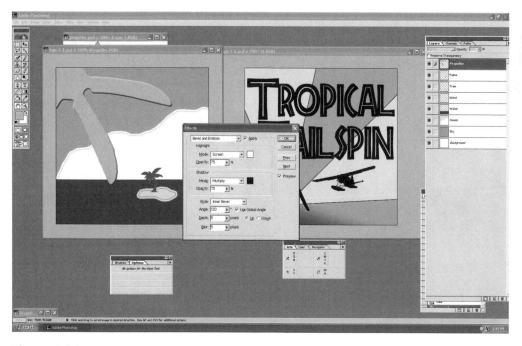

Figure 6.46
Bevel and emboss the blades.

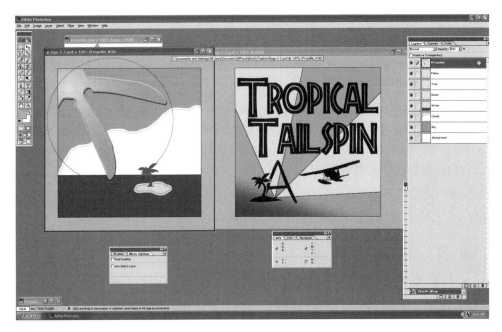

Figure 6.47
Try the Plastic Wrap filter.

Figure 6.48
Inner shadow plus an outer glow.

To do this, we'll copy the Propeller layer. Right-click on the Propeller layer in the hierarchy and choose Duplicate Layer. This will create a new layer called Propeller Copy (see Figure 6.49).

Next, we'll use the Elliptical Marquee or Selection tool. This is located in the same place as the Box selection tool in Photoshop, simply Alt+left-click the Box selection tool to change it to Elliptical selection. Drag an elliptical selection from the approximate center of the image toward the upper-left corner, and be sure you're working with the Propeller Copy layer. You should see something similar to Figure 6.50.

With this selection made, delete the inside of the selection, leaving only the tips (see Figure 6.51).

Next, we will color the tips red. Choose Layer > Effects > Color Fill and choose the color red (see Figure 6.52).

Moving on to the last step, we need to add the embossed Tropical Tailspin text. To start this process, we'll use the Type tool with Arial font at a size of 50 points.

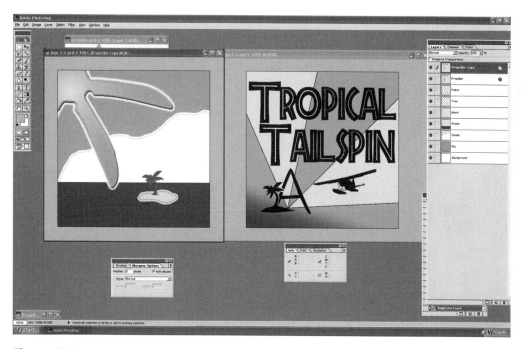

Figure 6.49
Duplicate the Propeller layer.

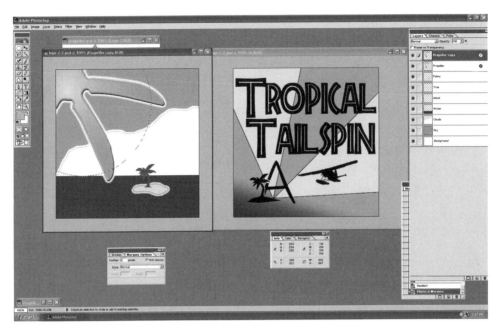

Figure 6.50
Elliptical selection.

Figure 6.51
Delete leaving only the tips.

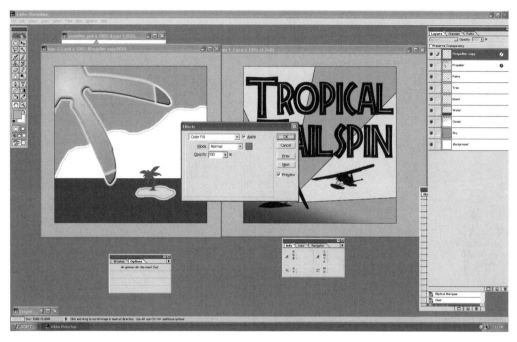

Figure 6.52
Color the tips red.

Type the word Tropical with these settings and place this text on the top blade (see Figure 6.53).

Next, do the same with the word Tailspin, but position the word closer to the bottom blade (see Figure 6.54).

Obviously, this text needs some serious work. Use the Rotation tool under Edit > Transform > Rotate on both layers to align them to the propeller blades (see Figure 6.55).

Things are looking cleaner in Figure 6.55, but the text just fades into the blade and is barely legible. The plan all along was to emboss the text so that it pushed up and out from the blade. To do this, choose Layer > Effects > Bevel and Emboss. This time, instead of using Inner Bevel as we did on the propeller itself, choose Outer Bevel, which enlarges the size of the text relative to the entire image. The result is an exaggerated text that looks like it's raised from the metal blade of the propeller. Its exaggerated look still lends itself well to the cartoony background, but it also has that bold appeal we were hoping to achieve (see Figure 6.56).

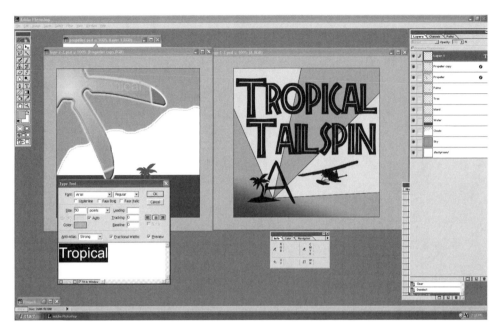

Figure 6.53
Tropical text on the blade.

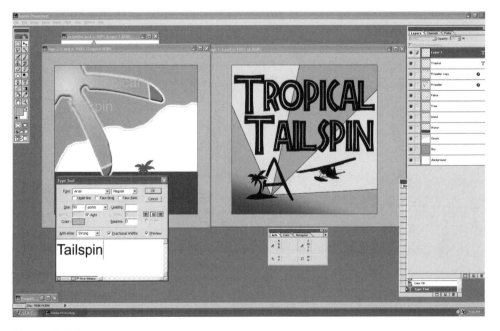

Figure 6.54
Tailspin text on the blade.

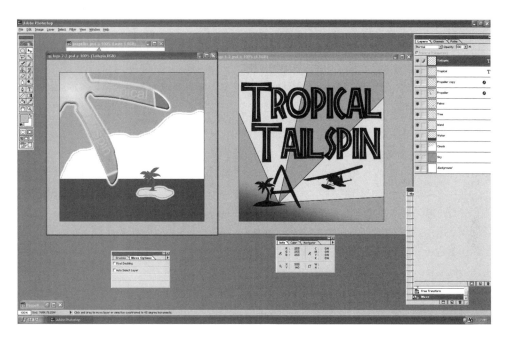

Figure 6.55
Rotated Tropical Tailspin text.

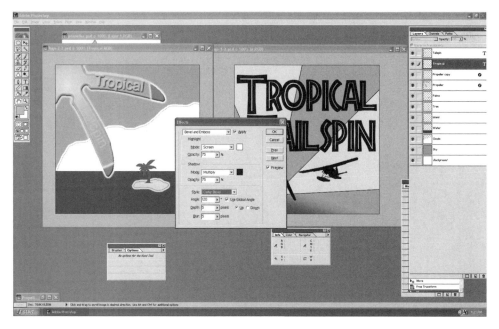

Figure 6.56
Tropical, beveled and embossed.

Once you apply the same Outer Bevel to the Tailspin text, you'll see that this concept does indeed have merit. Looking at both concepts side by side, it's plain to see that things can get confusing when choosing among your various ideas. At this point, neither image is truly polished, but both are certainly still candidates for the final logo (see Figure 6.57).

There is a really important lesson to take away from looking at these two logo examples. We hit on this briefly before, but elegance in design is something that cannot be overstated. When I woke up the morning after creating both of these designs, it was very clear that the starburst design was far more effective at this point than the propeller design. I truly believe that we can all create whatever it is that we envision, but the question is how long it will take. I'm not a particularly skilled artist. Yes, I create concept art all the time, and sometimes my art actually sneaks its way into production (though it's usually called out by critics). For me to use the second design, I would have to spend a lot more time on it (and it was already about four times as time consuming as the first logo), or I would have to hire someone with better artistic skills than I have to bring it up to production level for the game's release. At this point, we are still just talking about concept

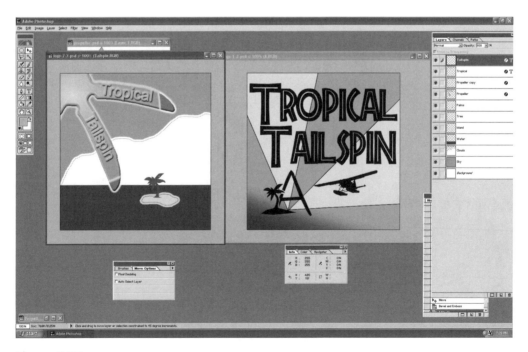

Figure 6.57
Both first revision concepts side by side.

art, so it's fine to experiment with various ideas. But if you're trying to make the most efficient use of your time, choosing something like the first logo is a wise decision.

Choosing simplistic concepts for your art, design, and even gameplay mechanics can help you make your product shine. You might not create an industry-changing game, but more than likely you'll get positive reviews for creating a simple, polished experience rather than a complex yet unpolished one. In Chapter 1 we talked about the equation for kinetic energy, which is equal to half the mass of an object multiplied by its speed (or even better its velocity) squared. I like to apply this concept to everything in life.

In this instance, the amount of game energy is equal to half the mass of your knowledge or budget multiplied by how quickly you can create something relevant and deliver it to the market. If you think of the *velocity* term as how quickly and accurately you place your product on the market, then you realize that it's more important to place something relevant on the market in a timely manner than it is to rely on a huge knowledge base or deep-pocketed development budget.

Something relevant can be *Modern Warfare 2* or *Flight Control,* complex or simple. The major point is that the equation must always be balanced. If you attempt to put something out with the energy of *Modern Warfare 2* alone, you're probably not going to fare too well. People will look at the equation and clearly see that it's unbalanced. Either you will deliver a terrible experience in a timely fashion, or you will deliver a good experience too late, when it's no longer relevant to the market. On the contrary, you could develop something simple and come away with a very balanced equation. Players will appreciate that balance. If you don't promise the world, no one will care when you don't deliver it.

Relating this back to the concept art, my particular skill level deems that I must keep things simple and even vague to create a polished presentation. If you're a skilled artist, perhaps you can up the ante and deliver something with more detail. If you are not, that doesn't mean you cannot create your own art, it simply means you must scale your art to keep the equation balanced. Purposely keep your concepts simple, and you can still find success.

3D Digital Concept Art

Now that we've done some hand-drawn sketches, researched icon designs, and even created two digital logos, it's time to talk about 3D concept art. If you've ever seen a game prototype, you know it's not pretty. Typically, 3D concept art consists of primitive shapes slapped together in a simple environment just to get a feel for things like camera position, speed, and general scale. For *Tropical Tailspin*, things won't be any different. The first draft is going to be ugly.

To generate the first concept scene for *Tropical Tailspin*, we're going to open Unity again. Once Unity's back up and running, create a new project and import iPhone Standard Assets.unityPackage (see Figure 6.58).

Inside the Unity iPhone Standard Assets folder is another folder called Example Scenes. Inside that folder is a scene called Water. This scene is a tropical scene complete with water, blue skies, and several islands. It's nowhere near production quality (meaning the quality of what we'd release on the App Store), but for the purposes of the proof of concept it works beautifully. The other thing we need is a water plane. For the proof of concept, we will construct the water plane out of Unity primitives. You'd be surprised how well you can model with Unity alone. You won't get production-quality results on most game types, but for quick 3D concept art, primitives are wonderful.

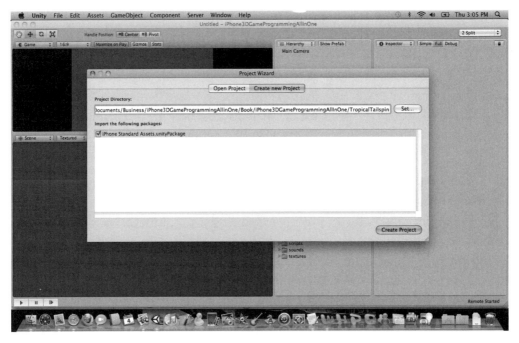

Figure 6.58
New Unity project, import iPhone standard assets.

The first step in creating the primitive-based seaplane is to organize the new project properly. Although we are just beginning our first Unity game, it's important to implement solid organizational constructs to ensure that the project will stay tightly tuned throughout development. To begin, we will create another folder in the Project view called Tropical Tailspin. Create the new folder by right-clicking within the Project view (but not on one of the pre-existing folders) and selecting Create > Folder from the pop-up menu. After creating the new folder, we'll have to name it properly. You can rename a folder by left-clicking on it and then pressing Enter/Return to focus on and edit the name of the folder (see Figure 6.59).

Inside this main Tropical Tailspin folder, we will also create several other subfolders. Any game project requires assets, including scripts, models, textures, sounds, GUIs, scenes, and prefabs. Scripts control the game logic and coordinate the experience. Models, textures, and sounds create the aesthetics of the experience. GUIs (graphic user interfaces) allow the users to navigate the game menus and customize their own experience. Prefabs are custom combinations of scripts, models, textures, sounds, GUI elements, and more that are easily reused and

Figure 6.59
Create a folder specifically for *Tropical Tailspin.*

repurposed within the project. When building games with Unity, some of the objects you want to model will be complex, but you'll want to re-create them multiple times in various scenes. Prefabs are a great way to populate your levels or scenes with complex custom objects.

For now, we need only three folders within the Tropical Tailspin folder. Left-click on the Tropical Tailspin folder to highlight it and then right-click on it and choose Create > Folder from the pop-up menu. After creating each new folder, left-click on it and then press Enter/Return to name the folder properly. For this simple 3D concept, we need only the Scenes, Scripts, and Prefab folders (see Figure 6.60).

We will now begin creating a scene. The first step is to open the example scene that comes with the Unity iPhone standard assets package located under iPhone Standard Assets > Example Scenes > Water within the Project view. This example scene is perfect for a proof of concept scene (see Figure 6.61). How lucky can we get?

With the scene open, we're going to begin building the conceptual aircraft out of primitives. The first step is to choose GameObject > Create Empty from the main

Figure 6.60
Create three new subfolders.

Figure 6.61
Welcome to *Tropical Tailspin* version 0.01.

menu (see Figure 6.62). This creates an empty object or transform in the scene and will form the basis for the airplane. I use the terms *object* and *transform* interchangeably in this instance because the most basic functionality of a game object is its transform component, which cannot be removed. This object will serve as a transform (a component consisting of a position, rotation, and scale) that other visual game objects will be parented to. Unity's parenting system works on the basis of a game object's transform, not the root game object itself. We will append the visual elements to this empty transform in relative space to keep things simple.

With the new empty game object created, highlight it in the Hierarchy view and press Enter/Return to rename it Airplane (see Figure 6.63).

Now that we have the base transform object renamed, we can begin appending each component of an actual aircraft to the airplane. Highlight the Airplane game object in the Hierarchy view and then choose GameObject > Create Other > Capsule from the main menu (see Figure 6.64).

If the new Capsule object did not become parented to the Airplane object, drag and drop it there now (see Figure 6.65).

Figure 6.62
Create an empty game object.

Figure 6.63
Rename GameObject to airplane.

Figure 6.64
Create a Capsule game object.

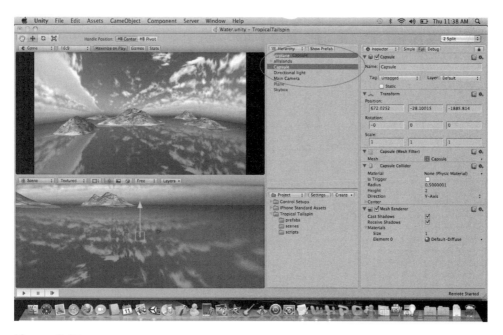

Figure 6.65
Attach the new capsule to the airplane.

Now that the capsule is attached to the airplane, it will become the primary component of the plane, better known as the fuselage. The fuselage is what other components like the wings, tail, and pontoons are mounted to. It's also what carries the passengers. Now, rename Capsule to fuselage.

Something you'll notice is that the fuselage is oriented vertically. This is perpendicular to the primary airplane transform. Rotate the fuselage 90 degrees about its X-axis to align it properly as a fuselage to the primary Airplane transform (see Figure 6.66).

The fuselage is aligned, but it isn't proportional to a typical fuselage, which is longer and narrower than the default capsule shape. To adjust for this, change the scale along the Y-axis from 1 to 3 (see Figure 6.67).

Now the fuselage is closer to what a traditional aircraft would look like. Of course, it still doesn't look like an airplane because we haven't added wings or a tail. To remedy this, we'll add a primitive set of wings. Select GameObject > Create Other > Cube (see Figure 6.68).

Figure 6.66
Align the fuselage.

Figure 6.67
Stretch the fuselage.

Figure 6.68
Create a cube for wings.

Parent the Cube object to the Airplane object by dragging and dropping it in the Hierarchy view. With the cube attached to the airplane, rename it Wings.

The wings still look like a cube, and as such, its proportions are again not correct to represent the wings. As we did with the fuselage, scale the wings, only this time scale them along the X-axis by 10 and along the Y-axis by 0.1. Also, if the position of the wings isn't dead center (0, 0, 0), change that as well (see Figure 6.69).

Now we're beginning to see the basic shape of an airplane come into focus. Obviously, this is still really rough, even for concept art! Let's add a few more details so that at least it's unmistakably an airplane, albeit an ugly one.

If you know anything about aircraft, then you know that there's typically a smaller set of wings at the rear of the plane. This tiny set of wings is called the horizontal stabilizer. (For prototype purposes, we'll call it the elevator, which is the moving flap attached to the horizontal stabilizer.) To create the elevator, we'll simply duplicate, rescale, and reposition the main set of wings to accurately portray an airplane's elevator.

Figure 6.69
Change the proportions of the wings.

First press the key combination Cmd+D to duplicate the wings. Next, rename the new set of wings to Elevator (see Figure 6.70).

Now change the position and scale of the elevator's transform to (0, 0, -2) and (3, 0.1, 0.5), respectively (see Figure 6.71).

With the wings and elevator in place, the crude shape is looking almost like an airplane. By adding the vertical stabilizer (we'll call it the rudder for now in Figure 6.72), we should be able to get started with general gameplay prototyping!

To create the rudder, you can either create a new cube as you did before or duplicate the elevator, which is probably the easier of the two options. Once the object has been duplicated, rename it Rudder.

With the rudder created and labeled, it's time to change its orientation and position to look something like a real plane's vertical stabilizer/rudder. Change the rudder's position and scale to (0, 0.5, 2) and (0.1, 1, 0.5), respectively (see Figure 6.73).

Figure 6.70
Rename the duplicate set of wings from Wings to Elevator.

Figure 6.71
Change the size and position of the elevator.

Figure 6.72
Duplicate the elevator and rename it Rudder.

Figure 6.73
Orient the rudder.

Now we have a solid concept locale and the first conceptual 3D model. The environment was a lucky break because the Unity team included it as a free asset with the software package. Creating the primitive plane was a little more difficult, but not by much, because the development environment supported all the functions we needed to create it out-of-the-box. One last step we can take at this point is to create a prefab out of the 3D concept airplane. To do so, right-click on the Prefabs folder in the Project view and select Create > Prefab from the pop-up menu.

Next, rename the prefab Airplane (see Figure 6.74).

Finally, drag the Airplane object from the Hierarchy view onto the newly created prefab to fill it with the contents of the concept plane (see Figure 6.75).

Finally, save this scene as tropical001 in the Scenes folder we created by selecting File > Save Scene As from the main menu (see Figure 6.76).

Figure 6.74
Rename the prefab.

Figure 6.75
Drag and drop the Airplane game object onto the Airplane prefab.

Figure 6.76
Save the scene as Scenes/tropical001.

Conclusion

Concept art is truly one of the more important (and fun) parts of developing a game. As you can tell, it's a long process that might last months, depending on the complexity of the game you're creating. At this point, you've got the necessary skills to communicate your vision in a crude manner. In the chapters ahead, we'll begin to make that vision come to life and then polish it so that it is understandable and enjoyable to new players.

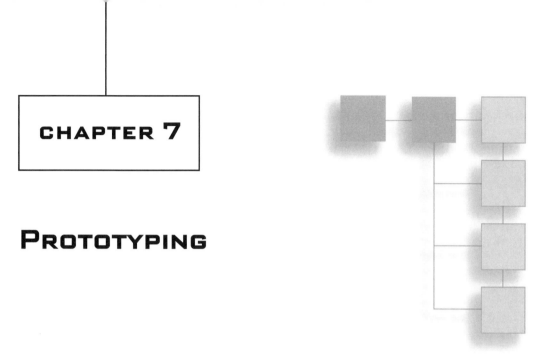

CHAPTER 7

PROTOTYPING

Prototyping (or as I like to call it, codesketching) is the programming equivalent to concept art. During this process, you will experiment with the various input methods we covered in Chapter 5 and create an interface with which the player can interact with your game. Some of the concepts you create when prototyping will go out the window as soon as the first player takes control of the game. Other ideas may stay in until the very end, only to be cut due to some unforeseen reason. Still other ideas will make their way from prototype all the way to production. Of course, the point of prototyping is to come up with the core interaction of your game, as well as creating as many iterations of that core interaction as possible. The more ideas you have and implement, the more good ideas will make it off the chopping block unscathed.

At the end of the previous chapter, we used the Scenes and Prefabs folders we created, but we never used the Scripts folder. That's because we needed to add a little foreshadowing to this book and create a solid segue into this chapter! *Scripts* are portions of programming code that bring the game world alive. A game world ocean has no motion without some programming potion.

Preconceived Notions

If you've played purposeful flight simulators like Microsoft's *Flight Simulator* or Laminar Research's *X-Plane,* or flown a Banshee in *Halo,* you have some notion of how flight works. On that note, it's important to run with your preconceived notions about a subject so that you can explore what you already know first and break that down into code. Chances are that most games fudged some real-world mechanic for the sake of gameplay or even technology limitations.

The first flight simulator I really enjoyed was *Pilotwings* for the Super Nintendo Entertainment System. Due to technology limitations, you couldn't do a flip in that game. Of course, the game we're holding up as a design example for our sample game is *Wii Sports Resort's* flight model. In *Wii Sports Resort,* you can do flips, but there are some other funky mechanics going on that are not accurate from a real-life physics perspective. Since we're programming a simulator, I think it's important that we at least realize what's fake and what's real in our knowledge base so far.

Let's begin creating a prototype that is based on our preconceived notions and see what we come up with. After creating this prototype, we'll then challenge ourselves to make it better by doing some real research. The important thing is sifting through your current knowledge base and separating the truths from the fallacies and then understanding why some falsehoods are good for gameplay.

Version 0.01

When creating a complex game simulator, it's important to set the scope correctly. Starting with a version number like 0.01 indicates that you intend to revise this prototype 100 times before you get to version 1.00, which is what players will experience. Iteration is a very important aspect in game development. The greater the number of iterations you make on a game or system, the better it can be. As you develop new iterations, the complexity of your game will increase, and as it does, it's important to keep it organized. When one aspect of the system gets too big, it's probably time to break that chunk off into its own subsystem. A flight simulator is a complex system that contains many subsystems. We'll likely create a single script that will yield something resembling a flight simulator but in no way will be representative of the final game players will experience.

Logical Analysis

Preconceived notions aren't worth much if you can't analyze and utilize them logically. Let's analyze some of our preconceived notions on flight simulators. First and foremost should be the concept of flight in general. We're playing a flight simulator; we're up in the air flying. Perhaps we should ask if we are flying backward, forward, or side-to-side. If we were building a helicopter simulator, the answer might be different, but airplanes generally just fly forward. Of course, *forward* is a relative term. The question now is: How do we change direction?

You may not realize it, but we've already identified several forces that act on an airplane just by asking a few fundamental questions that have nothing to do with the specifics of an airplane's mechanical systems. By asking yourself a series of simple questions, you can derive much without ever looking at reference material.

The first observation we made is that airplanes move forward as they fly (and if they aren't, then they're crashing, unless you're simulating a Harrier). Why is this? The answer is that the plane's propeller or turbine causes a force, and typically the propeller or turbine is aligned with the body of the airplane. So the first force acting on an airplane is the force caused by its engine(s) and propeller or turbine. This force is a three-dimensional vector aligned to the direction of the engine and scaled to the magnitude of the force.

The second observation we made is that forward (relative to the world around us) can change. This means that we can point the airplane in a new direction. Moving the airplane forward was pretty easy; there's an engine pointing a certain direction, and the airplane gets pushed in the direction the engine is facing. Changing the direction the airplane is facing is a bit more difficult. Perhaps at this point you're picturing little engines or propellers pointing in every direction. This idea isn't really too far from the truth.

The physicist Sir Isaac Newton created a law that stated that for every action there's an equal and opposite reaction. This applies to the airplane because, as the airplane moves forward faster and faster due to the engines' thrust, more and more force is applied to the airplane's body as a result. The action in this case is the thrust; the reaction is increased airflow and friction over the surfaces of the airplane as the airplane moves faster and faster. Depending on the shape of the surface on a particular part of the airplane, another force in a new direction is spawned. It's as if the original force branches out along the surfaces of the airplane. If the surfaces of the airplane are manipulated appropriately, then the airplane will change direction.

An analysis of preconceived notions has given us a decent description of how an airplane moves and changes direction, which by and large is all that it does! Now that we have described in words what an airplane does, let's create version 0.01 of the game based on this analysis of our preconceived notions and see what that gets us.

If you haven't already done so, open the Tropical Tailspin project in Unity. We're going to create a simple script that applies forces to the airplane in the manner that we described in our logical analysis.

To begin, right-click on the Scripts folder in the Project view under Tropical Tailspin > Scripts and choose Create > JavaScript from the pop-up menu (see Figure 7.1).

Now change the name from NewBehaviourScript to flight001 by right-clicking on the script and then pressing Enter/Return to modify the name (see Figure 7.2).

This script will contain the logic that flies the airplane. The JavaScript code we're going to write is just a simpler form of our logical analysis that essentially creates the rules of the simulation. Initially, the code will cover only a rudimentary part of the simulation, but as we learn more by observation, logical analysis, and research, the simulation will become more complex, and we'll create more JavaScript files to deal with the complexity.

Figure 7.1
Creating the first JavaScript file.

Figure 7.2
Rename the JavaScript flight001.

One thing you should note from the previous paragraph is the order in which we will deal with the creation of the simulation. First is observation, second is logical analysis, and third is research. To many people this might seem backward. Typically, we go to school first, talk about things, and then take the field trips to observe what we learned about. Of course, that system of learning and implementing knowledge was created before computers.

With the advent of the computer, everyone can seek out and experiment in real time on a subject by choosing individual paths. With that in mind, it makes sense to make observations about a subject, derive the mechanics driving the subject, and finally research the topic to see what other people observed when you cannot figure out a certain aspect of the subject you are trying to simulate. I find research without observation and logical analysis to be empty because there's no foundation for the bricks to be laid upon.

In the beginning of this book, I stated that we would create a game using a top-down perspective, which means that we're going to start by observing that which has already been built and then break it down to see how it was accomplished. PC flight simulators based on real flight have been around since the 1970s, when Bruce Artwick created the original *Flight Simulator* as his master's thesis. The bottom line is that everything we're going to cover in this book has already been created. The problem is that most of it hasn't been explained in such a way that would make it easily harnessed for independent commercial game development. That's the task this book aims to cover, and the method outlined previously is how we're going to get there.

With the script created and properly named, it's time to put what we have already observed into code. We stated that the engine creates a force that thrusts the plane forward. With that in mind, the first part of the code should address this force.

Inside `flight001.js` add this line:

```
private var forceThrust : Transform;
```

You may have noticed that we have typed the variable `forceThrust` as a `Transform`, which is a way of representing position and orientation data, not force data. Typically, force data would be typed and stored as a `Vector3`, but in this case, we're doing something special. It would be pretty easy to knock up a pseudo-flight simulator in Unity by applying some forces to the center of a rigidbody physics object. The result would not fly like a real plane. Instead, we are going to use a more detailed approach that accounts for the surface of the airplane. The variable `forceThrust` is a `Transform` type because we're going to apply a force at a certain point relative to the airplane's center of mass. This will create a more realistic flight model.

We will also be applying forces caused by the surface structure of the airplane. This method will result in realistic flight behavior even if we apply it only in a simple manner.

Before we continue to analyze the first flight model revision, we'll need to add a few more elements to the airplane model in the Unity Editor. In Chapter 5, we added all the major visual elements, which made the placeholder look something like an actual plane. Now we need to add the first few mechanical elements, which will make the placeholder behave something like an actual plane.

To begin, we'll add a series of game object transforms around the airplane, which will act as force points for the major components of the plane. First, click GameObject > Create Empty from the main menu (see Figure 7.3).

Afterward, drag and drop the new game object onto Airplane. When you do this, Unity will prompt you that you will lose the prefab connection by adding to the airplane. When it does this, just click Continue. When we are done with the

Figure 7.3
Create an empty game object to represent the first force point.

additions, we will simply drag and drop the new airplane onto the old airplane prefab in the Project view to update the old prefab with the new additions.

Now it's time to rename the game object something relevant, such as `force-Thrust`. You can either highlight the object and click on it once or highlight it and press Enter/Return to rename it (see Figure 7.4).

Now we've created the first force point. We need four more force points for our first prototype, so highlight the `forceThrust` object and press Command+D four times to duplicate the object (see Figure 7.5).

After duplicating the `forceThrust` object four times, rename the duplicates `forceWingLeft`, `forceWingRight`, `forceTailLeft`, and `force-TailRight` (see Figure 7.6).

With the duplicates renamed, we have the organizational basis for five force points on the plane representing the wings, tail, and engine. The only problem is that right now these force points aren't where they should be, so we need to move each one into an appropriate position. The `forceThrust` object was the first to be created, so it is the first one that we'll move. For now we'll assume that the thrust is generated from an engine directly at the rear of the airplane, so position `forceThrust` at (0, 0, −2) (see Figure 7.7).

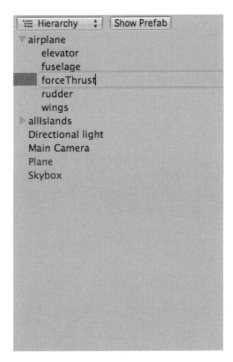

Figure 7.4
Rename the game object `forceThrust`.

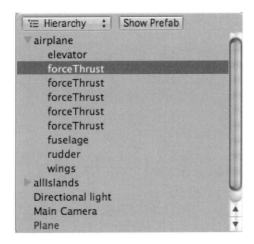

Figure 7.5
Duplicate the `forceThrust` object four times.

Figure 7.6
Rename the duplicates.

Figure 7.7
Position `forceThrust` at (0, 0, −2).

Next, move the wing force objects into position. Move `forceWingLeft` to $(-3, 0, 0)$ and then move `forceWingRight` to the opposing $(3, 0, 0)$ position (see Figure 7.8).

Our final version 0.01 force point move is to position `forceTailLeft` at $(-1, 0, -2)$ and `forceTailRight` at $(1, 0, -2)$ (see Figure 7.9).

Now that the force point objects are in place, we need to add one more component to the Airplane object, a Rigidbody. We're going to add the Rigidbody to the plane so that the force points will have a physics base to connect with and affect change. Rigid bodies, in general, refer to the concept of a physics-enabled object. To add this component to the Airplane object, choose Component > Physics > Rigidbody from the main menu (see Figure 7.10).

With the visuals, force points, and Rigidbody component attached to the airplane, we are now ready to dive into our first script. I'll warn you now to prepare for a bumpy ride! Let's look at our version 0.01 prototype code. You can access this code from the Tropical Tailspin project on the CD-ROM.

Figure 7.8
Position the wing force point objects.

Figure 7.9
Position the tail force point objects.

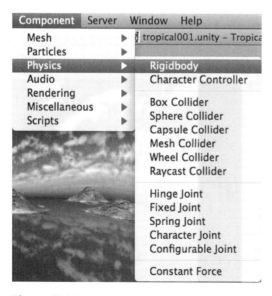

Figure 7.10
Add a Rigidbody component to Airplane.

```
private var forceThrust : Transform;
private var forceWingLeft : Transform;
private var forceWingRight : Transform;
private var forceTailLeft : Transform;
private var forceTailRight : Transform;
private var thisTransform : Transform;
private var thisRigidbody : Rigidbody;
function FixedUpdate()
{
    var accel : Vector3 = iPhoneInput.acceleration;

    thisRigidbody.AddForceAtPosition( thisTransform.forward * 100,
forceThrust.position );

    thisRigidbody.AddForceAtPosition( thisTransform.up * accel.x,
forceTailLeft.position );
    thisRigidbody.AddForceAtPosition( thisTransform.up * accel.x,
forceTailRight.position );

    thisRigidbody.AddForceAtPosition( thisTransform.up * accel.y,
forceWingLeft.position );
    thisRigidbody.AddForceAtPosition( thisTransform.up * -accel.y,
forceWingRight.position );
}
function Start()
{
    forceWingLeft = transform.Find( "forceWingLeft" );
    forceWingRight = transform.Find( "forceWingRight" );

    forceTailLeft = transform.Find( "forceTailLeft" );
    forceTailRight = transform.Find( "forceTailRight" );

    forceThrust = transform.Find( "forceThrust" );

    thisTransform = transform;
    thisRigidbody = rigidbody;
}
```

You'll notice that we have seven variables at the start of the program. These are all listed as private. What this means primarily to you as a Unity programmer is that they are not accessible in the Unity Editor. Instead, we have initialized these variables by using the `transform.Find()` method inside the `Start()` callback. If we were to remove the `private` prefix from those variables, we could remove the code from within the `Start()` callback and set the values of each variable manually from within the Unity Editor. In this instance, it's not crucial to set the variables manually, and as we iterate or create new levels of a game, it can become tedious to set variables like these manually. Depending on the application, it may be better to set the variables manually, but not in this case.

Beyond the scope of the variables, let's see what they stand for. Five of the variables are transforms that contain positions where a force will be applied to the airplane. We have all the basic points on the plane covered here: the wings, the tail, and the engine. Beyond that, we have `thisTransform` and `thisRigidbody`. These variables are references to the main Airplane object itself, which this script will be attached to. The reason we don't just call transform or rigidbody is because it is faster to cache references to these objects local to the script than to search for them each time we want to use them. Tiny optimizations like that can dramatically increase performance on a device like the iPhone.

If this is your first time looking at game/simulation code, it might be a bit daunting, but it doesn't have to be. Unity makes things pretty easy. The basic premise of Unity is that all pieces of a game are comprised of a component system that lets you drag and drop small portions of code onto a game object like the airplane. Within those small portions of code, you can create variables and functions and access Unity callbacks. *Callbacks* are functions that the Unity engine itself calls from within its main loop. The process, in simplest terms, is that you create a script, add your own variables/functions, add Unity-defined callbacks, and then drag and drop that script onto a game object. You can then attach many script components onto your objects to increase the complexity of their behavior.

Getting back to the `flight001.js` code, we have yet to cover the `FixedUpdate()` callback. It is used when you want a certain portion of code to be executed the same number of times each second. For physics simulations like a flight model, this is very important. If operations are not performed with precision, the simulation can become unstable. Within the `FixedUpdate()` callback, we have what amounts to six lines of code. The first line grabs and stores the current iPhone accelerometer data into a Vector3 called `accel`. The next five lines each apply a force at a position relative to the center of the main airplane on its Rigidbody component.

For now, let's examine one of those lines more closely.

```
thisRigidbody.AddForceAtPosition( thisTransform.up * accel.x,
forceTailLeft.position );
```

This line of code applies a force at the left portion of the tail. The first parameter passed into the call to `AddForceAtPosition` is the force. In this instance, we apply a force in the up direction relative to the airplane's primary transform, and we multiply that by the accelerometer input. This means that if you tilt the iPhone forward or back, more force will be applied, and that force could be either up or down because `thisTransform.up` multiplied by a negative accelerometer value creates a force pointing down relative to the airplane.

This first iteration is very basic. It applies forces only to five points on the airplane, and we haven't done much to account for air friction, throttle, or landing. With any game, you have to start somewhere and see if you're on the right track. You want to keep each untested code segment as simple as possible but not simpler. In other words, you want to meet your own personal goals for the current iteration of a prototype, and you want to do that as efficiently as possible.

Before we can begin actually testing this code, we need to do a few things in the Unity Editor. First, we need to drag and drop the script from the Project view onto the Airplane object in the Hierarchy view (see Figure 7.11).

You could run the game like this by pushing the Play button. (Make sure that you have your iPhone or iPod Touch running Unity Remote first.) If you do this, you'll notice that the airplane takes off but has no camera tracking, which makes it hard to see what's going on. To fix this, we have to make one more adjustment in the Unity Editor by dragging and dropping the main camera onto the Airplane object (see Figure 7.12).

One last tiny detail is that the camera is probably nowhere near the airplane, so you'll have to reposition it. Let's reposition the camera in a sensible place (now relative to the airplane since it's a child of the airplane instead of the origin) like (0, 5, −10). Also, change the camera's rotation to (20, 0, 0). With the camera in position, it's time for the first test run.

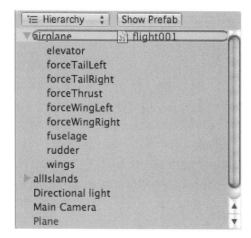

Figure 7.11
Drag and drop the script onto the Airplane object.

Figure 7.12
Drag and drop the main camera onto the Airplane object.

OK, I'm glad to see you're back. Are you feeling slightly queasy? As you will have noticed by now, this code doesn't do much for the fun factor of the game or our stomachs. This doesn't mean the code is useless; it just means that it's a little too simple for the task at hand. (In case you didn't realize it, writing flight sim code isn't for the faint of heart or stomach.) We're begging for version 0.02 code, but before we can write that we have to think about what's going awry in our version 0.01 code.

Version 0.01 is based on a few assumptions. For example, we have made the assumption that the wings, tail, and engine are all force points on a plane. This is a fine assumption. One thing we didn't do, though, is account for any sort of air friction in the first model. This could be the reason why the simulation is so uncontrollable. To fix this, we're going to add some friction with the Unity Editor (see Figure 7.13). Drag and Angular Drag represent air friction in the Rigidbody component. Drag is linear, which slows things down on a straight path, and Angular Drag slows things down that are spinning about an axis of rotation.

If we go back and run the simulation again, you'll notice that things are much easier to control, but there are still a few things wrong. First of all, the left and right roll controls are reversed. Secondly, we never positioned the airplane in a synchronized position, so you may be running into an island or the ground itself! First, let's find a good position for the airplane so we can eliminate any problems that may arise from starting position. A solid initial transform is (600, 200, −1500) with zero degrees of rotation on all axes (see Figure 7.14).

With the airplane positioned properly, let's go into the script and reverse the `accel.y` values so that the left wing uses the negative sign and the right wing goes positive.

```
thisRigidbody.AddForceAtPosition( thisTransform.up * -accel.y,
forceWingLeft.position );
thisRigidbody.AddForceAtPosition( thisTransform.up * accel.y,
forceWingRight.position );
```

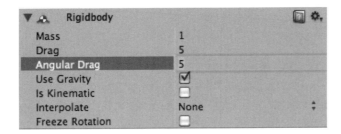

Figure 7.13
Change the Drag and Angular Drag to 5.

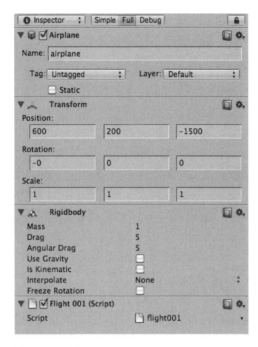

Figure 7.14
Position the airplane properly.

Also, just for the sake of fewer variables to contend with, let's remove gravity from the simulation for now by unchecking the Gravity flag on the airplane's Rigidbody component.

If you go back and run the simulation, you'll notice that things are much more controllable. There are still a few issues before we move on to version 0.02. When creating different versions of a prototype, it's important to achieve a clean version of the current incarnation before moving on to the next version. In this case, our version 0.02 will build upon a working version 0.01, but we won't move on until version 0.01 is a solid representation of what we were shooting for in the first place.

The last little detail you might notice about this version is that the reflections in the scene don't function correctly. The Unity team created the reflections for this sample scene, and they don't account for camera rotation. For our prototype, we don't need the reflections, so we will remove them so that the prototype is less disorienting. With that in mind, highlight the Main Camera object in the

Hierarchy view, right-click on the Render Water script component, and choose Remove Component (see Figure 7.15).

Of course, the Render Water script isn't the only script associated with the reflections. Also remove the iPhone Water script from the plane game object (see Figure 7.16).

With the reflection scripts removed, there's one last step we need to take. Highlight the Main Camera object and set its Clear flags to Solid Color. You should now get a much less disorienting view, which will be good when it comes time for your first testers to experience the game. At this point, we are now ready to close the door on version 0.01 and move on. Save the current scene (tropical001), duplicate it by pressing Command+D, and then open the new scene, tropical002 (see Figure 7.17).

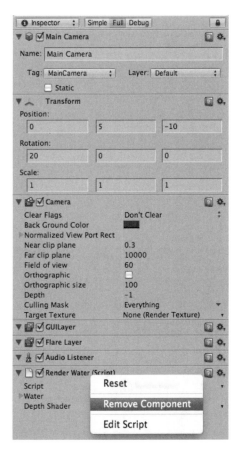

Figure 7.15
Remove the Render Water script component.

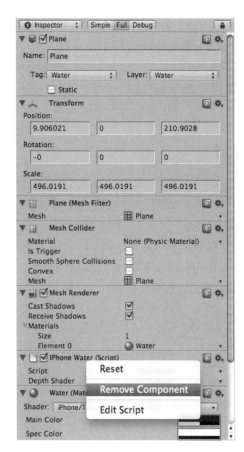

Figure 7.16
Remove the iPhone Water script component.

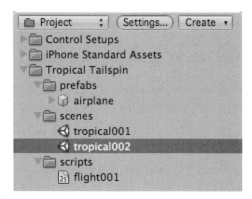

Figure 7.17
Save tropical001, duplicate it, and open tropical002.

With our new tropical002 scene open and ready to go, there are a few things we need to consider. We have created the basis for a viable flight simulator that acts according to relative forces, which is realistic. The problem is that the model is still simplistic and not based on much more than general knowledge and logic. To step up the prototype, we're going to have to do some research on general aviation mechanics, look at diagrams, and perhaps play some other flight simulators.

Research

Before we continue vigorously beating away at the keyboard, we're going to have to do some research, much like we did to aid the concept art. In this case, we're not just interested in photographs to help us see how things should look, instead we need schematics, abstract mechanical descriptions, and some prior examples of good flight simulators to compare the example game with. To create believable motion in games is an art. Initially, you may think that it's all based on scientific equations, but just like brush strokes on a canvas, it's how the science is applied that makes a game fun and accessible. Some of the most scientifically accurate physics simulations are also some of the most infuriating to play because the physics don't always transcend the input method of a game. To meld the input and the science, it's important to understand what you are trying to simulate on multiple levels: visually, conceptually, and interactively. Only by getting a complete understanding from multiple intellectual vantage points can you really nail gameplay time and time again.

For *Tropical Tailspin,* we need to first research general aviation mechanics. Without understanding and seeing the parts of a plane that make it fly, we cannot begin to program a more accurate and complex version of the prototype. To achieve a greater understanding, we're going to do some quick Internet searching and also play the most successful flight simulator for the iPhone, *X-Plane.*

A quick Google search for flight mechanics will get us started. The first entry in the search list is none other than a link to Wikipedia (the entry is "titles aircraft flight mechanics"), and it's chock-full of great information that will help us go from developing the simulator in layman's terms to developing the simulator definitively. If you read the entry you'll notice some similarities between the terminology we used when creating the airplane placeholder and a description of the real thing. As I outlined previously, it's very useful to gather information from multiple perspectives when creating a simulation. With that in mind, another useful Google search for "airplane parts" turns up a link to NASA's Web site and the image seen in Figure 7.18, which yields great insight into the mechanical design of an airplane through the use of a descriptive diagram.

From the airplane parts diagram, we can begin to properly lay out and label the model, which will serve as a reference for the production model we put in the game. Furthermore, as we learn more about the parts of an airplane, we'll create more complex code to simulate its flight. As the code base grows, we can break off chunks into smaller components that may very well line up one-to-one with the real parts of a plane.

Currently, the crude airplane model consists of four parts: the fuselage, wings, elevator, and rudder. By looking at the airplane parts diagram, we can see that a few of these elements are part of the whole, but that some of them are merely subcomponents and not the actual base parts of the plane. For example, the rudder and elevator are movable subcomponents of the vertical and horizontal stabilizers, respectively. On the opposite end of the spectrum, we added wings to the model and gave the airplane the ability to roll. Looking at the diagram, we can see that the plane would not be capable of roll without the ailerons, which are

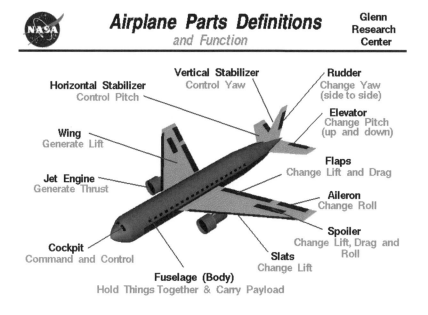

Figure 7.18
Airplane parts.

Figure 7.19
Duplicate the wings twice

subcomponents of the wings. As we expand the simulation, we'll want to cover these intricacies with both the code and the visuals.

To begin this process, let's add ailerons to the wings and add the vertical and horizontal stabilizers to which we will attach the elevator and rudder. First, highlight the wings and then press Command+D to duplicate them. Do this two times (see Figure 7.19).

Once the wings are duplicated, we can rename the duplicates `aileronLeft` and `aileronRight` (see Figure 7.20).

As we said, an airplane's ailerons are actually a subcomponent of the wings. Let's copy this hierarchy with the model by dragging the ailerons onto the wings, causing a parent/child relationship. Click on one of the ailerons and then press Command+left-click on the other to highlight both. Once both ailerons are highlighted, drag them together onto the wings (see Figure 7.21).

Adding the ailerons has added to the accuracy of the simulation quite well for now. Now let's create the vertical and horizontal stabilizers and then attach the rudder and elevator to them. The easiest way to do this is to duplicate the current rudder and elevator, since they are more representative of the stabilizers currently. Highlight either the rudder or the elevator and then press Command +left-click on the other to grab them both. Then press Command+D to duplicate them (see Figure 7.22).

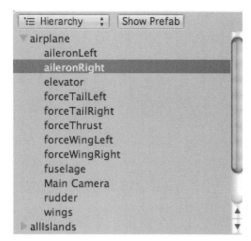

Figure 7.20
Rename the duplicates.

Figure 7.21
Attach the ailerons to the wings.

After creating the duplicates, rename one of the rudders `stabilizerVertical` and one of the elevators `stabilizerHorizontal` (see Figure 7.23).

You may have noticed that at times we name the objects in a seemingly backward fashion. For example, we named the vertical stabilizer `stabilizerVertical`. The reason for this is to make finding the objects in the hierarchy a bit easier. The basic premise of this naming convention is to place the more common term first.

Figure 7.22
Duplicate the elevator and the rudder.

Figure 7.23
Rename the duplicates `stabilizerVertical` and `stabilizerHorizontal`.

Both of the stabilizers will be listed together, so we don't have to go searching for all stabilizer objects; they are all in the same part of the hierarchy because Unity organizes the Hierarchy pane alphabetically.

Now that we have these duplicates made, it's time to place the rudder and elevator appropriately within the hierarchy. Drag and drop the Elevator object onto the horizontal stabilizer, or `stabilizerHorizontal` object (see Figure 7.24).

Figure 7.24
Drag and drop the elevator onto the horizontal stabilizer.

Then drag and drop the rudder onto the `stabilizerVertical` game object (see Figure 7.25).

With the new components, we have a very nice hierarchy defined, but it's not complete. Each of the major components containing a subcomponent, such as the wings containing the ailerons or the horizontal stabilizer containing the elevator, is actually a subcomponent of the fuselage. With that in mind,

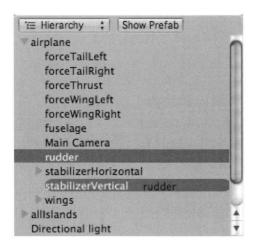

Figure 7.25
Drag and drop the rudder onto the vertical stabilizer.

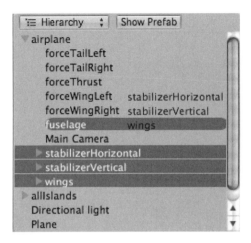

Figure 7.26
Drag and drop all major components onto the fuselage.

Command+left-click on the wings, horizontal stabilizer, and vertical stabilizer; then drag and drop all of them onto the fuselage (see Figure 7.26).

Organizing components as we just did not only keeps your project clean, but it also lends itself very well to a physical understanding of the components involved in a complex system. You can organize many things as we just did, from character models to city models. The small details get placed into larger objects. This is known as *abstraction,* and it's what allows us to manage complexity easily.

Now that we have done some noninteractive research and also some reorganization based on that research, it's time to do some interactive research. Maybe you've played a flight simulator at one time or another and perhaps even one of the many great flight simulators already available for the iPhone. In fact, the most popular and successful flight simulator for the iPhone platform is *X-Plane. X-Plane* uses blade-element theory to power its flight model. The *X-Plane* Web site (www.x-plane.com/pg_Inside_Mobile.html) actually gives us a description of the method employed to power the *X-Plane* simulator, which is quite fascinating. The flight model we're employing isn't quite as complex, but the basic fundamentals are the same.

With that in mind, we're going to use *X-Plane* as our benchmark. If *Tropical Tailspin* can even come close to the feel of *X-Plane,* then chances are we can reach and provide a fun experience for a great many players. If you haven't already, pick up a copy of *X-Plane* and dig in. (There are both free and paid versions for the Mac, PC, and iPhone.)

The first thing to notice is that *X-Plane* isn't very flashy. *X-Plane*'s creator, Austin Meyer, is more concerned with creating a realistic simulation. With that in mind, *X-Plane* features real planes, gauges, HUDs, and maps. The most detailed element of *X-Plane* isn't something you can see but rather something you can feel—its flight model—and it's a work of art.

When players get hold of your game, the first thing they want to experience is the simple act of controlling something new. The key word there is *controlling*. If players can't get a good feel for the controls in the first few seconds of their experience, none of the other details really matter. Whatever game you're creating, make it easy to control first and foremost and then add the details. It's always good to find something to use as a benchmark. In the example game's case, *X-Plane* provides the perfect benchmark of how to port a real flight simulator onto a small mobile device. Of course, our main concerns with *X-Plane* are its physics and controls.

You may be thinking about our commitment to create a game similar to *Wii Sports Resort's* flight model. We aren't dropping that concept at all. We are still creating a game based on an island-hopping seaplane with casual flight appeal. However, we aren't making a Wii game, and *X-Plane* represents a better flight model than *Wii Sports Resort*. Therefore, we are going to examine the best parts of each game to create something new and unique.

Getting back to *X-Plane* (hopefully you've played it by now), we need to pay close attention to a few key elements. First of all, the game uses a combination of touch and tilt controls, but once you're up in the air, the game is mainly about easy, free-flowing tilt controls with the touch buttons fading out after a few seconds of play without any screen input. That's when the feeling of flight really comes alive as you bank, roll, and climb through the air. We want to replicate the feeling of exhilaration associated with flight, and *X-Plane* already does it really well, so it's the perfect research subject. The last part of *X-Plane* that needs to be examined is the graphic effect of the forces acting on the plane. All versions of *X-Plane* include a special mode that graphs 3D vectors on top of the airplane's wings, tail, and engines to show the effect of these parts on the airplane's flight model. Look at Figures 7.27 and 7.28 to see the forces acting on the wings and tail of the plane as it climbs and dives.

You'll notice that in *X-Plane* there are quite a few more force points on each contact surface of the plane. The greater the number of force points, the more

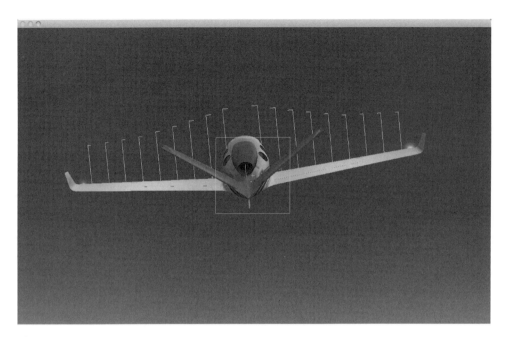

Figure 7.27
Climbing forces.

Figure 7.28
Diving forces.

accurate the simulation will be. *X-Plane*'s Web site claims that 10 force points per blade achieves a very high degree of accuracy, on par with simulations using many more force points.

Note

> From the *X-Plane* Web site: Ten elements per side per wing or stabilizer is the maximum, and studies have shown that this provides roll rates and accelerations that are very close to the values that would be found with a much larger number of elements.

X-Plane achieves very realistic results using up to 10 force points per wing or stabilizer and integrating those forces 15 times per second. We did something very similar with our first prototype, but we also let Unity's built-in physics engine contrive the simulation quite a bit. Now it's time to step things up a notch.

Version 0.02

When you create your first entirely independent game, be prepared to do many tiny revisions. For now, I'm going to spare you some of the more mundane details and pull out a version of the prototype that feels a great deal like *X-Plane* for the iPhone. This is our version 0.02.

Before we actually see the code, there are a few changes we need to make to the scene. First, we're also going to use a fluid third-person camera instead of a rigid one for version 0.02. To set the scene up for this, we need to detach Main Camera from Airplane and create a new empty game object, which will become the camera pivot point or the position the camera will always try to drift toward (see Figures 7.29–7.30).

With the new empty game object created, drag and drop it onto the airplane.

Finally, rename the new game object cameraPivot, as shown in Figure 7.31.

Once the cameraPivot is ready, go ahead and position it at (0, 5, −10).

In addition, before proceeding remove all Collider components from the airplane. Each mesh that we added (fuselage, wings, `aileronRight`, `aileronLeft`, `stabilizerHorizontal`, `stabilizerVertical`, elevator, and rudder) contains a collider of some sort. Select each mesh from the Hierarchy

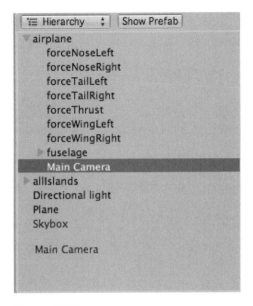

Figure 7.29
Detach Main Camera from Airplane.

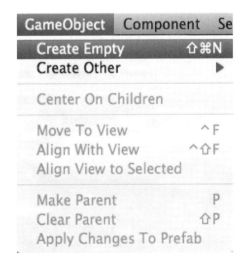

Figure 7.30
Create an empty game object to be a camera pivot.

Figure 7.31
Rename the new object cameraPivot.

view and then right-click on its Collider component and select Remove
Component (see Figure 7.32).

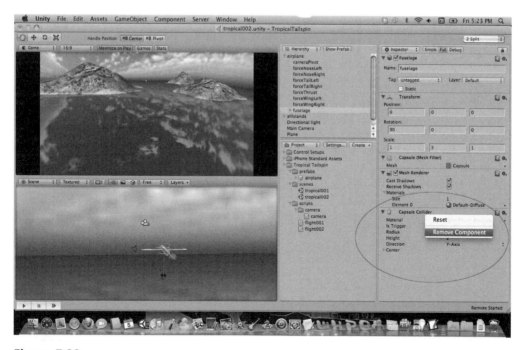

Figure 7.32
Remove all Collider components from airplane mesh game objects.

Now the scene is set to connect to the new code. Here is the code for flight002.js and camera.js. These two scripts give us a good-feeling flight model and a fluid third-person camera. Read on to find out how they work.

```
private var forceWingLeft : Transform;
private var forceWingRight : Transform;
private var forceTailLeft : Transform;
private var forceTailRight : Transform;
private var forceNoseLeft : Transform;
private var forceNoseRight : Transform;
private var forceThrust : Transform;
private var thisTransform : Transform;
private var thisRigidbody : Rigidbody;
private var thisGravity : Vector3;
private var myPitch : float;
private var calPitch : float;
private var offsetPitch : float;
private var calibrationZ : float;
function FixedUpdate()
{
if ( iPhoneInput.touchCount > 0 )
setCalibration();
var accel : Vector3 = iPhoneInput.acceleration;

if ( calibrationZ > 0 )
    myPitch = -Mathf.Atan2( accel.x, accel.z ) * Mathf.Rad2Deg;
else
    myPitch = Mathf.Atan2( accel.x, -accel.z ) * Mathf.Rad2Deg;

calPitch = ( wrapAngle( offsetPitch ) - wrapAngle( myPitch ) ) / 360;

thisRigidbody.AddForceAtPosition( thisTransform.forward * 2000,
thisTransform.position );

    //Get the angle between our velocity and the front of the wing
    var angleOfIncidence = Vector3.Angle( thisTransform.forward,
thisRigidbody.velocity );

    //Taking the Sin of the Angle of Incidence will yield 0 at 0 degrees
difference
```

```
    //and 1 (representing full friction at 90 degrees). This is what chan-
ges the direction
    //of the plane's velocity vector.
    var wingFriction = 0.1 + Mathf.Abs( Mathf.Sin( angleOfIncidence ) );

    //Add a small amount to the accelerometer values if they are equal
to zero
    var accelX = calPitch;
    if ( accelX == 0 )
        accelX += 0.1;

    var accelY = accel.y;
    if ( accelY == 0 )
        accelY += 0.1;

    var relativeLeftWingPosition : Vector3 = thisTransform.position -
forceWingLeft.position;
    var relativeRightWingPosition : Vector3 = thisTransform.position -
forceWingRight.position;

    thisRigidbody.AddForceAtPosition( thisGravity + ( -thisRigidbody.
GetPointVelocity( forceTailLeft.position ) * 0.1 ) + ( ( -thisTransform.up
* 4 * -accelX ) * wingFriction ), forceTailLeft.position );
    thisRigidbody.AddForceAtPosition( thisGravity + ( -thisRigidbody.
GetPointVelocity( forceTailRight.position ) * 0.1 ) + ( ( -thisTransform.
up * 4 * -accelX ) * wingFriction ), forceTailRight.position );
    thisRigidbody.AddForceAtPosition( thisGravity + ( -thisRigidbody.
GetPointVelocity( forceNoseLeft.position ) * 0.1 ), forceNoseLeft.posi-
tion );
    thisRigidbody.AddForceAtPosition( thisGravity + ( -thisRigidbody.
GetPointVelocity( forceNoseRight.position ) * 0.1 ), forceNoseRight.po-
sition );
    thisRigidbody.AddForceAtPosition( thisGravity + ( -thisRigidbody.
GetPointVelocity( forceWingLeft.position ) * 0.25 ) + ( ( thisTransform.up
* 2 * -accelY ) * wingFriction ) - thisTransform.forward * re-
lativeLeftWingPosition.y * thisRigidbody.velocity.magnitude * 0.001,
forceWingLeft.position );
    thisRigidbody.AddForceAtPosition( thisGravity + ( -thisRigidbody.
GetPointVelocity( forceWingRight.position ) * 0.25 ) + ( ( thisTransform.
up * 2 * accelY ) * wingFriction ) - thisTransform.forward * relativeR-
ightWingPosition.y * thisRigidbody.velocity.magnitude * 0.001, for-
ceWingRight.position );
```

```
}
function setCalibration ()
{
    var accel : Vector3 = iPhoneInput.acceleration;
    calibrationZ = accel.z;

    if ( calibrationZ > 0 )
        offsetPitch = -Mathf.Atan2 ( accel.x, accel.z ) * Mathf.
Rad2Deg;
    else
        offsetPitch = Mathf.Atan2 ( accel.x, -accel.z ) * Mathf.
Rad2Deg;
}
function Start ()
{
    forceWingLeft = transform.Find ( "forceWingLeft" );
    forceWingRight = transform.Find ( "forceWingRight" );

    forceTailLeft = transform.Find ( "forceTailLeft" );
    forceTailRight = transform.Find ( "forceTailRight" );

    forceNoseLeft = transform.Find ( "forceNoseLeft" );
    forceNoseRight = transform.Find ( "forceNoseRight" );

    forceThrust = transform.Find ( "forceThrust" );

    thisTransform = transform;
    thisRigidbody = rigidbody;

    thisGravity = Vector3 ( 0, -9.8, 0 );

    setCalibration ();
}
function wrapAngle ( angleToWrap : float )
{
    return 180 - angleToWrap;
}
```

As you can see, our version 0.02 prototype is much more complex than version 0.01. This code, along with a few changes to your scene, actually nets something that feels similar to *X-Plane.*

In addition to our version 0.02 flight model, we've also changed the camera behavior. The new camera code that follows creates a smooth third-person camera that isn't fixed rigidly to the airplane.

```
var target : Transform;
var pivot : Transform;
private var thisTransform : Transform;
function LateUpdate()
{

    thisTransform.position += ( pivot.position - thisTransform.posi-
tion ) * 10 * Time.deltaTime;
    thisTransform.LookAt ( target.transform.position + target.forward
* 0 );
}
function Start()
{
    thisTransform = transform;

}
```

Code Analysis

As we've already discussed, version 0.02 is quite a bit more complex than version 0.01. The first big change you'll notice is that we've added two new force points: forceNoseLeft and forceNoseRight. We've done this because we have added gravity to the simulation but not just to the center of mass; we are applying gravity individually to all of the force points. Without gravity applied to the nose of the airplane, the simulation wasn't balanced. On a real airplane, gravity would be integrated over the whole of the airplane's mass, not just at its center.

You'll also notice that we added the variables myPitch, calPitch, offsetPitch, and calibrationZ. These variables are used to calibrate your i-device, as shown in Chapter 5. Inside the FixedUpdate() callback, we have a conditional that checks for a screen touch. If the screen is touched, then the setCalibration() function is called and adjusts the basis angle for the airplane's pitch controls. Beyond that, we grab the current iPhone input accelerometer reading and store it into a Vector3 variable called accel. Once we get the current accelerometer value, we get the current pitch of the device, accounting for the direction the screen is pointing (calibrationZ). Finally, we grab the calibrated pitch, which is the difference between offsetPitch (acquired whenever calibration is done) and the current `myPitch` variable, all divided by 360.

With all the calibrated accelerometer work done, we then move on to applying the proper forces to the airplane. The first force we apply is the thrust force, which is equal to the airplane's current forward vector multiplied by 2,000. The next step is to calculate the angle of incidence between the velocity vector and the airplane's forward-facing vector. This is crucial because if you think about an airplane carefully, you'll realize how it carves through the air. The airplane's ailerons and elevator cause the airplane to change its orientation, but the difference between the angle of the airplane's orientation and the direction it's traveling causes different degrees of friction, which in turn cause the airplane to slow down severely when, for example, the airplane's orientation becomes perpendicular to its velocity. That's where the next line of code comes in, which sets a variable called `wingFriction`, equal to the sum of 0.1 and the absolute value of the sine of the angle of incidence. This means that there's very little friction when the plane's body and its velocity are aligned and full friction when the velocity and the body intersect each other.

The next few lines of code increment the accelerometer values slightly to ensure that no zero values are passed into the force point calculations. If one of the accelerometer values is set to zero, then whole portions of the code to follow might become equal to zero and cause the forces to be unbalanced or inaccurate.

What follows is a series of forces applied to the force points we laid out in the Unity Editor. This version of our prototype is far more complex than the first. In the Unity Editor, we've removed any sort of angular drag on the core rigid body, which now acts mostly as the center of mass. The first thing we do in this process is to grab the relative position of the wing-based force points. The reason for this is that we are going to apply drag based on these positions; doing so drastically alters the simulation. Without that calculation, the airplane doesn't change its heading as it banks. Depending on what flight games you've played before, this may seem acceptable. Many flight games allow the player to roll and then pitch to change heading or use the rudder to change heading. Real airplanes do in fact change their heading as they bank.

As was stated, this prototype is quite a bit more complex than the previous incarnation. Let's break them down now. The force point calculations begin on the tail of the airplane. The first step we take is to add gravity to the force being applied. The next step is to calculate the point velocity of each tail force point. The point velocity yields both the linear and angular velocity of the point relative to the rigid body. The point velocity is then multiplied by a factor of 0.1; ultimately this part of the equation creates the angular drag on the airplane. After applying gravity and angular drag to the airplane, we need to add lift and also factor in the wing friction we discussed earlier. To add these factors, we take the inverse of the airplane's upward orientation vector, multiply it by 4, and then multiply by the inverse of the accelerometer reading's X component (up is down and down is up to an airplane's flight yoke). Finally, we multiply all of that by the wing friction we calculated earlier. It should be noted that some of the arbitrary numbers we've multiplied by in this code have been derived through experimentation. Try changing these hard-coded numbers to see what effect it has on the flight model.

The next couple of lines apply the forces of gravity and angular drag to the nose of the airplane. These lines of code are quite simple. Their sole purpose is to counterbalance the forces being applied to the tail of the airplane. As we stated before, in real life, forces are integrated throughout the entire volume of a physical object's mass. These lines of code are a simple way to create that sort of balance.

Now we move on to the forces applied to the wings. These calculations are very similar to those applied to the tail. The first part is identical as we apply gravity. Then we apply angular drag. The biggest difference here is that when calculating angular drag on the wings, we use a factor of 0.25 instead of 0.1. This is logical because the wings are quite a bit larger than the elevator. The increase in surface area warrants an increase in drag coefficient.

The next part of the calculation accounts for lift, which in this instance is applied directly along the upward-facing vector of the airplane's body. The big kicker with this part of the calculation is that we multiply one wing by the inverse of the accelerometer reading's Y component and the other by the accelerometer reading's standard Y component. The opposing application of force causes the airplane to roll with the actual direction that the iPhone or iPod Touch is rolled. Finally, we again multiply all of that by wing friction.

The rest of the code behind this prototype consists of the calibration function, the start callback, and a utility function that simply returns the difference between 180 degrees and a passed angle. We covered calibration in Chapter 5, but for the sake of thoroughness, we'll do it again here.

This function first gets the current accelerometer reading and stores its Z component into the variable `calibrationZ`. This tells us whether the iPhone's screen is facing up or down. Depending on that, we make some subtle changes to the calculations used to figure out the offset pitch. To get the offset pitch, we use the `ATan2` function, which is used to get the angle in radians whose tangent is equal to parameter 1/parameter 2. (Draw a triangle if you have to.)

Once we have the angle in radians, we multiply by the math constant `Mathf.Rad2Deg` to get the angle in degrees. The last piece of this prototype code is the start callback. The start callback simply initializes the force points, primary transform, rigid body, and gravity, and calls `setCalibration()` for the first time. It's important to initialize variables such as transforms and rigid bodies because it's expensive in terms of processing power to look them up dynamically every time you want to reference them at run time. Looking them up and storing a reference to them at startup significantly increases performance on the iPhone.

That wraps it up for version 0.02 of the prototype flight model, but we still have some camera code to cover. The camera code is quite simple. The basic concept is to point the camera at a target, all the while having it attempt to position itself at a certain point that is always moving. This code creates a tethered camera effect whereby the farther the camera is from its desired position, the faster it moves to get into position. The camera always points at its target, keeping it centered onscreen. The code contains two variables, `target` and `pivot`, which are both transforms. `target` is where the camera points, and `pivot` is where the camera attempts to position itself. Both of these variables are assignable from the Unity Editor, and you will receive an error if either is not assigned properly. The target of the camera is obviously the `airplane` game object, and the pivot is the `cameraPivot` game object.

In this code, we use the `LateUpdate()` callback because we want the effects of the camera code to take place after everything else. This strategy creates smoother camera movement and rendering. Inside the `LateUpdate()` callback, we add the difference between the pivot's position and the camera's transform position, multiplied by 10, and then multiplied by delta time (time change since the last frame) to the current camera position to move the camera closer to its desired position.

Then we use the simple `LookAt()` function from the `Transform` class to keep the camera looking at its target. We also add the target's forward-facing vector to its position, so the camera looks slightly ahead of the airplane's center if so desired. In this example, we've multiplied by zero, so the camera points directly at the airplane, but for fun, you can plug in different values (or even expose the variable in the Unity Editor) and see how it affects the view. Lastly, we have a start callback, which just sets a variable local to this script to the transform of the object to which the script belongs.

Conclusion

We have now set up a fully playable 3D flight simulator based on very realistic physics principles. The result allows us to bank, flip, and do barrel rolls. This prototype is not to be confused with a complete and dynamic flight engine, but rather, it is the basis for one in the future. It is a very good base for a simple one-off game concept like *Tropical Tailspin*. Before we begin extending the prototype into a game, we must first do some play testing and iterating to make sure that our foundation is already appealing to others.

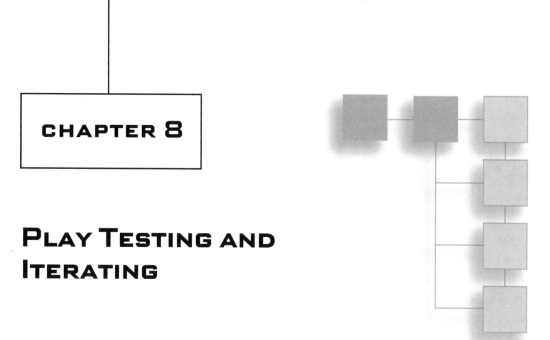

CHAPTER 8

PLAY TESTING AND ITERATING

By now we have covered a great deal of iPhone development. We know the ins and outs of the hardware, we know how to use all of the great software provided by Apple and Unity, we've learned a thing or two about concept art, and we've even put together a fully playable flight simulator prototype. It is almost show-time, but before we go uploading anything to iTunes Connect, we'd better get some opinions on the foundation of the game. Then we have to sift through them carefully to decipher what people really want across the board. Many times people will say one thing, but that's not actually what they want. It's our job as game developers to read between the lines and deliver the fun that other people crave. Sometimes, you'll realize that a concept you've tried to communicate doesn't come across to the player or that your prototype isn't technically polished enough to be intuitive. At other times, your art won't be clean enough to be functional as a form of communication. If you haven't noticed already, communication is a big part of game development. I'd go so far as to say that game development is just another language with which we can communicate ideas. If you notice that players aren't getting your message, you have to clarify that message. That is what gameplay testing accomplishes. Take your prototype, show it to players, but be aware that often what they communicate back to you has nothing to do with what they want from your game and more to do with what they didn't understand about it. It's a fine line to walk, but hopefully we can make it easier with some solid examples.

Testing Criteria

Before we start putting the new prototype in people's hands, we have to come up with some criteria for the play test. We have certain goals for *Tropical Tailspin*. First, it has to be easy to pick up and play. Second, it has to go beyond any other flight simulator tutorial on the iPhone (such as the simple flight demo that comes with Unity). Third, it has to contain a gameplay mechanic, even if it's a simple one like finding all the landmarks in *Wii Sports Resort*. Finally, we really want this game to feel solid and prove that at least the theory behind the flight model is capable of producing an experience that feels like the ultra-popular *X-Plane* series. With all of that said, we need to address each of these issues with questions aimed at the play testers.

The first goal is pretty easy. When people get their hands on *Tropical Tailspin*, can they begin doing loopty-loops without getting too frustrated? This test is simple and requires us only to see how someone reacts emotionally. If he cracks a smile, we're good to go.

The next goal is a bit more complex. We have to show someone who is tech savvy the flight simulator and, for example, the flight demo built into Unity. We need to approach someone who might be interested in demos and see if he thinks what we're doing constitutes a great improvement on previous example games.

The third is also pretty universal. Anyone who had fun with *Wii Sports Resort*'s flight mode should be able to give feedback on the gameplay concept. We have to add some quick gameplay mechanism to the prototype that simulates what the play testers can expect from the final game. On one hand, the concept of flying about and finding way points should be pretty simple and carefree for players, but it should at the same time give them a feeling of exhilaration as they explore and find new items. On the other hand, this means that we have to add some actual gameplay code for the play testers to interact with besides the flight model.

Our final goal is to engage players in a head-to-head playoff between the prototype and *X-Plane*. Obviously, *X-Plane* is far superior, but we have to know if players even see the potential for the game to appeal to players who greatly enjoyed *X-Plane*. The play testers should be able to give us some solid feedback on this matter. Have we engaged their imaginations?

Prepping the Prototype

Now that we have identified some bullet points for the testing, it's time to prepare the game for the play test. For the most part, the game is ready to be tested, but we still need a few more steps of iteration to test the basic gameplay.

The first thing we need to do is add some way points to the game for players to fly around and collect. For the purpose of this play test, we'll be using the old coin cliché. We can add a very simple coin counter GUI object, and players must attempt to fly around the environment and collect all the coins. In addition, we may want to add some form of collision to the airplane and environment to give the game some challenge or at least remove the feeling that the game is buggy because the airplane can pass through objects.

To begin, we'll add some coins. If you haven't already, open up the Unity Editor and, using the Scene view, zoom over to the center island hillside. Now create a cylinder (see Figure 8.1).

Once the cylinder is in view (you may need to zoom in a bit more), rotate it 90 degrees about its X-axis and then scale it up by a factor of (10, 0.1, 10),

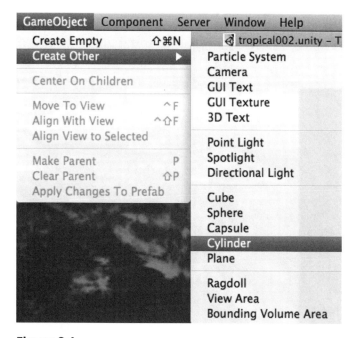

Figure 8.1
Add a cylinder that will become a coin.

as shown in Figure 8.2. This rotation and scale should net us something that looks like a large white piece of wafer candy.

Now that the shape is correct, let's get a material to match. Under the Tropical Tailspin folder in the Project view, create a new folder called Materials. Do this by right-clicking on the Tropical Tailspin folder and then choosing Create > Folder from the menu. Then do a slow double-click on the folder or highlight it and press Enter/Return to rename it Materials (see Figure 8.3).

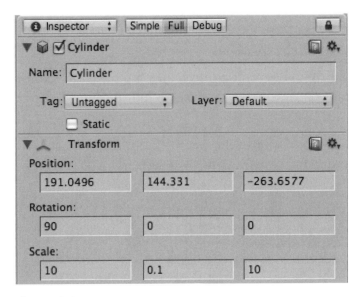

Figure 8.2
Rotate and scale the cylinder.

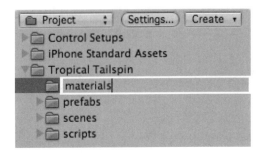

Figure 8.3
Create a Materials folder.

Now that we have a place to put the new material, it's time to create the material. Right-click on the Materials folder and choose Create > Material from the menu (see Figure 8.4).

When the new material is created, rename it Coin (see Figure 8.5).

After the material is renamed, it's time to make it look right. With the Coin material highlighted in the Project view, click on the color bar (which is white initially) on the far right panel. A Color Picker will pop up (see Figure 8.6).

The quick fit for a coin, of course, is the color yellow. Choose the yellow prefab color from the Color Picker. Once you've chosen the color, you can close the

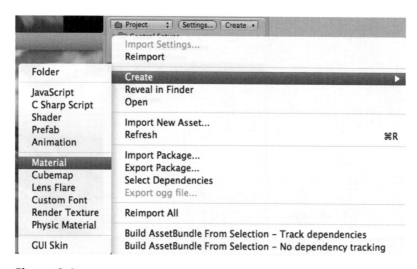

Figure 8.4
Create the new material.

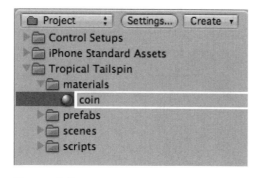

Figure 8.5
Rename the material Coin.

Figure 8.6
Color Picker.

Color Picker window. The final step is to drag and drop the new Coin material onto the cylinder in the Scene view (see Figures 8.7 and 8.8).

Now that the cylinder looks pretty *coiny,* we can go ahead and rename it Coin as well (see Figure 8.9).

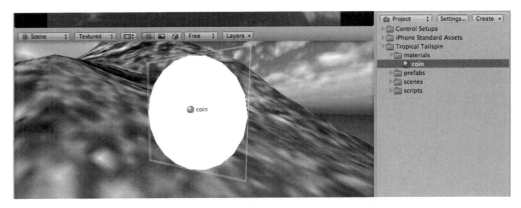

Figure 8.7
Drag and drop the Coin material.

Figure 8.8
Poof, you're King Midas.

Now we want to populate the whole environment with coins, which means we need a coin prefab to quickly and easily drop new coins into the scene. Right-click on the Prefabs folder in the Project view and choose Create > Prefab from the menu (see Figure 8.10).

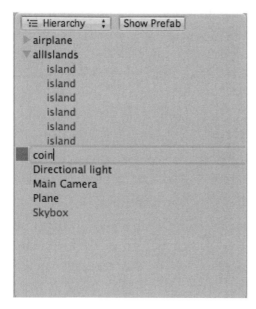

Figure 8.9
Rename the cylinder Coin.

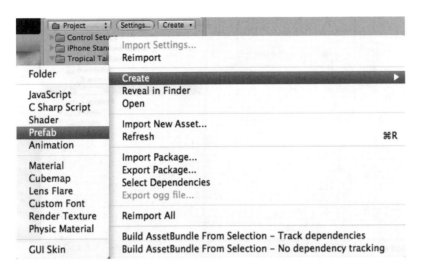

Figure 8.10
Create a new prefab.

Rename the new prefab Coin and then drag and drop the Coin object from the Hierarchy view onto the Coin prefab in the Project view (see Figure 8.11).

Now that we're ready to begin dragging and dropping coins, it might be a good time to do a bit of project cleanup. As your game projects become increasingly complex, it's a good idea to create new folders to keep things orderly. At this point, we're collecting multiple types of prefabs and scripts, which are placed somewhat haphazardly. To clean things up, let's add a folder within the Scripts folder called flightModel and two folders within the Prefabs folder called Airplane and Environment (see Figure 8.12).

Once you've created the new folders, drag their respective prefabs and scripts to them. This will create a more organized Project view. Also create a new Airplane2 prefab, because we changed the original 0.01 prototype airplane quite a bit. After the prefab is created, drag and drop the current airplane onto the new prefab (see Figure 8.13).

Now that the Project view is clean and we've got a coin in the level, it might be time to move on to version 0.03 of the game prototype, since we're moving on from our focus on the basic flight mechanics. Save this scene as tropical003 (see Figure 8.14).

Before we start littering the landscape with coins, let's run the game once and see how solid the scale of the coin is and if it seems to be manageable to fly into.

Figure 8.11
Drag and drop the Coin game object onto the Coin prefab.

We want it to require skill to run into a coin, but not too much. The challenge of running into a coin should merely engage the player but not break the feel of the game.

On first approach, it's pretty clear that the coin is too small a target to be fun. Let's scale the coin up to (100, 1, 100) and try again (see Figure 8.15).

Figure 8.12
Folder fun.

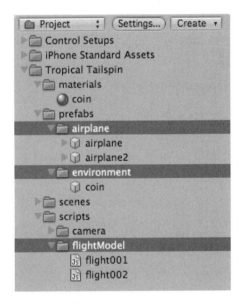

Figure 8.13
A little housecleaning.

With the coin scaled up by 10, I was able to run through it on my first try. We'll have to see what the play testers do, but for now it seems like we have a decent scale. It's important to point out that the model game on *Wii Sports Resort*'s flight mode does not require players to touch the way points they collect, only get close to them.

Figure 8.14
Save as tropical003.

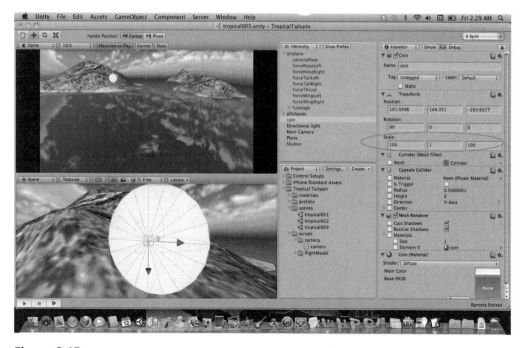

Figure 8.15
The coin was too small.

To complete the version 0.03 prototype, we need several coins, collision detection, and a coin counter displayed onscreen. We'll begin by adding collision detection to the islands. Select each island and then add mesh colliders by selecting Component > Physics > Mesh Collider from the main menu (see Figure 8.16).

Next, we need to add a collision method for the airplane. At first, a large box collider seems like an easy solution, but it doesn't work. The problem with

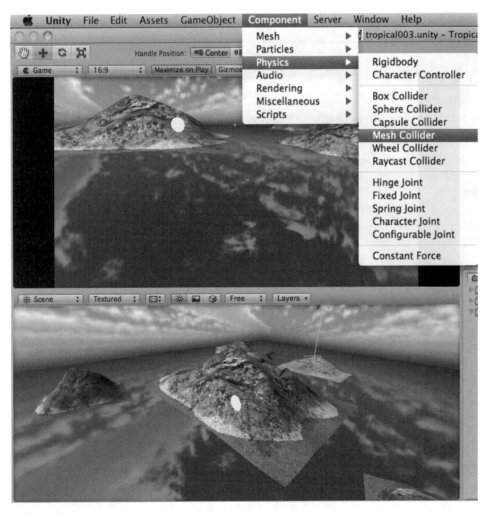

Figure 8.16
Add mesh colliders to the islands.

adding a box collider to the airplane is that it changes the physics of the flight model. To overcome this, we're going to need a bit of special sauce.

A variety of methods are available to handle collisions between the airplane and the environment. At this point, we simply want the quickest solution to detect a hit. The special sauce we need is this Update() callback code added to the flight002 script.

```
function Update()
{
  var hit : RaycastHit;
  var layerMask = 1 << 2;
      layerMask = ~layerMask;
  if ( Physics.Raycast ( thisTransform.position, thisTransform.forward,
hit, 10, layerMask ) )
      Debug.Log ( "Crash" );
  if ( Physics.Raycast ( thisTransform.position, -thisTransform.forward,
hit, 10, layerMask ) )
        Debug.Log ( "Crash" );
  if ( Physics.Raycast ( thisTransform.position, thisTransform.up, hit,
5, layerMask ) )
      Debug.Log ( "Crash" );
  if ( Physics.Raycast ( thisTransform.position, -thisTransform.up, hit,
5, layerMask ) )
      Debug.Log ( "Crash" );
  if ( Physics.Raycast ( thisTransform.position, thisTransform.right,
hit, 10, layerMask ) )
      Debug.Log ( "Crash" );
  if ( Physics.Raycast ( thisTransform.position, -thisTransform.right,
hit, 10, layerMask ) )
      Debug.Log ( "Crash" );
}
```

This code sends raycasts out in six directions around the airplane and lets us know if we've come too close to any scenery. A *raycast* is a linear method for determining collision. A ray is essentially just a line in 3D space with a start and end point. We can then search our scene geometry to find out if this ray intersects anything between the starting position and ending position. The way that Unity handles its raycasting parameters in this example is to accept a starting position, a direction vector, a reference to a RaycastHit object, a distance or length to run along our direction vector, and a layermask (in case we want to limit what we search for to speed things up). Right now, we're just recording a Crash line to the debugger log, which is a useful tool for letting us know that some condition was met without having to create a complex reaction. Once this code is added, we can save this script as flight003 and make the appropriate changes to the scene tropical003 so that the script and the scene versions are synchronized. That is, we remove the old flight002 script component from the Airplane game object and add the flight003 script to it. Once this is done, a message will pop up in the bottom-left corner of the Unity Editor that says *Crash* when you come too close to or run through the scenery (see Figure 8.17).

Notice how Figure 8.17 showed only the Game view. You can use the Maximize on Play button just above the Game view if you want to focus only on that, ignoring the rest of the Unity Editor. It's useful for taking screenshots.

Of course, we can't just stop at printing the word Crash. Now we need to find out what we're about to crash into. If we're about to crash into the ground, we need to blow up; if we hit the water, we need to make a splash; and if we crash into a coin, we need to pick it up.

To do this, we're going to need another function. This time the function won't be a callback but instead a custom function. Add this `handleRaycasts()` function to the flight003 script.

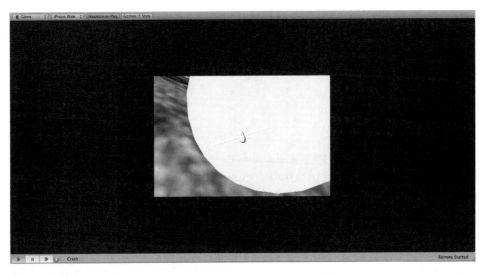

Figure 8.17
Crash in the debug log.

```
function handleRaycasts ( theHit : RaycastHit )
{
    switch ( theHit.transform.name )
    {
        case "coin" :
            Destroy ( theHit.transform.gameObject ) ;
            Debug.Log ( "Collected a coin!" ) ;
            break;

        case "water" :
            Debug.Log ( "Splash" ) ;
            break;

        default:
            Debug.Log ( "Crash" ) ;
            break;
    }
}
```

Once that is done, replace all the lines in the Update() callback that contain Debug.Log. ("CrashDebug") with handleRaycasts (hit) so it looks like the code below.

```
function Update ()
{
    var hit : RaycastHit;
    var layerMask = 1 << 2;
    layerMask = ~layerMask;
    if ( Physics.Raycast ( thisTransform.position, thisTransform.
forward, hit, 10, layerMask ) )
        handleRaycasts ( hit ) ;
    if ( Physics.Raycast ( thisTransform.position, -thisTransform.
forward, hit, 10, layerMask ) )
        handleRaycasts ( hit ) ;
    if ( Physics.Raycast ( thisTransform.position, thisTransform.up, hit,
5, layerMask ) )
        handleRaycasts ( hit ) ;
    if ( Physics.Raycast ( thisTransform.position, -thisTransform.up,
hit, 5, layerMask ) )
        handleRaycasts ( hit ) ;
    if ( Physics.Raycast ( thisTransform.position, thisTransform.right,
hit, 10, layerMask ) )
```

```
        handleRaycasts( hit );
    if ( Physics.Raycast( thisTransform.position, -thisTransform.right,
hit, 10, layerMask ) )
        handleRaycasts( hit );
}
```

Before running the game again, there's one last change we need to make. The water is still called Plane in the scene. Rename it Water (see Figure 8.18).

Now we have some options as to what we can collide with. Currently, the results of the collisions are pretty boring, but we can fix that. The most interesting reaction we have is the coin collision, which not only prints "Collected a coin!" to the debugger but also removes the coin from the scene. The Destroy() command will remove any game object from the scene. Use it wisely.

Now that we can collide with coins and remove them from the scene, it's time to add the coin counter to the game. This involves adding a new empty game object called GUI to the scene. We will then attach a script to the GUI game object containing an OnGUI() callback that counts up all the coins in the scene and prints the number onscreen. We worked with the OnGUI() callback in Chapter 5, but to reiterate, GUI stands for *graphic user interface*. Unity's GUI class contains functionality to print text onscreen, create windows to contain the text, and even to add scrollbars, buttons, and checkboxes. The GUI system provides a really nice interface for us to allow players to control the parameters of the game, like options screens, for example, although the GUI class can be used for much more.

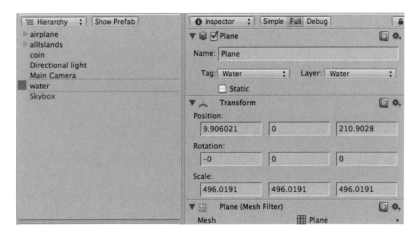

Figure 8.18
Change Plane to Water.

Begin by adding a new empty game object to the scene and renaming it GUI. Position the new GUI object at (0, 0, 0) for organizational purposes (see Figures 8.19–8.21).

Now we're going to need the script to drive the new GUI object. In the Project view, create a new folder under scripts called GUI.

Within the new GUI folder, create a new JavaScript called `coinCounter`.

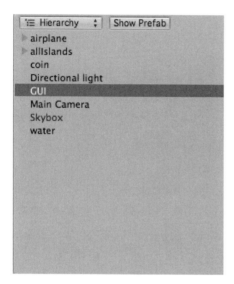

Figure 8.19
Create the GUI game object.

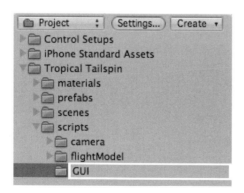

Figure 8.20
Create a GUI scripts folder.

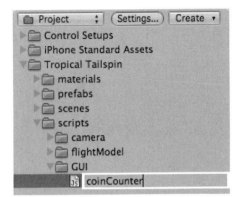

Figure 8.21
Create the `coinCounter` script.

With the new script created, open it up with Unitron and add the following code:

```
private var coinsBegin : int;
private var coinsCurrent : int;
function OnGUI()
{
    coinsCurrent = 0;
    var coinObjects = FindObjectsOfType( GameObject );
    for ( var coinObject : GameObject in coinObjects )
    {
        if ( coinObject.name == "coin" )
          coinsCurrent++;
    }

    GUI.Label( Rect( 0, 0, 320, 20 ), "Collected " + ( coinsBegin - coin-
sCurrent ) + " of " + coinsBegin + " coins!" );
}
function Start()
{
    var coinObjects = FindObjectsOfType( GameObject );
    for ( var coinObject : GameObject in coinObjects )
    {
        if ( coinObject.name == "coin" )
          coinsBegin++;
    }
}
```

After the code has been added, save the script and then drag and drop it onto the GUI game object in the Hierarchy view (see Figure 8.22).

Once the Script component has been attached, you'll see a small blurb of text in the upper-left corner of the game screen that tells you how many coins you've collected and how many coins are in the whole scene. This is a real milestone. Our simple prototype now has some semblance of gameplay!

Now we need to add some consequences for crashing. At this leg of the race, we don't need anything too fancy, but something to add a bit of challenge to the prototype would be to restart the level if you crash. This is a very simple

Figure 8.22
Drag and drop the `coinCounter` script onto the GUI game object.

mechanism and isn't remotely polished, but it will showcase a few important programming aspects.

The basic premise we're going to follow is to destroy the Airplane game object upon a collision, print a "Crashed" message onto the center of the screen, and, finally, let the player tap the screen to retry. Adding this sort of mechanism will have a few branching effects. For example, by destroying the Airplane game object, we will cause an error in the camera script as it attempts to look at and follow the airplane. To handle this, we will have to add a check to the camera script to make sure that the target and pivot both exist before attempting to access them. If either the target or pivot doesn't exist, then it is considered to be null by the program. *Null* is the absence of data.

Let's begin by modifying that camera script to handle a null-case scenario. Change the public variable initializations and the `LateUpdate()` callback to look like the following code:

```
var target : Transform = null;
var pivot : Transform = null;
function LateUpdate()
{
    if ( pivot != null )
        thisTransform.position += ( pivot.position - thisTransform.
position) * 10 * Time.deltaTime;

    if ( target != null )
        thisTransform.LookAt ( target.transform.position + target.
forward * 0 );
}
```

With these changes, we can even set the target and pivot fields to None in the Unity Editor without throwing an error. We are well within our rights to destroy the Airplane object upon crashing into the water or into anything else via the default case in the flight003 script component's `handleRaycasts()` function. Let's modify that code to match the following:

```
function handleRaycasts ( theHit : RaycastHit )
{
  switch ( theHit.transform.name )
  {
    case "coin":
```

```
      Destroy( theHit.transform.gameObject );
      Debug.Log( "Collected a coin!" );
      break;

   case "water":
      Destroy( gameObject );
      Debug.Log( "Splash" );
      break;

   default:
      Destroy( gameObject );
      Debug.Log( "Crash" );
      break;
   }
}
```

You'll now notice when running the game with Unity Remote that you can crash into the water or one of the islands. The reaction to a crash is still quite simplistic, but we have eliminated the ability to fly through objects unscathed. Now we can add the last bit of functionality to allow us to have a small yet fully functional game. To do this, we need to send a message to the GUI game object. Before we can send a message to the GUI object, however, there are some preparations we must make. First, we need to add a public reference to the GUI object from the flight003 script. To do this, add the following line of code at the top of the script:

```
var gameObjectGUI : Transform = null;
```

This new public variable will store a reference to the GUI game object. With this variable in place, we can now add the next line of code to both the water switch condition and the default switch condition.

```
gameObjectGUI.SendMessage( crash );
```

Before this code will function, we need to add a `crash()` function to a script attached to the GUI game object, which will receive the message.

We use Unity's `SendMessage()` function in this case because we cannot call custom script functions directly from a Transform game object's Script component, only functions that belong to built-in Unity classes. For example, we could easily call `gameObjectGUI.LookAt()` because `LookAt()` is a function of the Transform class. The `SendMessage()` function will look through all the Script components attached to a game object and call the function name passed for each script that contains a function with that name. Thus, any other scripts attached to `GameObjectGUI()` that contain a `crash()` function will also be called. The `SendMessage()` function is a good way to call any custom script function. Alternatively, we could use something like this code snippet:

```
var script : crash = gameObjectGUI.gameObject.GetComponent( crash );
script.crash();
```

Because this functionality is quite different from the `coinCounter` script, it would be wise to create an additional script to encapsulate this functionality. Be warned that, should we add too many scripts with `OnGUI()` callbacks, it could hurt the performance of the game. At this point, we should be fine, but in the future we may consider consolidating the code down to one script to control all of the GUI functions. For now, let's move on and create a new script called `Crash` in the GUI Scripts folder (see Figure 8.23).

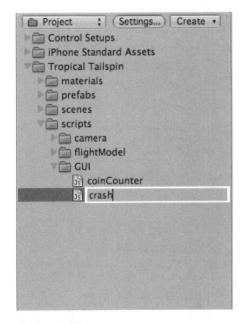

Figure 8.23
Create a `Crash` script in the GUI Scripts folder.

After the script is created, open it and add the code below.

```
private var crashed : boolean;
function crash()
{
    crashed = true;
}
function OnGUI()
{
    if ( crashed )
        GUI.Label( Rect( Screen.width / 2 - 50, Screen.height / 2 - 10, 100,
20 ), "You crashed! Tap screen to restart." );
}
function Update()
{
    if ( iPhoneInput.touchCount > 0 && crashed )
    {
        Application.GarbageCollectUnusedAssets();
        Application.LoadLevel( 0 );
    }
}
```

Before we can run the game again, we need to make a few adjustments in the Unity Editor. First drag and drop the new `Crash` script onto the GUI object (see Figure 8.24).

With the script safely attached, we can set the `gameObjectGUI` reference of the airplane's flight003 script component to the GUI object (see Figure 8.25).

We need to choose File > Build Settings and then click the Add Current Scene button so Unity recognizes the scene as level 0. Now if we run the game with Unity Remote, we'll be able to crash and restart to try again. At this point, it's safe to say that we can populate the locale with coins and begin testing the game. To do this, we should first drag and drop the coin onto its prefab because it has been modified since we originally created the prefab (see Figure 8.26).

Since the prefab has been updated, we can simply drag and drop the prefab into the Scene view to populate the locale with coins (see Figure 8.27).

The new coins will be placed in front of the camera by a distance of several hundred units. You can also choose one of the existing coins in the scene and

Figure 8.24
Drag and drop the `Crash` script onto the GUI game object.

begin duplicating and dragging it by pressing Command+D and then using the widget in the Scene view to move the new duplicate to the desired position. Create eight coins using this method to populate the locale with landmarks for the player to fly to and collect (see Figure 8.28).

The gameplay is basic, but we have all the elements: control, challenge, and feedback. At this time, we should be clear to get some play testing reactions and see if we're on the right track. To do this, we're going to employ three testers: Evan, Leroy, and Rich. These guys are going to put the prototype through its paces, compare it to *X-Plane, Wii Sports Resort,* and the original Unity flight demo and offer feedback on what we've done so far.

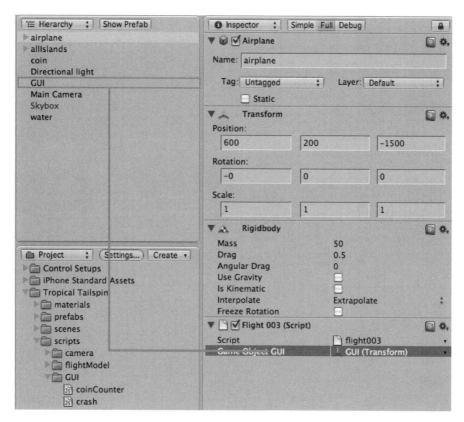

Figure 8.25
Set the `gameObjectGUI` reference to the GUI game object.

Evan, the first tester, is a fairly typical game player. He doesn't have any development experience but has been there through every game I've ever made (even the really bad ones). His initial impression of *Tropical Tailspin* started off a little rough as he wasn't sure whether the airplane was supposed to align directly with the device or not. After a few seconds, he figured out that the airplane wasn't snapped directly to the iPod Touch he was playing on and then proceeded to do a barrel roll, at which point he said, "Yeah, this is cool, and it's easy enough to figure out." He was delighted at the fact that you could do flips and barrel rolls even if there was no other gameplay to speak of. After letting him take a spin with *Tropical Tailspin*, I booted up *X-Plane* on the same device and let him take control mid-flight in the third-person perspective so the experience would be as close as possible to the prototype. *X-Plane* has a lot of features that the prototype doesn't have and won't ever have, and the biggest reason we're using *X-Plane* as a

Figure 8.26
Drag and drop the Coin game object onto the Coin prefab once again.

benchmark is for its relaxing, fun, yet realistic flight model. He said this is basically the same thing.

Evan got the point of the game quickly and got roughly the same feeling for the controls from the prototype as he did with *X-Plane*. This is a big victory for the prototype, but, of course, all was not well. Evan commented about the graphics (which we all know are terrible in the prototype) and the fact that there wasn't much to do. Overall, he said he'd be pretty happy if he could make something like *Tropical Tailspin* by reading this book. Since our main goal with *Tropical Tailspin* isn't to sell the game itself, this opinion is exactly what we're looking for.

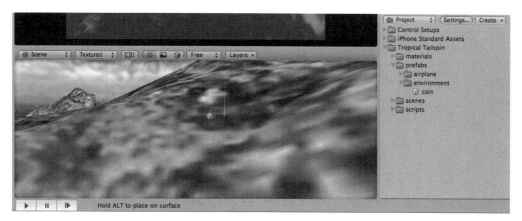

Figure 8.27
Drag and drop the prefab into the Scene view.

Our next tester, Leroy, is more technically savvy and not much of a player, and he has done some game development of his own. Leroy's first impression of the game was very similar to Evan's. The fact that this simple demo already allowed him to do flips and barrel rolls was paramount. He was impressed, but not being much of a portable guy, he wanted to hook it up to a PC and a joystick. His comments about the graphics were similar to Evan's.

Our primary reason for bringing Leroy into the test wasn't to get his opinion as a player looking to possibly develop, but more as a developer and flight aficionado who's been around the block a few times. Thus, Leroy had to compare *Tropical Tailspin* to *X-Plane* solely for the feel of the flight model. His impressions were also favorable. He noted that the graphics in the prototype were lacking but that the flight mechanics were very close.

Our final tester, Rich, is a hardcore player and also a developer. We want to get his opinion on both sides of the fence. Not surprisingly, his reaction was similar to the other two testers. The prototype is a fine proof of concept with good basic flight mechanics, but it lacks the polish of the current Unity flight example. All those who participated in the testing process agreed that a more polished flight example would go a long way in proving that this book was a worthwhile investment.

One area of contention for all the testers was coin collecting. When we set out to make this example game, we decided to use *Wii Sports Resort*'s flight mode as our gameplay foundation. Currently, *Tropical Tailspin*'s coin collecting requires too

Figure 8.28
Islands full of coins.

much precision to be fun. In *Wii Sports Resort,* you aren't required to hit the landmarks, just get near them. Our game will have to follow suit and perhaps add something more precise as an added challenge but not as the base gameplay element.

Conclusion

We've created a playable 3D game demo with physics, touch and tilt input, accelerometer calibration, collision, GUI code, objectives, and penalties. We are well on the way to submitting our example game to Apple for final approval. Of course, as the testers noted, the current prototype, though functional, leaves a lot to be desired in terms of presentation, compared even to the flight example that ships with Unity. Though we've bested its physics with a more realistic flight model, we still have a lot to do before it will represent a good selling piece for this book. Now it's time to take the tester's advice and begin creating the production art. When we finish the next chapter, we should have a good-looking game that will strike anyone as a polished example of what's possible on the iPhone.

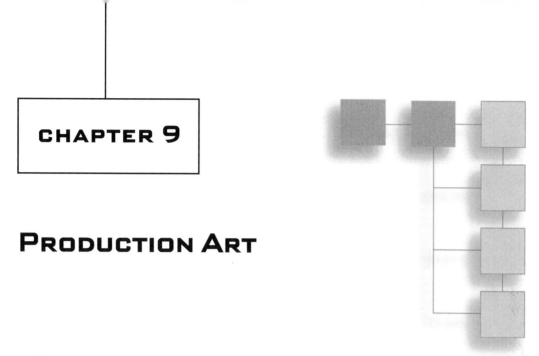

CHAPTER 9

PRODUCTION ART

Adding production-level art to a 3D game is a massive challenge and can be tackled in a variety of ways. For our example game, we have to consider the constraints we have been dealt. First of all, we are dealing with a free game. This doesn't free us from having to deliver high production values, but it does lower expectations a bit. Doing a 3D game doesn't mean we have to compete with the AAA titles of the iPhone world. We need to create attractive visuals that cover the subject matter. We need a seaplane model to replace the primitive-based placeholder, an attractive island locale with some interesting landmarks, and a nice GUI front end to bring the package together. There are some details to each of these components, such as particle effects, rigging, animation, alpha channels, and more, so we really have a lot to cover before this game can reach production-level quality. Let's get started.

The first aspect we're going to cover is the airplane model. Due to the current constraints, we're going to first look and see if someone else has crafted an adequate model to fit the game design. In some instances, reinventing the wheel is necessary, but in this instance, we should be able to find a nice model, do a little work to it, and then release it into the game world successfully.

One of the best places to find decent models is TurboSquid.com. They have a solid selection, and they provide information about the models, such as whether or not they are rigged, animated, or textured, and also how many polygons the models consist of. The iPhone hardware is pretty limited, and the recommended polycount for 3D scenes is 10,000, although I've created scenes with up to 25,000 that play fairly well. For this game, we want things to play very smoothly, due to the nature of the game. Flight games require a lot of precision, and the higher the frame rate, the more precise the controls will feel for players. Also, we want to reserve processing power for other game elements such as physics.

If we search TurboSquid for "seaplane," we get decent results. Some of the seaplanes in their catalogue are too serious and warlike, while others look like they are made from Lego blocks. Of the seaplanes that look appropriate, only one really fits the title and platform. The best model for us is seaplane1 by tom_drin. (see Figure 9.1) The look of the plane is whimsical but not unrealistic or exaggerated, and the polygon and vertex counts are well within our limits. Additionally, the price is right. When developing a game, you have to think about your budget and the realistic possibilities of iPhone sales. In this case, we're developing a free game, so our budget is zero, but depending on what you do with your time, it might be worth the $35 to pay someone else for a model, because chances are the model would take a number of hours or even days to re-create, depending on your skill level. In this instance, it's a good deal and will help keep the project on track for simultaneous release with this book. It should be noted that the author of the seaplane has agreed to allow us to distribute this seaplane model on the book's CD for educational purposes. Go ahead and put that $35 back in your wallet for now.

Of course, there will be some 3D work involved with the seaplane. As we can see from the description, it is not animated or even rigged. If we want it to feel alive at all, we'll need some propeller animation, which will involve rigging the propellers in a 3D modeling application. Furthermore, the texture looks fine, but we may want to spruce it up a bit with some tropical accents to make it look like a tour plane. Overall, that's work we will have to do no matter what, and a good 3D artist will charge approximately as much as this model costs in total, but on an hourly rate.

Now that we have chosen the airplane model, we still have about a million other elements we need to consider for the final game. The environment is a huge element, and more than likely we won't find anything useful on TurboSquid.com because the island isn't a generic object like a seaplane or a barrel.

If you search for the words "tropical island," you'll get a number of results, but none of them fit our iPhone game. Either they don't look any better than the

Figure 9.1
The seaplane model.

current prototype islands, or they are too detailed to be useful. The good thing about the search results is that they may give us ideas about what the islands should look like.

One of the island models in particular comes somewhat close to the character we're trying to achieve with *Tropical Tailspin*. The island model golfo by FraP is pretty good. It is too detailed for the game in terms of the polygon count, and it's in a format we can't use, but it's a fairly nice-looking model because of the archway, which harkens back to the concept sketch we drew in Chapter 6 (see Figure 9.2).

At this point, we need to either hire an environment artist or tackle the island model solo. Due to our particular format challenges, you probably already knew that we'd be tackling the bulk of the environment modeling in this book. Our game plan is to look back at the quick map sketch we drew and begin creating a 3D model (including an archway) to represent the base island, which is unique to *Tropical Tailspin*. After the base island is in place, we will use other, more generic items to fill in the details.

Figure 9.2
This island's got too many polygons.

As of this writing, Unity iPhone is at version 1.7, and, unfortunately, it does not support the terrain engine of its big brother, Unity or Unity Pro. Our only option is to use a third-party modeling tool to create the islands. The market is littered with 3D modelers that serve all functions, from general purpose to very specific uses. A fairly recent addition to the modeling world is new tools specifically created to simulate sculpting, as opposed to subdivision modeling or constructive solid geometry (CSG) modeling. Sculpting tools are a great fit for terrain modeling, and in fact, most game engines have built-in terrain editors with sculpting tools (Unity included). Since Unity iPhone's terrain support is not yet in place, we're going to need another solution. The solution we're going to employ for right now is Autodesk Mudbox (Autodesk.com), a super-simple tool that allows us to sculpt terrains quickly and easily and then export them to 3DS Max for detail work. Let's get sculpting!

When we open Mudbox to a blank scene, we'll begin by choosing Create > Mesh > Plane from the main menu (see Figure 9.3).

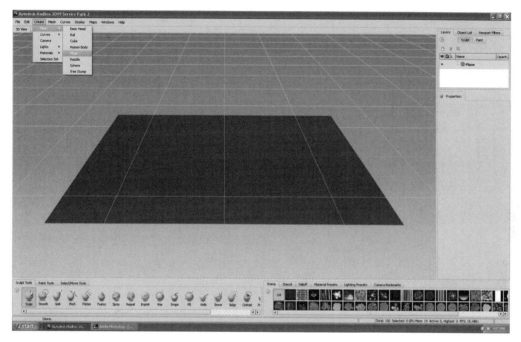

Figure 9.3
Create a plane.

You should now have a brown flat plane in the viewport. Select the Sculpt tool from the Sculpt Tools tab at the bottom of the screen. With this tool selected, move the mouse over the plane and click the left mouse button while dragging the mouse around to raise the vertices on the plane.

You might notice when using Mudbox that a message box pops up, telling you to press Shift+D to divide the mesh into finer polygons. This is just fine because the plane is currently very low poly. Press Shift+D and another message will pop up, telling you the new polygon count of the plane. We'll want to subdivide the mesh to 1,600 polygons, so do it twice. The reason we need to subdivide the plane is because the number of polygons determines how fine the detail level will be. If we want to generate subtle details in the curvature of the terrain, we'll need an appropriate number of polygons. In this instance, 1,600 gets the job done (see Figures 9.4 and 9.5).

We want to approximate what we originally created in the concept sketch from Chapter 6, and it should look something like Figure 9.6. To get this look, we used a Size setting of 10 and a Strength setting of 25.

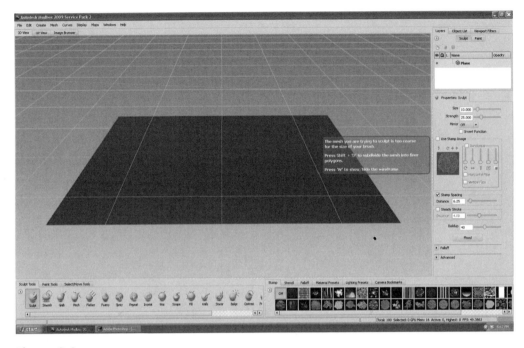

Figure 9.4
The plane isn't fine enough.

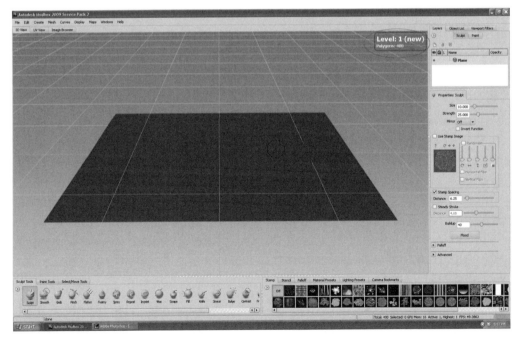

Figure 9.5
Subdivide 1 yields 400 polygons.

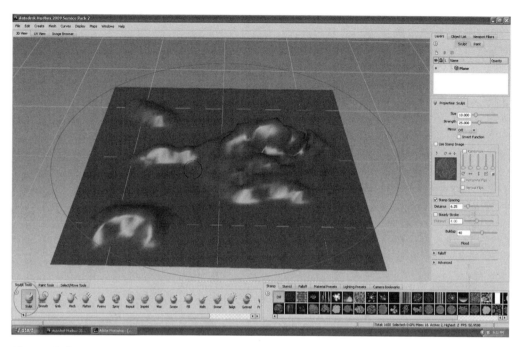

Figure 9.6
Use the Sculpt tool to approximate the concept map.

Once the map looks approximately like the concept map, we will need to smooth it out a little using the Sculpt tool and then add a few details, such as the lake on the big island. Now choose the Smooth tool from the Sculpt Tools tab at the bottom of the program and run the tool over the big island, especially where the lake should go. Also run it over the smaller islands, just on the top, to create a level area for some structures (see Figure 9.7).

After smoothing the islands, we're going to take it one step farther and flatten the areas where structures will appear. Choose the Flatten tool from the Sculpt Tools tab and flatten some ground where structures appeared in the concept drawing. Remember to keep some of the jagged edges where they belong. For example, in the concept drawing there's an indication of a rocky cliff face on the top-left island. Use the Flatten tool carefully to create an island shaped in such a way (see Figure 9.8).

Now we're going to add the lake by using the Sculpt tool inverted. Select the Sculpt tool from the Sculpt Tools tab and check the Invert Function option on the right side of the screen (see Figure 9.9).

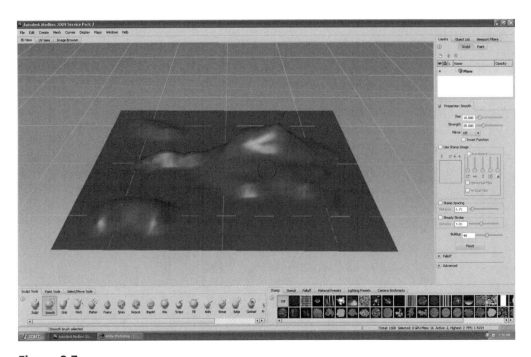

Figure 9.7
A smoother island chain.

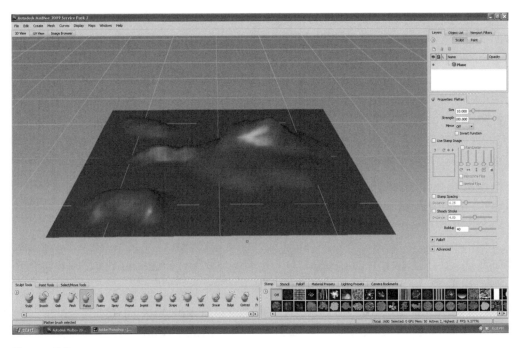

Figure 9.8
Carefully flatten the structure ground.

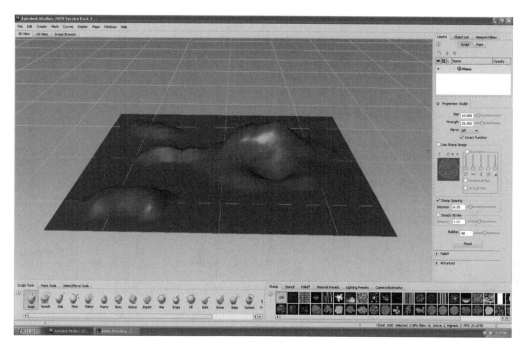

Figure 9.9
Inverse sculpt to create the lake.

At this point, the chain of islands is ready to be exported into 3DS Max for some detail work. Before we can export, though, we need to select the mesh from the Object List tab on the right side of the screen. Click on Object List and highlight the Plane object. After you have selected the Plane object, choose File > Export Selection from the main menu and save the object as `islandChain.obj` (see Figure 9.10).

Now that we have exported the island chain from Mudbox, we can import it to 3DS Max. Then we can add details such as the archway and also UV map the model so it can be properly textured. Once the arch is added and the object is UV mapped and textured, we can import it yet again (this time into Unity) and begin adding the details that will make up the final scene.

With 3DS Max open, click on the 3DS Max icon in the upper-left corner of the screen and select Import > Import (see Figure 9.11).

When you choose the Import option, a file browser will pop up. Navigate to where you exported your `islandChain.obj` model and select it for import. Then click on the Open button (see Figure 9.12).

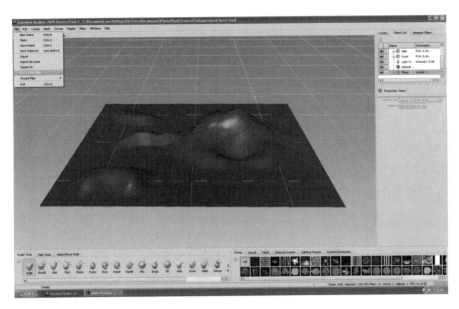

Figure 9.10
Export the selected plane.

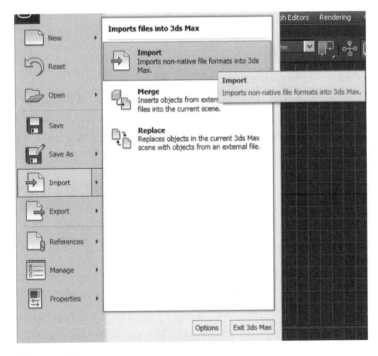

Figure 9.11
Import in 3DS Max.

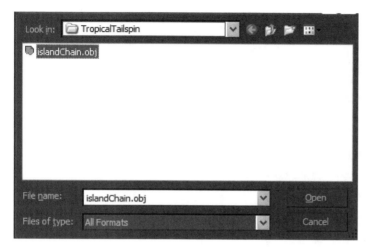

Figure 9.12
Import file browser.

When you click the Open button, an Import Options dialog box pops up. At this point, we're not going to change any of the options, but in the future we may want to convert its units, default axes, and much more (see Figure 9.13).

When you click Import, the model appears in the 3DS Max viewports, very much like it did in Mudbox, only now it is gray or white instead of brown. The good news is we can clearly see the geometry, and we can now prepare the model for some detail work.

The first thing we're going to do is add the archway detail. To prepare for this, we need to do a few things. Notice that the island mesh is called Plane_2. If we click on the Select Object button in the toolbar above the top-left viewport and then click on the island in one of the viewports, it will select the island mesh. Alternatively, you could click on the Select by Name button next to the Select Object button and choose Plane_2 from the list (see Figure 9.14).

Once the object is selected, either by using Select Object or Select from Scene, we can click on the Modify tab on the right side of the screen to change the object. In this case, we want to change the name from Plane_2 to islandChain (see Figure 9.15).

Now we're going to need a new primitive shape to use as a base for the carving operation, which will create the archway. Click on the Create tab next to the

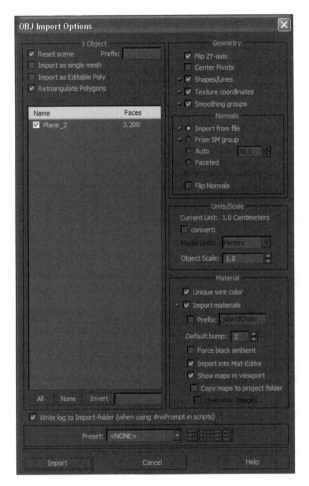

Figure 9.13
OBJ Import Options dialog.

Modify tab and choose Box. Zoom into the archway by using the arrow keys and the camera rotation widget in the upper-right corner of the Perspective view. Click and drag a box shape into the front of the archway. The first click and drag determines the horizontal size of the box; when you release the left mouse button, the height of the box is determined by dragging the mouse (see Figure 9.16).

After we've created a decent-size box in front of the archway, we'll have to rotate it into position and slightly alter its shape to make the perfect carving. Choose the Select and Rotate tool from the toolbar. Then select and rotate the box so

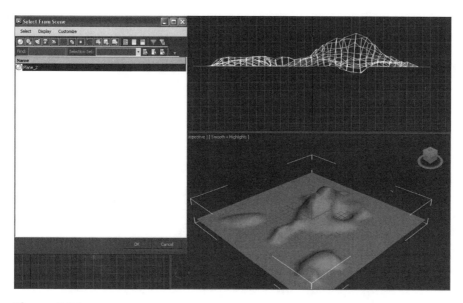

Figure 9.14
Select from Scene dialog.

that it fits through the space where the archway should be. You will probably have to also use the Select and Move tool to get it into perfect position (see Figure 9.17).

Figure 9.15
Change the name from Plane_2 to islandChain.

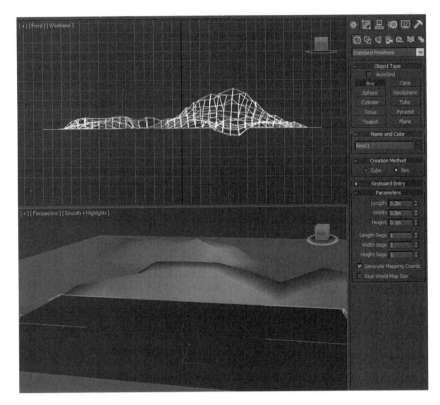

Figure 9.16
Create a box primitive in front of the archway.

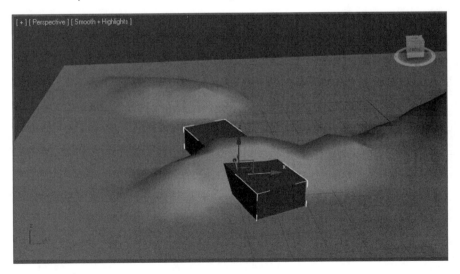

Figure 9.17
Move the box into position through the archway.

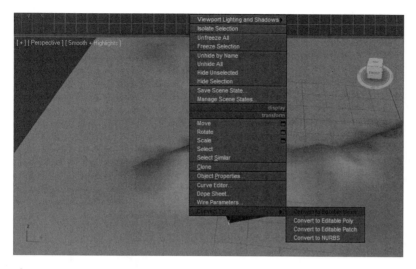

Figure 9.18
Convert to Editable Mesh.

With the box in position, we can now alter its shape slightly to get the perfect arch. Right-click on the box and choose Convert to Editable Mesh from the pop-up menu (see Figure 9.18).

Now we can alter it to a suitable shape for carving. Right-click on the box and select Cut Polygons from the pop-up menu. Click and drag from the nearest edge to the camera to the back edge of the box farthest from the camera. You should see a dotted line from front to back. Select Vertex Selection from the menu on the right to show two additional vertices between the top corners of the box (see Figure 9.19).

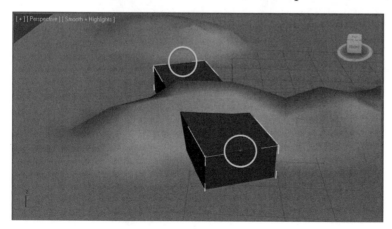

Figure 9.19
Cut creates two additional vertices.

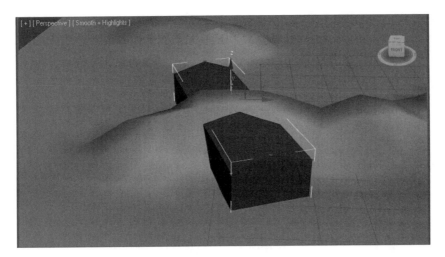

Figure 9.20
Raise the vertices.

Select both vertices by clicking on the first one and then Ctrl+clicking on the second one to highlight them. Then use the position widget to raise them up (see Figure 9.20).

Now we're going to expand the bottom of the archway. We can do this in a number of ways, but the easiest is to use Edge Selection and move the two bottom edges outward from the center of the arch (see Figures 9.21 and 9.22).

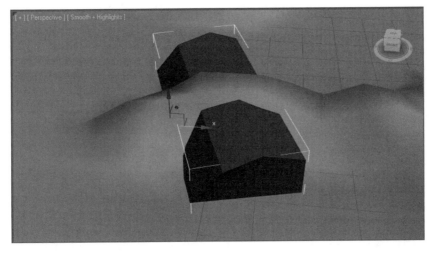

Figure 9.21
First the bottom-left edge.

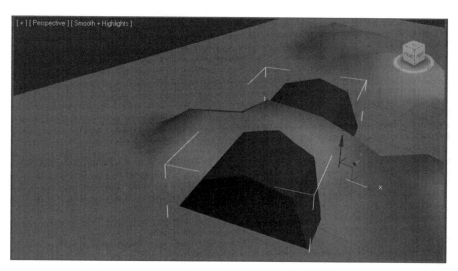

Figure 9.22
Then the bottom-right edge.

Now that the box is rotated, placed, and shaped appropriately, it's time to carve the archway. Select the islandChain object. Then change from Standard Primitives to Compound Objects on the Create tab on the right. Select ProBoolean from the Object Type tab (see Figure 9.23).

Click on Start Picking under the Pick Boolean tab on the right of the screen and then click on the box in the viewport. This will remove anything in the space occupied by the box, carving the archway into the island (see Figure 9.24).

We're going to remove any of the flat geometry or any geometry that penetrates the surface of the flat geometry, such as the lake. We're going to prep the islands for a reflection trick. If you think back to Chapter 7, we had to remove some reflection code from the demo because it wasn't suitable for camera rotation. Instead of debugging that code, we're going to use an old trick and mirror the geometry. For this trick to work, we need to see only the islands. We need to convert the island chain geometry to an editable mesh because at the moment it's set up for ProBoolean operations. Right-click on the island chain geometry and choose Convert to Editable Mesh from the pop-up menu. Then use face selection to highlight all the faces where water would be (see Figure 9.25).

Figure 9.23
Compound Objects > ProBoolean.

When all the water-covered faces are highlighted, press the Delete key to get rid of them (see Figure 9.26).

After the bulk of the faces are deleted, there will still be some geometry that appears below the surface of the island chain. We need to move up individual vertices to the level of 0 along the 3DS Max Z-axis. This way, when we mirror the

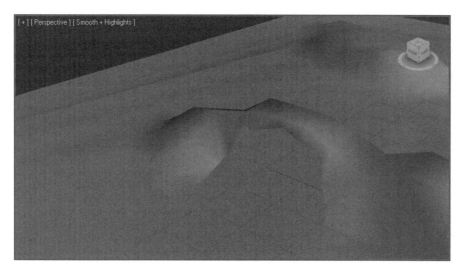

Figure 9.24
Archway carved.

geometry for the reflection, there won't be any strange faces poking up. You'll notice that we have this problem only around the lake. In the Perspective viewport, select all the vertices around the edge of the lake and align them flat whether they are above or below the Z-axis 0 mark (see Figure 9.27).

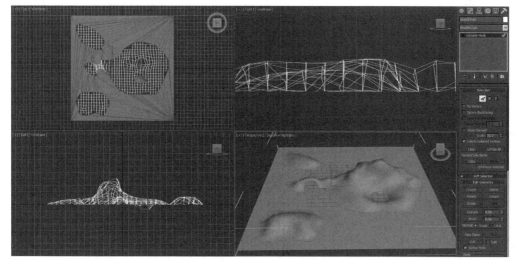

Figure 9.25
Highlight water-covered faces.

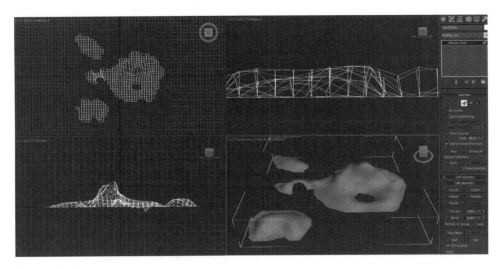

Figure 9.26
Delete water-covered faces.

With the water-covered faces removed and the lake edges aligned, we can mirror the geometry to create a reflection. We do this easily by using the Mirror tool on the main toolbar just above the top-right viewport. Clicking on the Mirror tool opens a dialog. Set the object up to mirror about the Z-axis and create a clone of the geometry. Also, adjust Offset so that the geometry meets cleanly (see Figure 9.28).

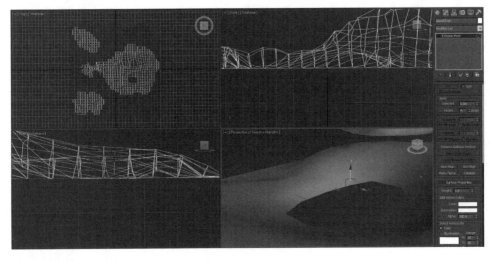

Figure 9.27
Flatten the lake's edges.

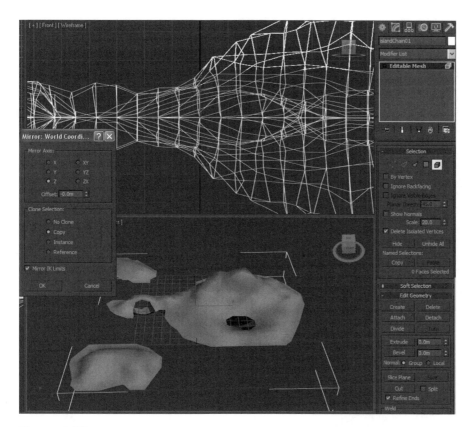

Figure 9.28
Mirror the geometry.

With the geometry carved, cleaned, and mirrored, we are ready to move on to texturing the islands with UV mapping. *UV mapping* and unwrapping is a process that allows us to transform a 3D model into a 2D flat surface with a coordinate system denoted by U and V instead of X and Y. This enables us to paint a 2D texture that will wrap around a 3D model, giving the model the desired look and feel, depending on the detail of its surface materials. This will give the islands the tropical look we want. The UV map will enable us to add grass, sand, and rocky faces to the island geometry. To begin, choose the main-Island object and use Select by Element from the menu on the right. Highlight all three islands (see Figure 9.29).

When all of the islands are highlighted, choose Modifiers > UV Coordinates > UVW Map from the main menu (see Figure 9.30).

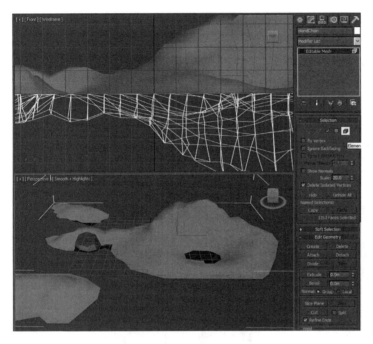

Figure 9.29
Highlight all three islands with Select by Element.

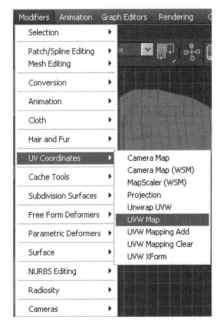

Figure 9.30
UVW Map.

Once the UVW Map modifier is applied, we can apply the Unwrap UVW modifier by choosing Modifiers > UV Coordinates > Unwrap UVW (see Figure 9.31).

Choose Edit from under the Parameters tab on the right and a window will pop up, showing the UVW mapping of the model. The wireframe image in that window will be the basis for how we apply textures to the model. We are going to export this image and use the image-editing tools to create a single texture that will be applied to the whole island chain. Click on Tools > Render UVW Template and change the settings in the Render UVs dialog box to a width and height of 1,024 (see Figure 9.32).

Click Render UV Template and save the image so you can open it with your image-editing software (see Figure 9.33).

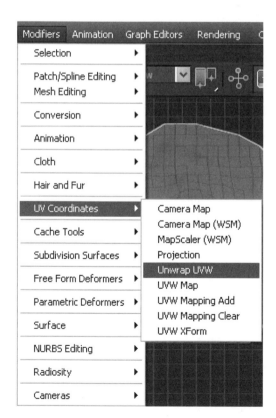

Figure 9.31
Unwrap UVW.

Figure 9.32
Render UVW Template.

Save the image as a PNG with 24-bit color and remove the alpha channel to make things easier in the image-editing software (see Figure 9.34).

After the image is saved, we can open it up in the image-editing software and begin applying color and texture to make the island come alive. Opening the UVW template in Photoshop, we get what looks like a wireframe aerial shot of the island (see Figure 9.35).

The job here is pretty easy. What we're going to do is paste in a series of other 1,024 × 1,024 texture maps to layers and erase the parts we don't want so that the layers merge down into one coherent texture. We've got a sandy texture, a more rocky texture, and a grassy texture that we're going to load in to map these islands (see Figure 9.36).

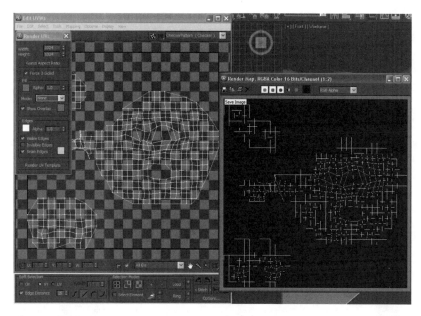

Figure 9.33
Change the settings, render the template, and save the image.

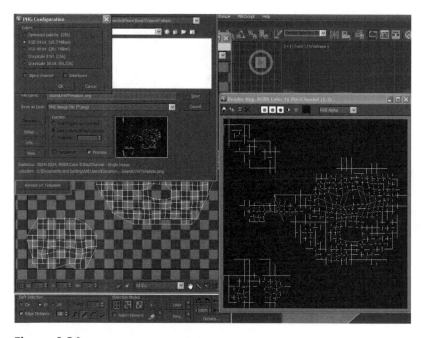

Figure 9.34
Save as a 24-bit PNG without the alpha channel.

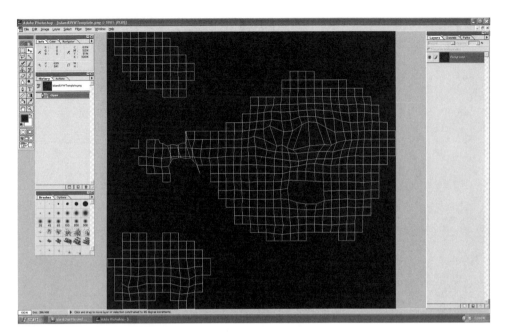

Figure 9.35
UVW template in Photoshop.

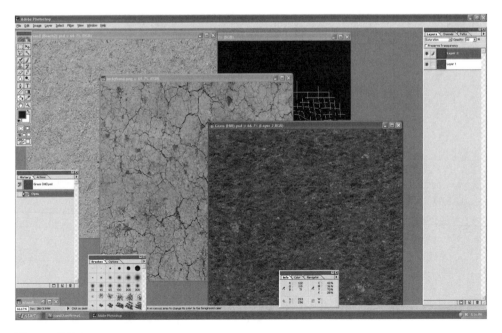

Figure 9.36
Three base textures.

We'll now copy and paste the three base textures into the UVW template and create a copy of the islandUVWTemplate background. When the copy is created, move it to the top of the layers and change its opacity so that you can see the next layer below it (see Figure 9.37).

Now we can begin work on the sand layer, which is just below the template copy. Choose the Eraser tool and erase sand from everywhere you don't need it. We'll want sand mostly at the edges of the islands, so erase the sand from the central areas. We'll also want the archway to be almost all rocky (see Figure 9.38).

The first pass exposes the rocky texture just beneath the sand, but now we want to begin erasing the rock where we want to see grass. This will apply to all of the flat top areas. The places we want to leave rocky will be the mountain, lake, archway, and the jagged face on the island to the northwest. We might place a few patches of grass on the mountain. We'll want to save this image in its layered form in case we want to make changes some time in the future. After saving it in a native layered format, we'll save it as a PNG file to be loaded into 3DS Max for texturing. Before we do that, hide the topmost layer, the background copy, exposing just the texture map (see Figure 9.39).

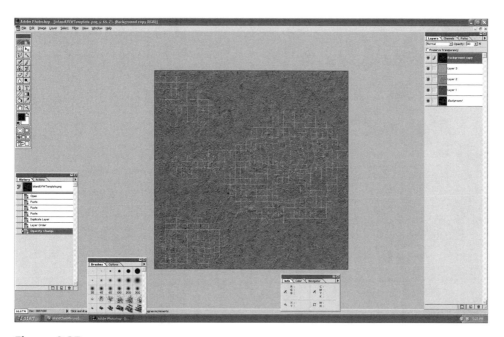

Figure 9.37
Copy the background, move to top, and change opacity.

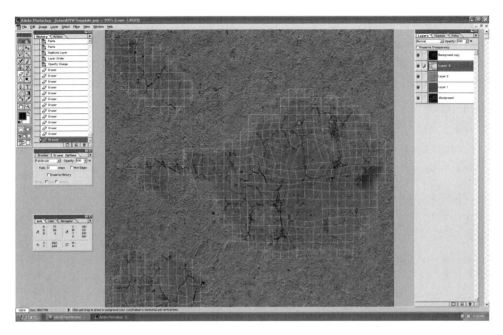

Figure 9.38
Erase the sand and expose the rock.

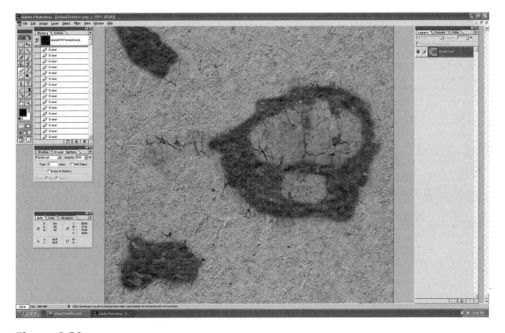

Figure 9.39
The bare texture.

Once the image is saved (islandTexture.png), we'll go back to 3DS Max and create a material to texture the island. This material will also transfer over to Unity. Remember that materials are a combination of textures, colors, and other specialized properties that create special rendering aesthetics. Press M to open up the Material editor and select the top leftmost material. The name is currently set to Default, but we can change that by clicking on the name and changing it to islandTexture (see Figure 9.40).

Figure 9.40
Change the material name.

After the material is renamed, extend the Maps tab and choose the island-Texture.png file as the Diffuse Color map (see Figure 9.41).

Another dialog pops up; choose Bitmap from the list of options and select OK (see Figure 9.42).

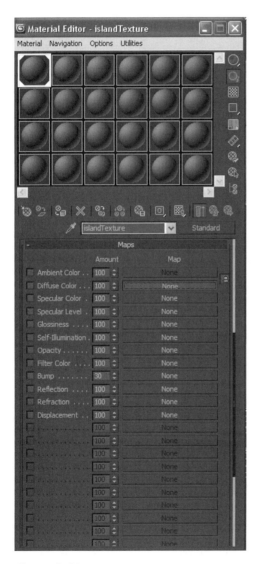

Figure 9.41
Click on the button labeled None next to Diffuse Color.

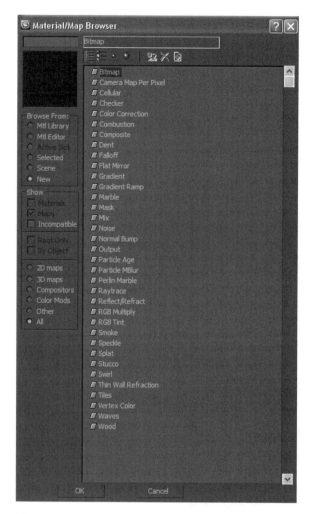

Figure 9.42
Choose Bitmap from a long list of options.

At this point, a file browser will open. Navigate to the location where you saved the `islandTexture.png` file and choose it (see Figure 9.43).

When we have selected a texture map for the material, we can drag and drop the material onto the island chain. To see the results of the mapping, press Shift+Q in 3DS Max to render the scene (see Figure 9.44).

The result of the render is decent, but we are missing something. The mirrored object isn't textured because we mirrored the object before doing the texture

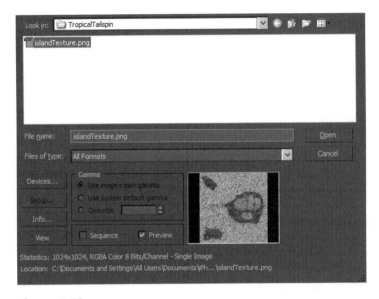

Figure 9.43
Choose the texture with the file browser.

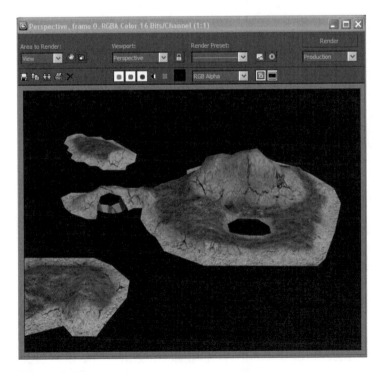

Figure 9.44
The render.

mapping. To remedy this, delete the island copy and redo the mirror operation on the base island. This quickly and easily replaces the original island copy with a textured one (see Figure 9.45).

The true test of the new island will be seeing it in action. Before we open Unity, we have to export the model from 3DS Max. Click on the 3DS Max icon in the upper-left corner of the screen and choose Export > Export (see Figure 9.46).

The exporter will bring up a file browser. Navigate to the place you want to save your model and save as Autodesk (FBX) (see Figure 9.47).

The last part of the export process brings up an FBX Export dialog with various options. The part we're interested in is embedding the media, which is under the Include tab. Expand the tab and check the box next to Embed Media.

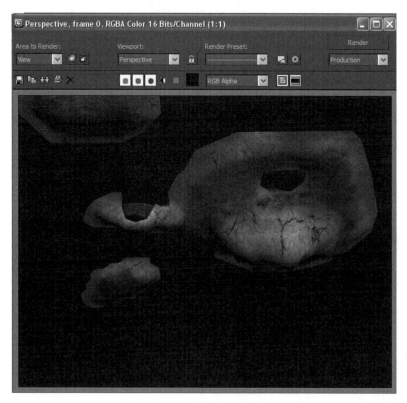

Figure 9.45
Textured reflection copy.

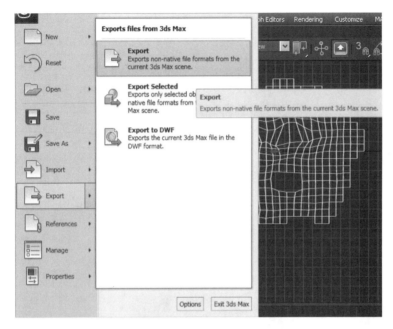

Figure 9.46
Choose Export > Export.

Figure 9.47
Save as an FBX file with the file browser.

Open Unity and change the scene to accommodate this new model. Open tropical003 and highlight the Allislands game object in the Hierarchy view and delete it by pressing Command+Delete. Then create a new folder within the Tropical Tailspin folder called Models (see Figure 9.48).

Within the Models folder, create another new folder called islandChain and then drag and drop the `islandChain.FBX` file into that folder (see Figure 9.49).

For easy readability and Unity compatibility, rename the `islandChain.fbm` folder Textures. The FBX file with embedded media creates this folder with the extension that stands for Film Box Media, but it's a lot easier just to call it Textures. With that done, drag and drop the new model into the scene (see Figure 9.50).

You'll have to scale it up 1,000 times for it to fit within the scene we already created. When you do that, it looks pretty good. You may also need to adjust the water plane's material. It should be set to iPhone/Transparent/Vertex Color with the color blue and an opacity of 10% (see Figure 9.51).

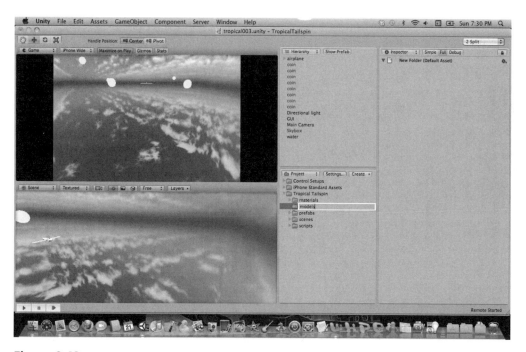

Figure 9.48
Delete the old islands and create new folder models.

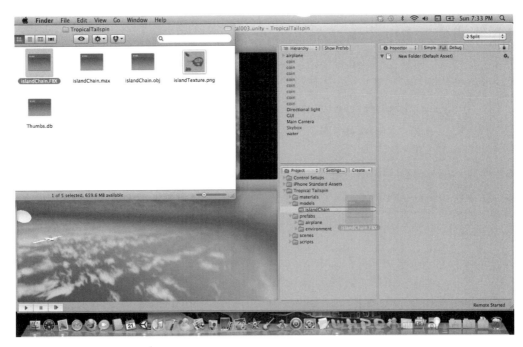

Figure 9.49
Drag and drop `islandChain.FBX` into the islandChain folder.

Figure 9.50
Drag and drop islandChain from the Project view to the Hierarchy view.

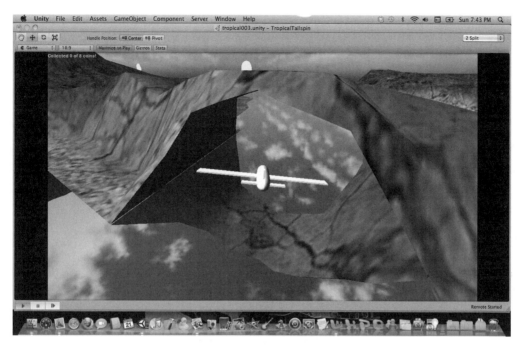

Figure 9.51
Look at that archway, with reflection.

Remember that you can find all of these files on the CD inside the Tropical Tailspin project.

We have made some improvements over the prototype already. The island chain looks decent, but we have a number of other details to add before it's ready for prime time. We haven't added the new seaplane model we acquired from TurboSquid. Second, we have to get rid of the static skybox you can fly into, and, finally, we need to add details and ambiance fitting a real game made to fit the template created by *Wii Sports Resort*'s flight mode.

To begin adding the next level of detail, we'll start with adding the new seaplane. We need to make some adjustments to the seaplane in a 3D modeling app first. Let's have a look at it in 3DS Max now. The reason we must open the model in 3DS Max or some other modeling tool is because the OBJ format isn't rigged to allow the propellers to spin.

When we open the file in 3DS Max, we need to do a few things. First, we need to change the scale of the seaplane from −132 in all directions to +132 in all directions. Next, we need to rotate the seaplane 180 degrees about its local Z-axis and then 180 degrees about its local Y-axis. Then we'll create three bones, one for each propeller and one for the rest of the seaplane body. To add these bones, click on Animation > Bone Tools > Create Bones from the main menu.

In 3D animation, *bones* are essentially the same thing as an empty transform in Unity that has other 3D objects parented to it. The difference is that a bone typically has vertices for children. Once a vertex is assigned to a bone, the vertex maintains its position relative to that bone as the bone moves. By creating a complex hierarchy of bones, incredibly complex 3D animations can be created. The human body doesn't work too much differently. The skin is attached to muscles and tendons, and those are attached to bones. In 3D animation, the mesh or visible geometry is considered the skin (see Figure 9.52).

Using the front viewport, click in the center of each propeller with the Create Bones option and click and drag a bone down the propeller blade facing down. You will have to click once, drag, and then click again to create a bone. The program automatically appends a second bone to the first. When you click to

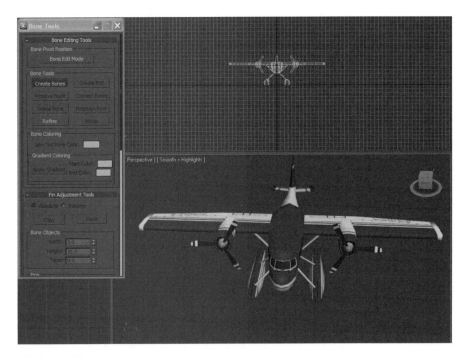

Figure 9.52
Create bones with the Bone Tools dialog.

complete your first bone, simply press Escape while drawing the second bone to exit the creation process. Create a bone for each propeller and a third bone to represent the rest of the plane (see Figure 9.53). You may notice some extra bones if you check the Select by Name list; if so, delete them.

Now that we have three bones created and aligned with the seaplane and its propellers horizontally, we need to align the propeller bones front to back. Use the left or right side view and, with the Bone Tools dialog, open the Bone Edit

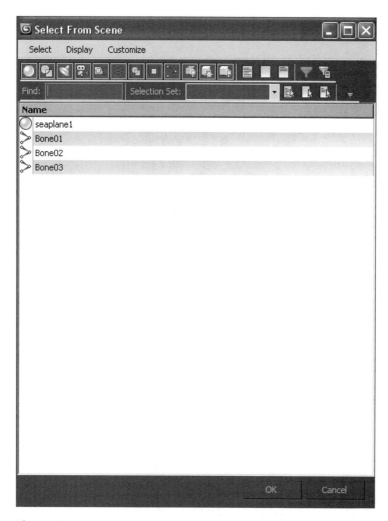

Figure 9.53
Create three bones in Front view and check the scene for extra bones.

mode and drag the bones toward the front of the plane so they are aligned with the propellers along this axis as well (see Figure 9.54).

With the bones in position, it's now time to turn the seaplane itself into a skin that can be deformed by the bones. To do this, choose Modifiers > Animation > Skin (see Figure 9.55).

Now we need to add the three bones to the modifier via the right panel under the Parameters expansion tab where it says Bones and has an Add button. Press the Add button and a Select Bones dialog pops up. Select all three bones and press the Select button (see Figure 9.56).

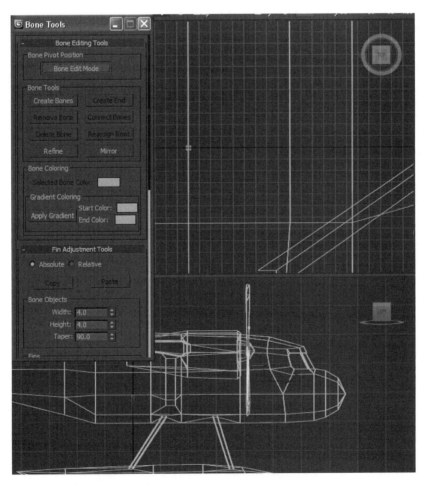

Figure 9.54
Move the bones toward the front of the plane in Left or Right view.

Figure 9.55
Use the skin modifier on the seaplane.

When the bones are first added, they will affect the wrong portion of the sea-plane. Since bones take direct control over vertices, we need to make sure that the correct vertices are assigned to the correct bones. We need to fix that so that

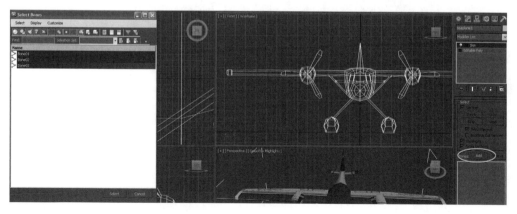

Figure 9.56
Add the three bones to the skin modifier.

the propeller bones only affect the propellers, and the central bone affects the rest. To do this, select the seaplane mesh, click on the Edit Envelopes button under the skin modifier on the right side, check the Vertices checkbox, and, finally, select Bone03 in the list. In addition, scroll down and make sure the only checkboxes checked under Advanced Parameters are Always Deform, Rigid Vertices, and Weight All Vertices (see Figure 9.57).

With Bone03 highlighted, move down to the Weight Properties section and click on Weight Table to open the Skin Weight Table dialog (see Figure 9.58).

With the dialog open, use the drop-down menu in the lower-left corner and choose Selected Vertices. Drag+select the whole plane in one of the viewports.

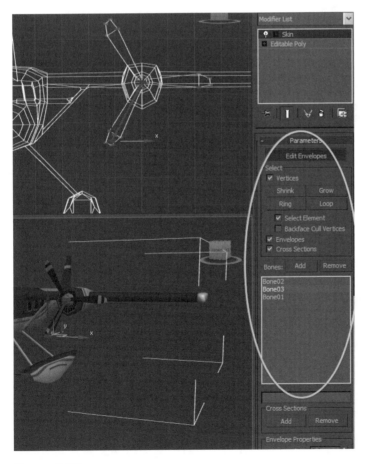

Figure 9.57
Edit Envelopes, select Vertices, highlight Bone03.

Figure 9.58
Skin Weight Table dialog.

Then choose Edit > Select All from the Skin Weight Table dialog's main menu and type **1** in the top bone position under Bone03 (see Figure 9.59).

Now using the Skin Weight Table dialog, switch to Bone02 and then use Selected Vertices in the bottom-left menu to highlight the tips of the left propeller in one of the viewports. Choose Edit > Select All and change the top bone under Bone02 to 1. The 1.000s in the Bone03 column will shift to the Bone02 column (see Figure 9.60).

Finally, choose Bone01 in the dialog and repeat the process, but this time select the tips of the right propeller to assign them to Bone01 (see Figure 9.61).

Before we continue any further, we need to do some quick organizational work with the bones. Use the Select by Name tool to select each of the bones separately and use the Right menu's Modify tab to rename them seaplane, propellerLeft,

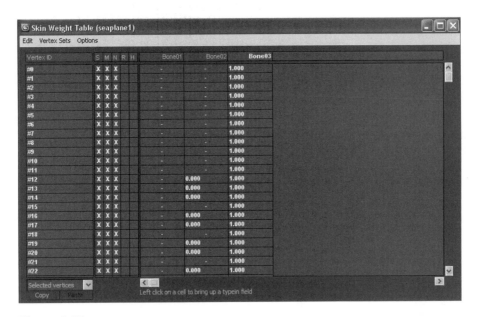

Figure 9.59
All vertex weights are assigned to Bone03.

and propellerRight. Also, rename the mesh seaplane1 seaplaneMesh. The Select from Scene dialog should look like Figure 9.62.

We just have one last thing to do, which is to link the bones in a proper hierarchy so that when the seaplane bone is moved, both propeller bones move with it. To do this, we will select the propellerRight bone (see Figure 9.63).

Click on the Select and Link tool on the far left above the top left viewport (see Figure 9.64).

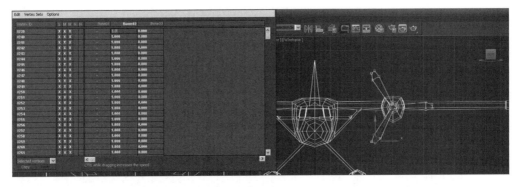

Figure 9.60
Assign the left propeller vertices to Bone02.

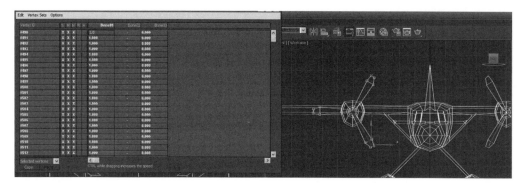

Figure 9.61
Assign the right propeller vertices to Bone01.

Reopen the Select by Name dialog (which will now be called Select Parent) and choose seaplane from the list. This will make the rightPropeller bone a child of the seaplane bone (see Figure 9.65).

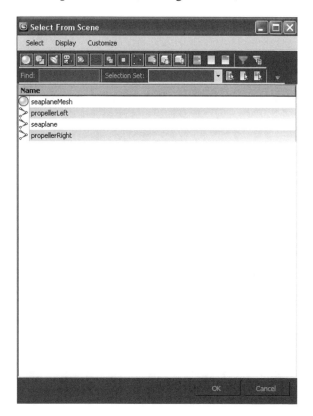

Figure 9.62
Renamed objects.

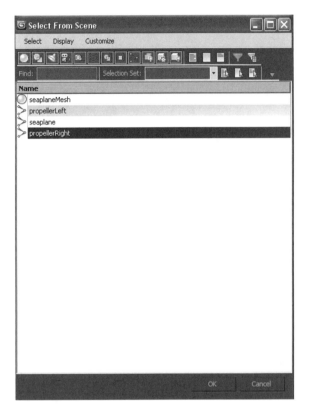

Figure 9.63
Select propellerRight.

Once propellerRight belongs to seaplane, deselect the Select and Move tool and open the Select by Name dialog again. Choose propellerLeft and link it to the seaplane bone as well. Both propellerRight and propellerLeft will appear under

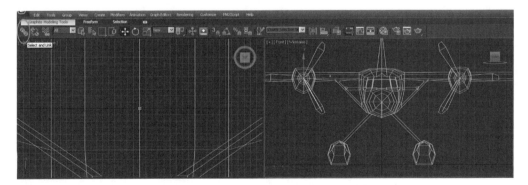

Figure 9.64
Select and Link tool.

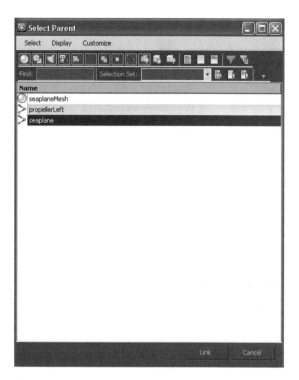

Figure 9.65
Choose seaplane from the Select Parent dialog.

the seaplane bone when you open the Select from Scene dialog with the Select by Name button (see Figure 9.66).

If we choose each of the three bones and move or rotate them, they should properly rotate their respective child bones and vertices. Now it is time to export and load it into Unity. Export to the FBX format again, following the same process we did for the island export, and then open Unity.

Create a new folder under Models called Seaplane. Open a Finder window and drag and drop the `seaplane.FBX` file into the newly created Seaplane folder (see Figure 9.67).

As with the island model before, rename the seaplane.fbm folder "Textures" for readability. Then drag and drop the seaplane model from the Project view into the airplane game object in the Hierarchy view (see Figure 9.68).

You'll notice that the airplane model is too large for the scene as it was originally laid out. Since the seaplane was modeled by someone else, it used a different scale

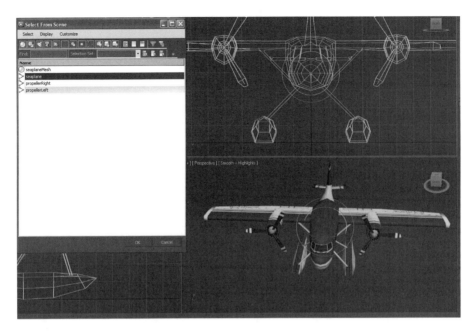

Figure 9.66
Both propeller bones are now children of the seaplane parent bone.

Figure 9.67
Drag and drop the `seaplane.FBX` file from the Finder window into Unity.

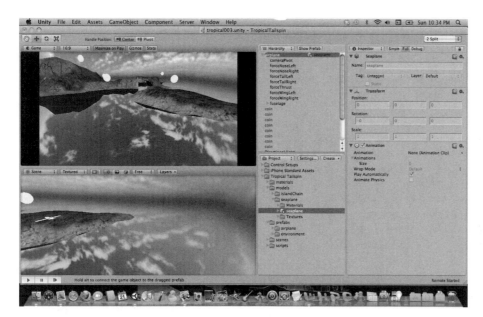

Figure 9.68
Drag and drop seaplane onto airplane.

than we did with the island and from the Unity scene we used as a basis for the prototype. To compensate, scale the seaplane down to (0.5, 0.5, 0.5) and also move it down along the Y-axis by 1 unit so that it is more centered about the old airplane (see Figure 9.69).

When the seaplane is in position, deactivate the old Fuselage object and all of the airplane parts we attached to it earlier. Highlight the fuselage and then uncheck the checked box at the top of the Inspector by its transform. A dialog box asking if you want to deactivate all of the children will pop up; choose Deactivate Children (see Figure 9.70).

Now that we have our cool new seaplane imported into Unity, we still need to add a few things to animate it. Create a new Script folder called Animation and then create a new JavaScript called propellerRotation (see Figure 9.71).

Open it up and add the following code:

```
function FixedUpdate()
{
   transform.localEulerAngles = Vector3 ( transform.localEulerAngles.x,
   transform.localEulerAngles.y, transform.localEulerAngles.z + 10 );
}
```

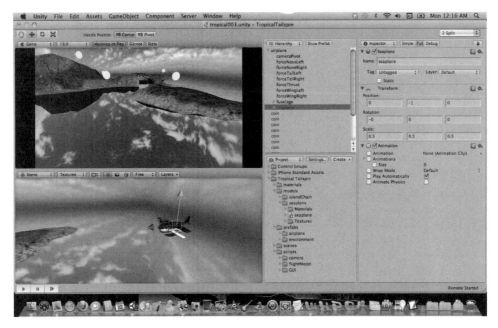

Figure 9.69
Scale and position the seaplane.

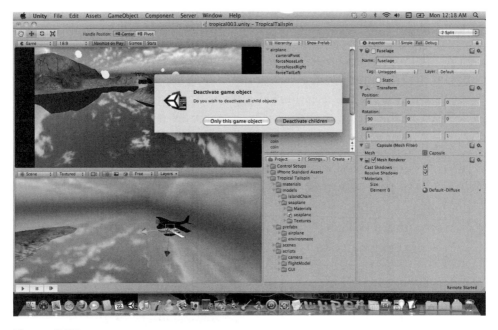

Figure 9.70
Deactivate Fuselage and all its children.

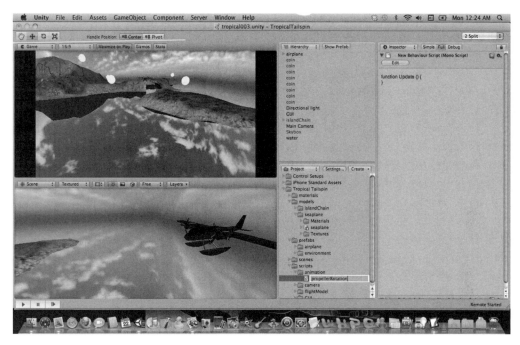

Figure 9.71
Create a propellerRotation script.

Save the script and drag and drop it onto both propellers (see Figure 9.72).

If we run the game using Unity Remote, we'll get a whole new experience with real sea plane, rotating propellers, and the new island chain. Save the open scene as Tropical004. We've definitely upped our game!

After a quick test run and saving, there are a few more changes we can make to improve the look of this scene. Move the directional light in the scene to (−1, 1, −1), set its rotation to (50, 25, 0), and duplicate it and move its duplicate to (−1, −1, −1) and set its rotation to (310, 25, 0). Change the Water material again so that it has 50% opacity. With these changes, the reflections become more visible, and the scene begins to pop. Feel free to experiment with the lighting and opacity yourself and see how these changes affect the scene. Many times what looks good is subjective or perspective-dependent (see Figure 9.73).

Although the scene looks better now, we're still a long way from the final look that *Tropical Tailspin* needs to create a compelling experience. To reach the next level, we need to replace the skybox, improve the scene's lighting, and add detail objects to make the locale interesting. Because we're on a tight schedule and a

Figure 9.72
Drag and drop the propellerRotation script onto both Propellers.

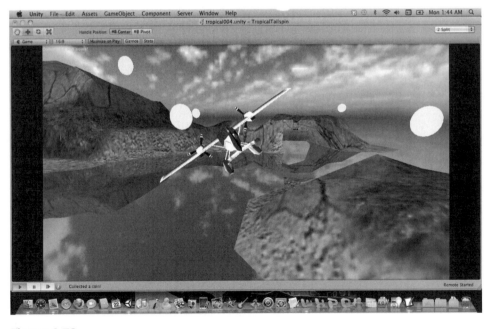

Figure 9.73
Scene adjustments make it pop.

tight budget, and because it's legal, we're going to use some of the detail models that the desktop Unity comes with to improve its included island demo. The island demo is free with Unity, and its assets are free to use on Unity projects, so we're in the clear. If you haven't already done so, download and install the free version of Unity from Unity3D.com or install it from the CD and grab the assets from Hard Drive > Users > Shared > Unity > Island Demo > Assets.

The assets we want to bring over are the trees, rocks, wrecks, cabanas, and bunker (which looks like ancient ruins). With a combination of these objects, we can create a very compelling scene. The folders we want from the Unity island demo can be seen as imported into the Tropical Tailspin project below (see Figure 9.74).

The first detail we're going to add is the bunker/ruins, which look an awful lot like the structure we placed on the southern island in the concept map. Drag the Bunker object into the scene and position it appropriately on the southern island. It should be noted that during the import process of these raw assets we will need to assign the proper textures and materials to the objects to get them working (see Figure 9.75).

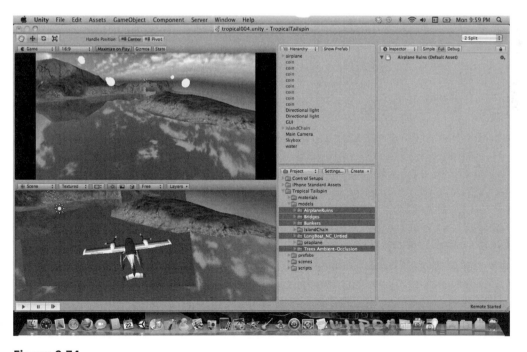

Figure 9.74
Our shamelessly ripped Unity assets.

Figure 9.75
The southern ruins in place.

The ruins are looking pretty lonely, though. Let's add some giant palm trees. Drag and drop the Palms model into the scene and duplicate it several times to create some decent foliage (see Figure 9.76).

Considering that we're going to need a lot of palm trees in the scene, create a Trees game object in which to encapsulate all of the palm trees. Create an empty game object, position it at the origin, and then drag all the palms into it. This will help clean up the Scene hierarchy. Duplicate more of the palms and place them around the lake on the big island (see Figure 9.77).

Now it's time to create a resort-looking area leading up to the archway. Create an empty game object called Resort and position it at the origin. Drag the cabana, footbridge, and boat into the Resort game object. Save the scene as tropical005 in case of any bugs, crashes, power failures, or other unexpected nastiness (see Figure 9.78).

After the scene is saved, feel free to duplicate the cabana containing the footbridge and boat a few times. Then we'll move on to the third island by creating

Figure 9.76
The palms.

Figure 9.77
More palms.

Figure 9.78
Cabanas, bridges, and boats, oh my!

an empty game object called Ruins. Add some of the busted bunker blocks, more trees, and the Spitfire airplane ruins (see Figure 9.79).

We've purposely made the Spitfire much smaller than the other objects because it should be similar in size to the seaplane. We decorated the island to be similar to the concept map and flew a bit by the seat of our pants, which is just fine. Sometimes, just getting creative with a quick layout can offer some huge benefits. In most cases, getting a map started is the hardest part, but once you begin, the juices start flowing, and new, unforeseen concepts begin to become part of the design. There's plenty of time to fix any huge leaps in logic. For now, save the map again and give it a quick play to see how the Spitfire looks in comparison to the seaplane (see Figure 9.80).

After a quick play, the Spitfire appears to be way too small in comparison. Whether or not that's actually true doesn't much matter because anyone who plays the game won't be able to perceive the exact scale. Let's scale up the Spitfire a bit to see the difference (see Figure 9.81).

Figure 9.79
Ruins—notice the scale of the Spitfire.

Figure 9.80
Small Spitfire.

Figure 9.81
Spitfire scaled to (500, 500, 500).

Now we'll show the Spitfire compared to the seaplane, in both large and small form (see Figures 9.82 and 9.83).

Although the original size we chose was a better representation of reality relative to the seaplane, it's near impossible to spot and would make for an annoying landmark.

Another problem we might face is more technical. At this point, we already have too many polygons and vertices for an iPhone game. By clicking the Stats button above the Game view, we can see what the scene has to process (see Figure 9.84).

Part of creating the production art is not just making it look good but also getting it streamlined and ready to run on an iPhone. It is best to have around 10,000 vertices or fewer. We can get away with more, but we'll have to test the game on a device before we know if we're taxing it too hard. For now, it's safe to assume we let our creative spark get in the way of practicality. To figure out what's giving us such trouble, we'll go through and deactivate the trees, resort, ruins, and main bunker game objects to find the culprit (see Figure 9.85).

Figure 9.82
Larger Spitfire.

Figure 9.83
Original Spitfire.

Figure 9.84
The Stats window.

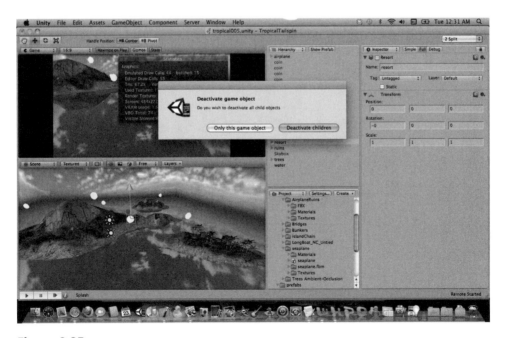

Figure 9.85
Deactivate the children, too.

With this test, we can see that the resort area is responsible for more than half the polygons and vertices in the scene, not to mention that it also dramatically increases the number of draw calls (crucial on iPhone hardware). To remedy this situation, we'll have to check each object in the resort individually. We find that the footbridges are worth about 20,000 vertices each. Although they are a very nice detail, they don't make the cut because they're just too resource intensive.

The only way to tell if we're really in the clear on the performance of the game is to test it on a device. To do this, we'll have to take a few steps in Unity and then a few more steps in Xcode. In Unity, choose Edit > Project Settings > Player to open the Player Settings Inspector on the right (see Figure 9.86).

In the Player Settings Inspector menu, change the bundle identifier to com.iphone3dgameprogrammingallinone.tt, change iPhone Application Display Name to Tailspin5, iPhone Stripping Level to Use micro mscorlib, iPhone Script Call Optimization to Fast but no Exception, and, finally, Default Screen Orientation to Landscape Left (see Figure 9.87).

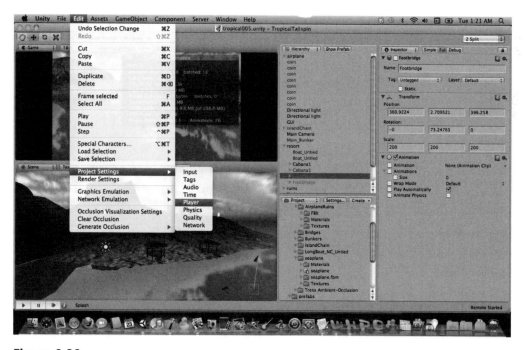

Figure 9.86
Open Unity Player Settings.

Figure 9.87
Change the Unity player settings.

After the player settings have been set, choose File > Build Settings from the main menu (see Figure 9.88).

The Build Settings dialog will pop up. Highlight and then delete any old scenes in Build Settings by pressing Command+Delete and click on the Add Open Scene button (see Figure 9.89).

Check the Compress Textures and the Strip Debug Symbols boxes to gain maximum performance. Click the Build & Run button to build the project and automatically deploy it to a properly provisioned iPhone or iPod Touch. The build process is the process by which all Unity code, textures, and models are converted to a format that will be acceptable for use on an actual device (see Figure 9.90).

After a few seconds of building in Unity, Xcode (the Apple IDE included with the iPhone SDK that you installed back in Chapter 2) will pick up the project. Once in Xcode the project will go through a few more building processes and an installation process, and finally you will notice the message in the lower-left

Figure 9.88
Open Build Settings.

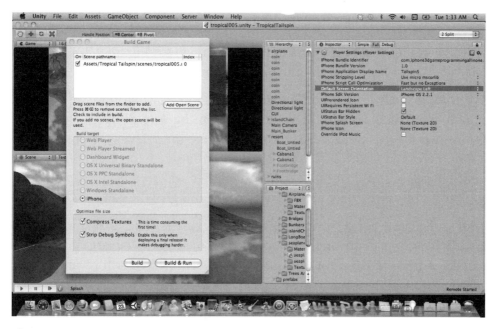

Figure 9.89
Add Open Scene.

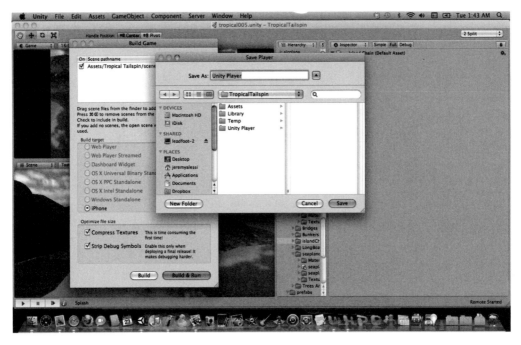

Figure 9.90
Save as Unity Player.

corner of the window that the application is running (see Figure 9.91). You can test *Tropical Tailspin* on a real iPhone or iPod Touch.

We have come a really long way! It won't be much longer before we're building the example game with Xcode for deployment on the App Store. We still have some more tweaking to do. After running the game on a device, it's readily apparent that the whole resort area is too resource intensive to be used. We need to remove it entirely or find another solution. Either way, we need to delete the Cabana objects, so we're going to deactivate them and give the game another test.

After testing the game again, we can see that things are better but that a problem still exists. If we run back through the objects and deactivate the large groups, we notice that the trees account for another 20,000 vertices. We don't want to take away all the detail in the game, so we cannot simply deactivate all the trees, but maybe we got a little duplicate-happy with them in the first place. Let's remove two bunches of palm trees from each island. We'll notice that the vertex count is down to 15,000, which should provide acceptable performance.

Figure 9.91
Xcode running.

There is one last optimization we need. On all of the island components, check the Static checkbox in the Inspector menu. These objects will be unmovable, but all objects that share the same materials will be combined into a single draw call. Even running Unity Remote, we notice that the Stats window reports a drop from 22 draw calls to 9 when the game is running (see Figure 9.92). Let's deploy the game to a device just to be sure.

Much better! Now that the scene runs well, we need to go back and add the last few details, such as a better skybox and lighting. Delete the old Skybox object from the Hierarchy view. Highlight the Main Camera and change Clear Flags to Skybox (see Figure 9.93).

We need to create a new folder under the main Tropical Tailspin folder called Skyboxes. Right-click on the new folder and create a new material called night-Sky. I have always loved the night flight mode of *Wii Sports Resort*, so we're going to mix things up a bit and do a night sky. When the material is named, change its shader to RenderFX/Skybox (see Figure 9.94).

Now we're going to go back to one of the image-editing tools and create a simple 256 × 256 black texture with a few white spots on it. Save the image as

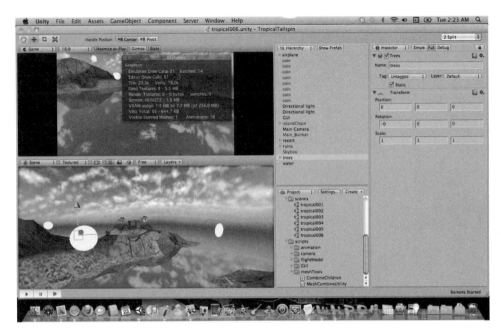

Figure 9.92
Static check non-moving objects.

Figure 9.93
Change Main Camera Clear Flags to Skybox.

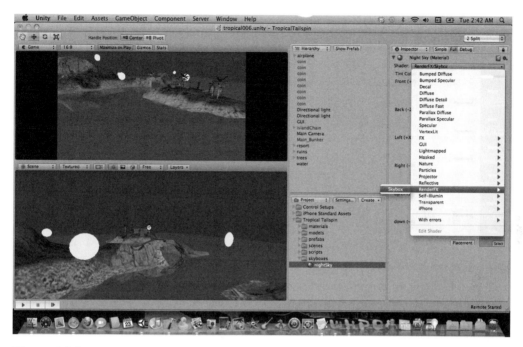

Figure 9.94
RenderFX/Skybox shader.

nightStars.png. Drag and drop the image into the Skyboxes folder (see Figure 9.95).

Once the texture is imported, change all six slots of the nightSky material to use the new texture. Set the texture's Repeat mode to Clamp in the Project view Inspector menu (see Figure 9.96).

Highlight the Main Camera game object and add a Skybox component to it (see Figure 9.97).

The last part of adding the skybox is to change the Material selector on the Main Camera's Skybox component to nightSky (see Figure 9.98).

The night sky is nifty, but it still comes off looking rather incomplete because there's a jagged edge where the plane ends and used to be met with the old static skybox. What we'll do to compensate for it is change the texture applied to the water to the SpotLight texture in the iPhone Standard Assets package (see Figure 9.99). This works because the spotlight texture is bright in the middle and black at the edges. With the proper shader applied to the texture, we get a material that

Figure 9.95
Import `nightStars.png`.

Figure 9.96
Change all Skybox slots to use `nightStars.png`.

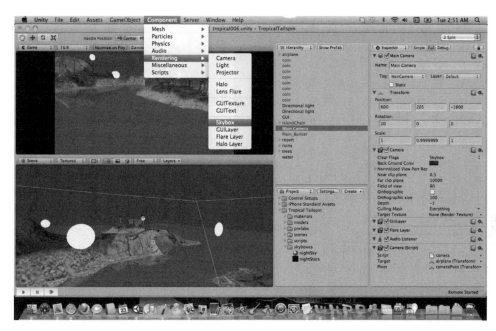

Figure 9.97
Add a Skybox component to Main Camera.

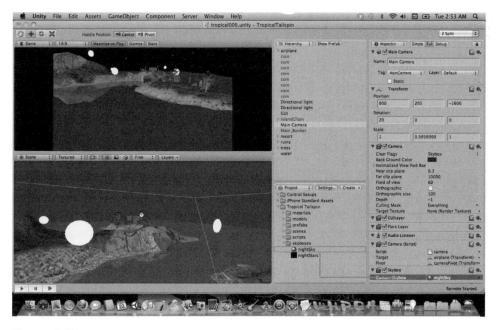

Figure 9.98
Change the Skybox component's material to nightSky.

Figure 9.99
Change the water's texture to SpotLight.

fades slowly from center to edge, ultimately removing the jagged edge where the water plane ends.

Now the jagged edge is removed, and the water fades to black at the edges, giving the illusion that light is generated from the center of the map and fades to pitch black off in the distance (see Figure 9.100). This is a neat effect that keeps us from having to worry about strange physical boundaries or geometric limitations. (After all, we are out of geometry.)

The only change we'll have to make is to add a check for an altitude below 0 because there won't be any colliders beyond the water plane. If the seaplane goes below an altitude of 0, we'll trigger a crash. That code will be reserved for the next chapter. For the production art to be completed, we need to make one last change. The dark blue water just doesn't look tropical. Change the water's color to cyan with the opacity at 100%. Now the locale looks to be surrounded by the bioluminescent water found around many real-world tropical islands (see Figure 9.101).

The very last thing we'll do is tone down the intensity of the down-facing directional light to 0.5. This gives the islands a slightly more natural look with the

Figure 9.100
Smooth transition into the night.

Figure 9.101
Bioluminescent water.

night sky backdrop. The lighting in this scene is completely exaggerated, but a combination of 0.5 at the top and 0.7 from below highlights the effect we're trying to convey and also allows the main islands to blend a bit better with the dark skybox. Save again as tropical007; we want to keep track of the changes so we can compare and contrast our decisions later.

Conclusion

Creating final game art is a very difficult, subjective, and time-consuming task. In this chapter, we covered a lot of ground, from purchasing prebuilt models to modeling, rigging, and texturing models. We also learned about the real-world performance of a Unity iPhone game and how to deploy the game to a device. Finally, we learned how to use a few neat tricks to circumvent the addition of boundaries to an "open-ended" world. We've created a game that looks somewhat close to the original template we set out for, but we still need to tie all the loose ends together.

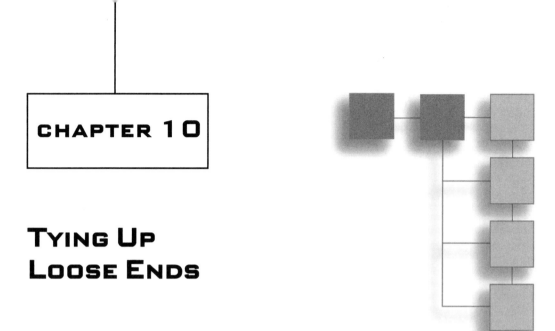

CHAPTER 10

TYING UP
LOOSE ENDS

We now have a functional game. However, we don't have a particularly fun or polished game. Our game is also still missing many basic elements such as the icon, splash screen, and title screen. It's close to deadline, and we have a game to deliver. How are we going to finish it? In this chapter, we're going to be crunching to tie up the loose ends, and some of it may not be pretty.

The first major element we need to improve to prepare *Tropical Tailspin* for prime time is the one basic gameplay mechanic. The floating coins in the game just aren't cutting it. We need to replace the floating coins with landmarks that don't require direct collision to be collected, and we need to give them descriptions to make them interesting. The first thing we're going to do in this process is remove the gold coins. Delete them all and then save the scene as tropical008.

Once the coins are removed, we need to create a new empty Game Object and rename it Landmark. This Game Object will be the parent object to a collection of waypoints that we'll position individually next to the lake, ruins, temple, boats, plane crash, and some others we haven't created yet. Afterward, we'll write a script that will determine if we've spotted a landmark and give us credit for it, much like the coins but more interesting, relaxing, and on target for our original goal.

After creating the Game Object, we need a landmarks script to help us determine if the player actually found a landmark and to trigger some sort of indication. Create a new folder under Scripts called Environment. Then we'll add a new

JavaScript file to the folder and also call it Landmark. Afterward, we'll add the
following code to the new script:

```
var description : String;
var findRange : float;
var seaplane : Transform;
private var thisTransform : Transform;
private var collected : boolean;
private var windowRect : Rect;
windowRect = Rect ( 0, 0, 480, 100 );
private var pointer : LineRenderer;
private var inRange : boolean;
function getCollected ()
{
  return collected;
}
function landmarkWindow ( WindowID : int )
{
  GUI.Label ( Rect ( 20, 10, 460, 90 ), description );
}
function LateUpdate ()
{
  if ( seaplane )
  {
    if ( Vector3.Distance ( thisTransform.position, seaplane.position ) <
findRange )
    {
      pointer.SetPosition ( 0, seaplane.position );
      pointer.SetPosition ( 1, thisTransform.position);
      inRange = true;
    }
    else
    {
      pointer.SetPosition ( 0, Vector3 ( 0, 0, 0 ) );
      pointer.SetPosition ( 1, Vector3 ( 0, 0, 0 ) );
      inRange = false;
    }
  }
}
function OnGUI ()
{
  if ( inRange )
```

```
  {
    windowRect = GUI.Window ( 0, windowRect, landmarkWindow, "LANDMARK
FOUND!" );
    if ( !collected )
    {
      collected = true;
      thisTransform.name = "Found" + thisTransform.name;
    }
  }
}
function Start()
{
  thisTransform = transform;
  pointer = GetComponent ( LineRenderer );
  pointer.SetPosition ( 0, Vector3 ( 0, 0, 0 ) );
  pointer.SetPosition ( 1, Vector3 ( 0, 0, 0 ) );
  pointer.SetWidth ( 0.1, 0.1 );
}
```

This code does the heavy lifting for our landmark system. It contains three editor-accessible variables: description, findRange, and seaplane. The description variable is a string that describes the landmark, findRange is the distance we want the seaplane to come within to find this landmark, and seaplane is a reference to the Airplane game object that the player controls.

The private variables consist of thisTransform, collected, windowRect, pointer, and inRange. The thisTransform variable we've been over many times. The collected variable is a flag to signal that the player has collected this waypoint. The windowRect variable contains the position and size of the window in which the landmark's description will fit. The pointer variable is a reference to a LineRenderer component, which we will attach to each landmark to be used as a pointer so the player knows for certain what he has found and where it is. Finally, inRange tells us whether the seaplane is in range or not because we use a distance check to figure out if the seaplane's in range or not, which we need to know in more than one callback function. Distance checks are fairly expensive, so it's better to check for distance once and store whether the seaplane is in range.

This script uses the LateUpdate() and OnGUI() callbacks. The LateUpdate() callback is used to position the vertices of the LineRenderer attached to the object so that they are positioned smoothly during gameplay. The OnGUI() callback is used to display the description window for each landmark. Finally, the Start function is used to initialize a few things, most notably the width of the landmark pointer to (0.1, 0.1). This makes the pointer look more elegant than the default size of 1 × 1.

Once the Landmark script is created and saved, drag and drop it onto the Landmark Game Object. Afterward, we'll attach a LineRenderer component to it. Once that's done we'll create a new prefab called Landmark inside the Environment prefab folder and then drag and drop the Game Object onto the prefab (see Figure 10.1).

After the Landmark prefab is done, we can drag and drop as many of them as we desire into our scene, positioning them near the visual landmarks. One thing to note is that during the positioning of the landmarks, we'll want to uncheck the Use World Space option of the LineRenderer component. If we don't, the landmarks all look like they are positioned at the origin. We can also name the landmarks in the Hierarchy view to distinguish them from each other. After positioning and naming them, we can then set their descriptions, find ranges, and link the Airplane game object to each of them in the Seaplane field (see Figure 10.2).

Figure 10.1
Landmark prefab.

Figure 10.2
All 10 landmarks.

Once we get the landmarks in place, we need a new landmarkCounter script to replace the old coinCounter script. Remove the coinCounter component from the GUI game object, create a new landmarkCounter script in the same folder as the coinCounter script, and then add the following code to the new script:

```
var landmarks : Transform;
private var landmarksBegin : int;
private var landmarksCurrent : int;
function OnGUI()
{
  landmarksCurrent = 0;
  for ( var i = 0; i < landmarksBegin; i++ )
  {
    if ( landmarks.GetChild( i ).name.Substring( 0, 5 ) == "Found" )
      landmarksCurrent++;
  }
  GUI.Label( Rect( 0, 300, 480, 20 ), "Collected " + ( landmarksCurrent ) +
" of " + landmarksBegin + " landmarks!" );
}
```

```
function Start()
{
  landmarksBegin = landmarks.childCount;
}
```

The only thing this script requires is a reference to the Landmarks parent game object. The code then runs through the landmarks to check their names. This is an instance where we're using a method from the Mono Project, which is Unity's backend codebase. The method Substring belongs to the String class under System. Read more about using these sorts of methods using the link www.go-mono.com/docs.

The basic premise of the landmark system is that once the player has found a landmark, the landmark's name changes to the string Found+*the landmark's name*. If the first five letters of the landmark's name are Found, then we count it in the loop.

With the 10 landmarks in place and the new scripts, we can now fly around the island, discovering new things along the way in a fashion similar to the template game *Wii Sports Resort*'s flight mode (see Figure 10.3).

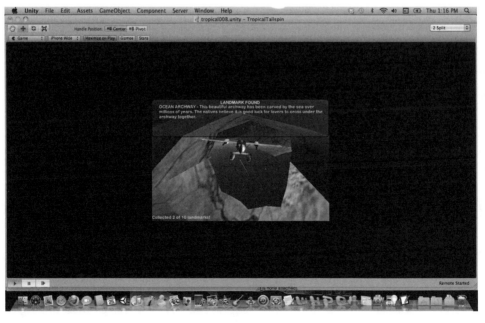

Figure 10.3
Discover the tropics.

At this point, the main gameplay mechanic is wrapped up, but there are still a few things we need to handle. First of all, none of the newly imported models contain collision. To fix this, we're going to right-click on Models in the Project view and choose Import Settings from the pop-up menu. Check the Meshes Have Colliders option in the Import Settings dialog (see Figure 10.4). Do this for the island chain and all major structures, such as the bunkers.

Once the colliders are in place, we can safely (or not so safely) fly into objects without players complaining that there's a bug! Of course, it's not very interesting just to crash and see the seaplane disappear. Now is the time for some particle effects and a prefab trick.

When using Unity, there are times that we'll want to use the same prefabs between multiple projects or pass them around to team members in a larger game situation. Unity provides a packaging system for such occasions. For example, we need an explosion, and the Unity Star Trooper example project (located under Hard Drive > Users > Shared > Star Trooper) comes with one. To get it, we'll need to export the prefab from that project.

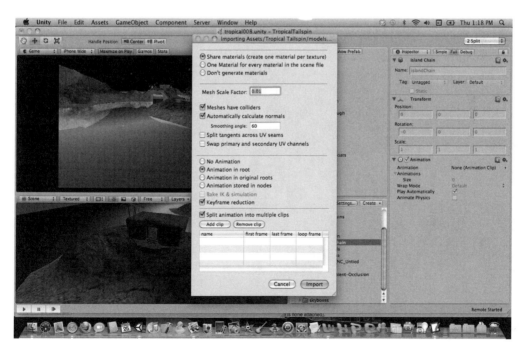

Figure 10.4
Add colliders using import settings.

We'll right-click the Explosion prefab that contains children in the Star Trooper project and choose Export Package (see Figure 10.5).

Then we'll save the package as `explosionPackage` in the root folder of the Tropical Tailspin project (see Figure 10.6).

Once the package is saved, we'll open the Tropical Tailspin project again and import the package by right-clicking in the Project view and selecting Import Package (see Figure 10.7).

A file browser will pop up; navigate to the Tropical Tailspin root folder and choose the `explosionPackage` file (see Figure 10.8).

The package will import the Prefabs folder over from the Star Trooper project. Move the Explosion prefab from there into a new Particles folder inside the Prefabs folder. Afterward, delete the imported Prefabs folder (see Figure 10.9).

Now we need to modify the flight collision code to take into account the instantiation of the explosion. *Instantiation* is the process of creating a new game object on the fly inside a script file. Prefabs provide a quick and easy way to

Figure 10.5
Export Package.

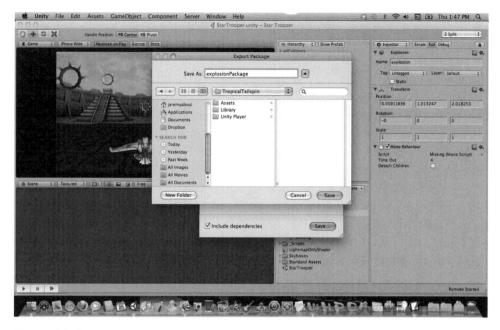

Figure 10.6
Save As.

Figure 10.7
Import Package.

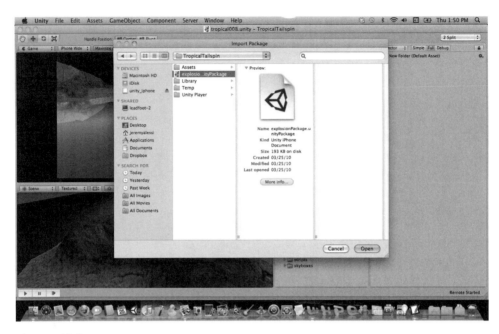

Figure 10.8
File browser.

Figure 10.9
Move Explosion from Prefabs to Particles.

spawn or instantiate new game objects dynamically. Add an editor-exposed variable called explosion, which will reference the Explosion prefab. Add the following code at the beginning of the flight003 script file:

```
var explosion : GameObject;
```

Then modify the handleRaycasts() function to look like this:

```
function handleRaycasts( theHit : RaycastHit )
{
  switch( theHit.transform.name )
  {
    case "coin":
      Destroy( theHit.transform.gameObject );
      Debug.Log( "Collected a coin!" );
      break;
    case "water":
      Destroy( gameObject );
      SendMessage( "crash" );
      Debug.Log( "Splash" );
      break;
    default:
      var explosionClone = Instantiate( explosion, thisTransform.posi-
tion, thisTransform.rotation );
      Destroy( gameObject );
      SendMessage( "crash" );
      Debug.Log( "Crash" );
      break;
  }
}
```

The important line to pay attention to is this one:

```
var explosionClone = Instantiate( explosion, thisTransform.position,
thisTransform.rotation );
```

This line dynamically spawns an explosion when the seaplane crashes into a solid object. Now we want to also add a splash particle effect for the water case. To do this, add a similar line inside the water case, but instead of referencing explosion, reference splash.

```
var splashClone = Instantiate( splash, thisTransform.position,
thisTransform.rotation );
```

Add another `GameObject` variable at the top of the script called `splash` that is also a public editor-exposed Game Object like `explosion`. Save this new script as `flight004.js`. Remove the old flight003 script from the Airplane game object, attach flight004, and save the scene as tropical009. Before we can continue, we need to duplicate the Explosion prefab and then make some adjustments to it.

```
var splash : GameObject;
```

If we expand the Splash prefab, we'll notice that it has a child object called Large Flames. This child has a Particle Renderer component with a material assigned to Fire Smoke (see Figure 10.10). Unity has a built-in particle system, and the Particle Renderer component is responsible for the visual representation of the particles.

Now we'll duplicate the Fire Smoke material and rename it Splash. Then we'll change its texture to smoketest2 (see Figure 10.11).

Figure 10.10
The Fire Smoke material.

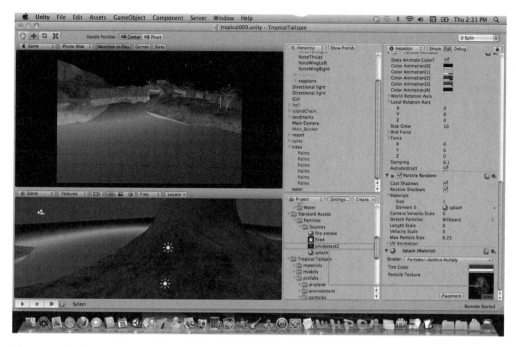

Figure 10.11
Change to the Splash material.

Make sure that all the fields of the new flight004 script component are set, as seen in Figure 10.12.

Now we have two distinct crash animations for water and solid objects. A problem that will arise is for crashes out at sea. We need to modify the flight004 code to account for an altitude below 0. Add the following code to the end of the `Update()` callback:

```
if ( thisTransform.position.y < 0 )
{
  var splashClone = Instantiate( splash, thisTransform.position,
thisTransform.rotation );
  Destroy( gameObject );
  SendMessage( "crash" );
  Debug.Log( "Splash" );
}
```

With this new bit of code, we safely account for the player being able to fly under the scene by flying out to sea and down below the islands. With these last few

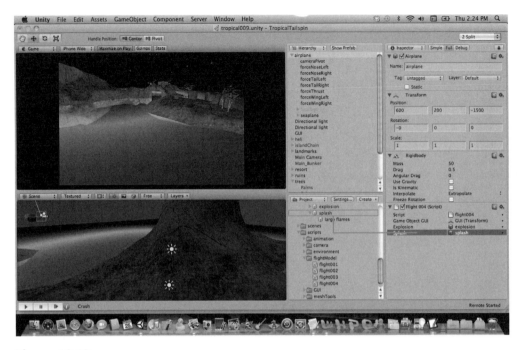

Figure 10.12
Set the fields of the flight004 script component.

changes, we've sealed off the environment and added a sense of plausibility to the game. The last element, which we've neglected to touch on at all, is sound. We need a propeller sound, acceleration changes, a crash sound, and a beacon sound for when we find landmarks. Unity provides a very simple interface that enables us to create complex 3D audio. Unity's Main Camera contains an audio listener, so we can drag and drop audio sources onto game objects. When we run the game, Unity calculates how the effects will sound in 3D space. In addition, we can tweak the settings of audio sources to get the game sounding rich.

The first step in adding sound effects to a game object is to give the game object an AudioSource component. Once there is an audio source attached to a game object, we can choose a sound file for the audio source, set it to play on wake, adjust the volume, and more. The first object we're going to attach an audio source to is the seaplane, the Airplane game object (see Figure 10.13).

It's nice having an audio source attached to the seaplane, but it's not much good unless we have a sound file to associate with it. There are many great sources for sound effects. There's an excellent online Web site called freesound.org. This

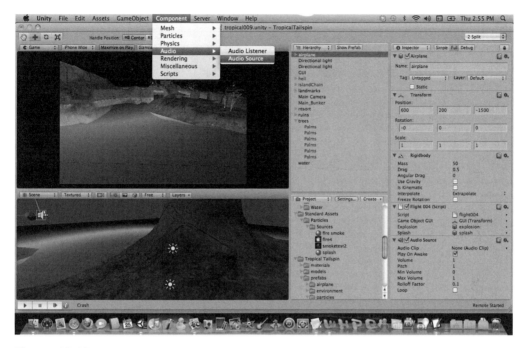

Figure 10.13
Add an AudioSource component to Airplane.

Web site operates under the Creative Commons license (read it), but essentially it boils down to using the sounds as you want for free but giving credit to the author. It's a win-win situation all around.

The sound effect we're going to use for the airplane is a derivative of Benbon-can's Aircraft Dive. We're going to take the sound effect into Audacity (a free sound-editing program available at Audacity.SourceForge.net) and remove everything but a small loop-friendly portion of the sound. We're going to delete everything but the first 5 seconds. If we hear any pops or sounds of discontinuity, we know it won't work in our game. A fairly safe technique is to get both ends of the sound graph (visible in Audacity) to roughly align with each other. Alter-natively, we might use the fade-in and -out filters built into Audacity to create smooth transitions within a sound wave (see Figure 10.14).

Once we're down to just the first 5 seconds, we're going to export the sound as `propellers.wav` and import it into the Unity project. Then we'll simply choose it as the AudioClip on the AudioSource component. When I create assets,

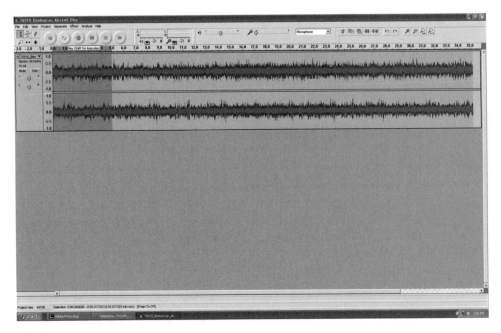

Figure 10.14
Edit sounds with Audacity.

I save copies of them both inside and outside of my Unity project. Unity has a great asset-management system that allows you to adjust assets without constantly having to access them in third-party tools, but sometimes you want to replace an asset, and Unity doesn't allow that. If you attempt to replace an asset with a newer one, Unity creates a new asset and appends an incremented index number to it. Therefore, when working with assets in rapid succession, it is best to keep your Unity project clean and tidy by working inside another folder with your third-party tools and dragging and dropping assets either into the appropriate Assets folder using OSX Finder or directly into the Unity Editor's Project view (see Figure 10.15).

Initially, you'll notice that the sound effect plays only once. For it to keep playing (as it would with propellers), we need to check the Loop checkbox. The sound effect is pretty convincing. Still, we need to add some variation to it as the plane changes altitude. Add the following line of code to the end of the `FixedUpdate()` callback in flight004:

```
audio.pitch = 1.0 − Mathf.Clamp( thisRigidbody.velocity.y / 100, −1, 1 );
```

Figure 10.15
Choose `propellers.wav` as the AudioClip.

This single line of code changes the pitch of the audio source according to the Y-component of the airplane's velocity. As the airplane increases its upward velocity, the sound of the propellers slows down, indicating a decrease in velocity as the airplane climbs against gravity. As the airplane dives, the sound of the propellers plays more quickly, emulating the sound of a traditional dive bomb maneuver as the airplane quickly descends toward the ground.

Now we need to attach audio sources (included in the Tropical Tailspin project) to the Explosion and Splash prefabs to account for crashes. For the splash sound effect, we're going to use duckboy80's SplashEdit, and for the explosion we'll be using digifishmusic's Missile Strike. The splash sound effect is fine, but the explosion effect needs to be trimmed down to when the missile strikes. Use Audacity to trim the effect. Once the effects are ready, import them into Unity and add the AudioSource components directly to the prefabs. Then set the AudioClip directly in the prefab (see Figure 10.16).

Once the AudioSource components are attached to the Crash particle effect prefab, the sound effects will play as soon as we crash without any further

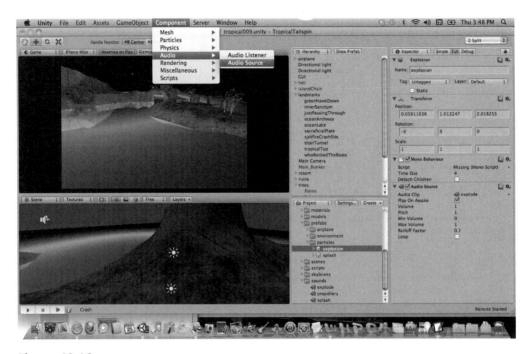

Figure 10.16
Add AudioSource components to Crash prefabs.

programming. Prefabs are fun, aren't they? The last bit of audio we need to add is the beacon sound when we're viewing a landmark. There are a few nice samples on freesound.org, but the one we're going to use is SfdAeroBeacon by Acclivity.

To use the beacon sound effect, we need to add some special script functionality to the Landmark script and also attach an AudioSource component to the Main Camera game object. We'll begin by adding an audio source to the camera. After adding the audio source, set the AudioClip to `beacon.wav` and uncheck the Play on Awake checkbox. Next, open up the `landmark.js` file and add the following code within the not collected conditional inside the `OnGUI()` callback.

```
Camera.main.audio.Play();
```

After making these last few changes, we finally have all of the elements of a 3D game intact: 3D models, GUI elements, physics, sounds, and most of all gameplay! We're darn close to being able to wrap up the project, but we still need to add a title screen and to get the icon into place. Before proceeding, we'll save the current scene and open a new one.

To handle the title screen, we're going to save the new scene as titleScreen. We're going to add a GUI folder to the project and a GUITexture game object to the new scene (see Figure 10.17). Then we're going to import a new image we made in the image-editing software that is a remix of the old *Tropical Tailspin* icon art. We'll set the GUITexture's Texture field to that of the new `titleScreen.png` image. We'll then change the Pixel Inset fields to (−240, −160, 480, 320) so that the GUITexture fills the entire iPhone screen.

Next, we're going to add some text telling the player to tap the screen to play. We'll add a GUIText game object to the scene (see Figure 10.18).

Now we'll set its Z-axis position component to 1 so that it appears in front of the background. We'll change its Text field to Touch to Play! so that players know what to do when this screen loads. Then we'll drag the `Jurassic.ttf` (true-type font) file we downloaded in Chapter 6 into Unity (see Figure 10.19).

Figure 10.17
Add a GUITexture title screen backdrop.

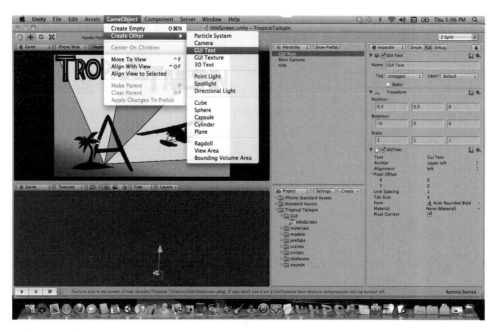

Figure 10.18
Add a GUIText object.

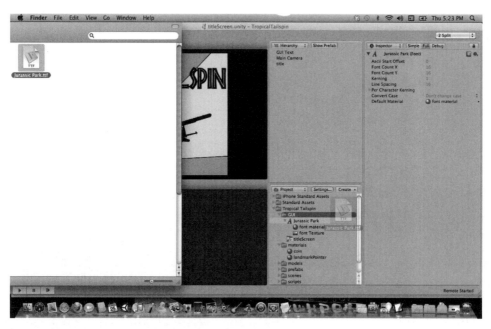

Figure 10.19
Import font.

Now right-click on it in the Project view and go to Import Settings to change the font size to something more legible, like 32 (see Figure 10.20). Then we can assign the GUIText to use the Jurassic font.

Our next objective is to place this text properly onscreen and give it some animation to call extra attention to it. Set the GUIText's Pixel Offsets to 330 and 32 (see Figure 10.21).

Now we're going to create a new script under the script's GUI folder called bouncingText.js. Add the following code to the script, save it, and then attach it to the GUIText game object:

```
private var baseX          : int;
private var baseY          : int;
private var sinScale        : float;
private var thisGUIText    : GUIText;
function Update()
{
  if ( !thisGUIText.enabled )
    return;
```

Figure 10.20
Font Import settings.

Figure 10.21
Position GUIText.

```
    if ( sinScale < 360 )
      sinScale += 10 * Time.deltaTime / Time.timeScale;
    else
      sinScale = 0;
    thisGUIText.pixelOffset.x = baseX + Mathf.Sin( sinScale ) * 5;
    thisGUIText.pixelOffset.y = baseY + Mathf.Cos( sinScale ) * 5;
}
function Start()
{
    thisGUIText = GetComponent( GUIText );
    baseX = thisGUIText.pixelOffset.x;
    baseY = thisGUIText.pixelOffset.y;
}
```

The first part of this script creates two variables to store the original size of the GUIText. The next variable, `sinScale`, is an incremental variable that adds up to 360 before being reset to 0. If we take the sine of this variable at any given time, it will result in a sequential process of growing and then shrinking. Inside the

Update() function, we can see where we increment the sinScale variable by 10 × Time.deltaTime * Time.timeScale. Time.deltaTime tells us how much time has passed since the last frame, and Time.timeScale tells us how fast the game is running compared to real time.

For instance, a value of 1 means we're running at real-time speed. A value of 0.5 results in a value two times slower than real time, which can be used to create slow-motion effects. After that, we set the pixelOffset sizes to be equal to the original size of our GUIText plus the Sin(sinScale) times 5 along the X-axis and plus the Cos(sinScale) times 5 along the Y-axis. Finally, the Start() function initializes the variables.

Once this script is attached to the GUIText game object, running the scene in the Unity Editor should net us some animated bouncing text. This text will be used to grab the player's attention after the initial splash/loading screen. Rename the GUIText game object touchToPlayText.

The final step to get past the title screen is to add a script called titleScreen.js to the GUI Scripts folder and then attach it to the titleScreen scene's Main Camera. The script should contain this very simple bit of code:

```
var touchToPlayText : GUIText;
function Update()
{
  if ( iPhoneInput.touchCount > 0 )
  {
    touchToPlayText.text = "L O A D I N G";
    Application.GarbageCollectUnusedAssets();
    Application.LoadLevel( 1 );
  }
}
function Start()
{
  iPhoneSettings.screenCanDarken = false;
}
```

The editor-available variable touchToPlayText provides a reference to a GUIText object in the title screen scene. The Update() function checks to see if the screen has been touched, upon which it sets the referenced GUIText object to say "L O A D I N G" and then runs garbage collection to clean up memory before finally loading the game environment. The `Start()` function just sets the `iPhoneSettings.screenCanDarken` variable to false so that the screen will stay lit even if it isn't touched for a while.

Before we run this, we need to make a few changes. Open the build settings and remove any levels already present by highlighting them in the list and pressing Command+Delete. Click on Add Open Scene to add the title screen (level 0). Then open tropical009 and add it as level 1 (see Figure 10.22).

Even though the title screen isn't a whole new locale, it is still considered a separate scene and level to Unity. If we want to create multiple levels or locales, we would do it in the same manner. The one thing we probably want to change in the structure of this game is to load level 1 upon a crash instead of level 0. There's no reason to return players to the title screen for this simple game. Inside the crash script (Tropical Tailspin > scripts > GUI > crash.js), change 0 to 1 in the `Application.LoadLevel()` call.

The last couple of things we need to add to wrap up our example game are the icon and the splash screen. The icon is what users will see on their iPhone or iPod

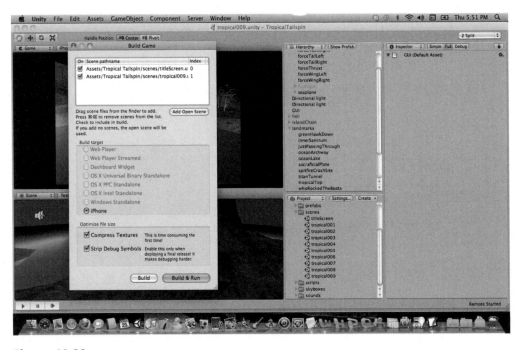

Figure 10.22
Multiple levels in the build settings.

Touch menu screens before launching an application. The splash screen is the very first screen a player will see when he launches an application. These can be set in the Project Settings > Player Settings Inspector menu, but first we need to import the icon file. Open the sunset logo design from Chapter 6 in the image-editing software, flatten the layers, scale the image to 57 × 57 pixels, and save it as `icon.png`. Import it into Unity in the same place as `titleScreen.png`. Export a copy of the title screen texture rotated 90 degrees clockwise and save it as `splash.png`. Set the splash screen and icon to `splash.png` and `icon.png`, respectively (see Figure 10.23).

Now it's time to build the game and deploy to a device for final testing. As we run through the game on a device, we need to create a list of final changes before we package the final game for submission to Apple. After that, we'll fix any minor glitches and run another round of gameplay testing.

Playing...

Please wait patiently...

Play testing...

Thank you for holding...

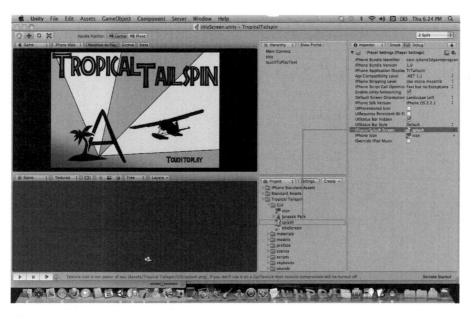

Figure 10.23
App splash screen and icon settings.

Processing...

Zeek ker bzzzzz bzzz bz bz bz (think 56k modem if you remember what that is)

Done...

After a number of play tests, there are many noticeable problems. First, the rendering speed is insufficient. To combat this, we need to add occlusion culling to the map to chunk it up. *Occlusion culling* is a process that creates a special visibility tree internally for Unity to hide or show objects, depending on where the camera is and what direction it's pointing. By automatically hiding much of the scenery when it's not visible to the camera, the game will run much faster. To do this, we need to add a ViewArea game object. We set the view area's size to (3,000, 1,000, 3,000) with a cell size of 500. This creates a grid of 72 3D boxes and determines what 3D models get drawn, depending on the camera's position. Then we need to run the occlusion algorithm by choosing Edit > Generate Occlusion > Build Release (see Figure 10.24).

Another step we can take to ensure the greatest possible performance is to change the fixed rate logic. Fixed rate logic is the speed at which the game logic runs, or how many times per second the `FixedUpdate()` function attempts to run. This is

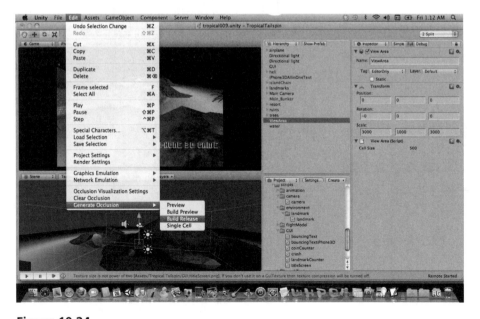

Figure 10.24
We generated occlusion after all.

different than frame rate, which is how many times per second the graphics are rendered to the screen. Typically, the frame rate is dependent on the logic rate, so it's important to run game logic as little as possible without ruining the gameplay. By default, the fixed rate logic in Unity runs at 50 times per second. By selecting Edit > Project Settings > Time from the main menu, we can change the fixed logic rate (fixed timestep). The default fixed timestep is 0.02 (there are 50 steps of that size in 1 second). If we change the timestep to 0.066, for example, we'll run the logic at 15 times per second instead of 50 because there are 15 0.066 second chunks in 1 second. The downside of this is that we need to go back and speed up the propellers! To fix this problem, change the propellerRotation script to the following code. The propellers will still spin the same amount no matter how much time passes, but on a machine with a lower frame rate, the animation may appear choppier. This code is located under Tropical Tailspin > scripts > animation.

```
function Update()
{
  transform.localEulerAngles = Vector3( transform.localEulerAngles.x,
transform.localEulerAngles.y, transform.localEulerAngles.z + 500 *
Time.deltaTime );
}
```

Now that we've fixed the propellers, we need to choose a reasonable fixed timestep. Currently, we have some fairly jittery camera movement because we chose to move the camera via LateUpdate(). If we shift the camera's movement into FixedUpdate(), we can lose the slight jitters that occur due to frame rate fluctuations. This will put more strain on the game. For example, if we put it into FixedUpdate() calls by using a fixed timestep of 0.02 seconds and we put the camera code into FixedUpdate() as opposed to LateUpdate(), all of a sudden on an iPhone 3G there's not enough time to render the Landmark information window in the OnGUI() callback. To fix this, we have to restructure the Landmark script as seen in this code. You can follow along or grab the latest landmark.js file from the Tropical Tailspin project.

```
var description : String;
var findRange : float;
var seaplane : Transform;
var textBox : Texture;
private var thisTransform : Transform;
private var collected : boolean;
private var pointer : LineRenderer;
```

```
private var inRange : boolean;
private var timeStamp : float;
function getCollected()
{
  return collected;
}
function FixedUpdate()
{
  if ( seaplane )
  {
    if ( inRange )
    {
      pointer.SetPosition( 0, seaplane.position );
      pointer.SetPosition( 1, thisTransform.position);
    }
    else
    {
      pointer.SetPosition( 0, Vector3( 0, 0, 0 ) );
      pointer.SetPosition( 1, Vector3( 0, 0, 0 ) );
    }
  }
}
function OnGUI()
{
  useGUILayout = false;
  if ( inRange )
  {
    GUI.Label( Rect( 10, 10, 480, 120 ), textBox );
    GUI.contentColor = Color( 0, 0, 0 );
    GUI.Label( Rect( 20, 20, 440, 100 ), description );
    if ( !collected )
    {
      collected = true;
      thisTransform.name = "Found" + thisTransform.name;
      Camera.main.audio.Play();
    }
  }
}
function Start()
{
  thisTransform = transform;
  pointer = GetComponent( LineRenderer );
```

```
  pointer.SetPosition( 0, Vector3( 0, 0, 0 ) );
  pointer.SetPosition( 1, Vector3( 0, 0, 0 ) );
  pointer.SetWidth( 0.1, 0.1 );
}
function Update()
{
  if ( seaplane && timeStamp + 0.5 < Time.time )
  {
    if ( Vector3.Distance( thisTransform.position, seaplane.position ) <
findRange )
      inRange = true;
    else
      inRange = false;
    timeStamp = Time.time;
  }
}
```

The big benefits of the changes are that we achieve smooth redraw animation of the line renderer by placing it in the FixedUpdate() callback, and we gain speed (and the GUI back) by placing the distance check in the LateUpdate() callback. That callback is the very last thing to be called, so we have shifted all of the time into other aspects of the program, placing the distance check last (it doesn't need to be checked at a constant rate or need smooth animation). This is an example of solid time integration. If we integrate the time in the right order, we can get exactly what we want out of the device.

Unfortunately, those small changes weren't enough to get Unity's window GUI working on slower devices consistently. In the Unity documentation, it says to always set useGUILayout to false. In the previous code, we could not do that because we needed to use Unity's window system. Now we're using a white texture with a text bubble–shaped alpha channel called textbox.png. This is a simple graphic that can be created in the image editor by painting a white box and then creating an alpha channel with a white center and curved corners. Alternatively, you can just grab the file from the Tropical Tailspin project on the CD. By ditching the window system, we can ensure that we have proper functionality even on slower devices. In addition, the new text box is easier on the eyes!

The next big problem after speed was a nasty case of z-fighting going on at the water's edge of all the islands. (The iPhone doesn't know which pixels to draw first.) The iPhone's z-buffer isn't great, and testing on a development machine with 32-bit color doesn't showcase the problems. Once I ran the game on my test device, however, I could see that the water and the edge of the islands were overlapping, constantly fighting to see which should be drawn first. This is called *z-fighting*, and it manifests itself in a rapid flickering rendering glitch. The solution to z-fighting is to create four cameras and use Unity's layer system to render the skybox first, then the mirrored reflection geometry, then the water plane, and finally the rest of the scene. By doing this, we tell Unity exactly in what order to draw the scene's geometry. Create three additional cameras, attach them all to the Main Camera, position them at (0, 0, 0), and set all the cameras' near/far clip planes to 1 and 3000.

Next, we'll remove all the audio listeners from each camera besides the Main Camera, and finally we'll remove the Skybox component from the Main Camera and add it to the skybox camera. Then we'll set the culling masks of the Main Camera to Default, the skybox camera to Nothing, the reflection camera to Water, and the water camera to TransparentFX (see Figure 10.25).

Figure 10.25
Camera culling masks.

The final step in the process is to set the layers of the objects we want to render. The reflection island geometry should be set to Water, the water plane geometry should be set to TransparentFX, and the rest should be set to Default. Unity provides a few layers by default. Layers are rendered beginning with layer 0 and then onward sequentially (see Figure 10.26).

Things look much better and run much more smoothly, but there is still a problem. The flight model is very slippery and imprecise because the amount of thrust being applied (2,000) is too strong. Lowering the value to 1,000 creates a more tightly controlled experience.

Another problem that pops up is with the imagery and textures. All the logo images, title screen, splash screen, and icon appear washed out on the iPhone. By increasing their contrast to 50 in Photoshop, we are able to maintain a bright vibrant look. We always need to keep an eye out for washed-out textures, those that have been compressed into ugliness, and textures that are just too big. On that last note, several of the textures in the scene are too large. The only texture that needs to be 1,024 × 1,024 is the island terrain texture. With Unity's

Figure 10.26
Game object layers for rendering.

import settings (right-click on a texture asset and select Import Settings), we can adjust every texture in the scene quickly and easily to something manageable by iPhone standards. Try to use textures that are under 256 × 256 pixels unless they are used on something very prominent, such as the island.

The very last piece of the puzzle for now is to add a blurb of text and a link to purchase this book online. To do this, we need another font (BeyondControl from 1001fonts.com in this case), a GUIText object, and a script not only to drive movement but to open a URL when touched. The following code drives the iPhone 3D Game Programming All in One text object.

```
private var baseX : int;
private var baseY : int;
private var sinScale : float;
private var thisGUIText : GUIText;
private var timeStamp : float;
function Update()
{
  if ( !thisGUIText.enabled )
    return;
  if ( sinScale < 360 )
    sinScale += 10 * Time.deltaTime / Time.timeScale;
  else
    sinScale = 0;
  thisGUIText.pixelOffset.x = baseX + Mathf.Sin( sinScale ) * 5;
  thisGUIText.pixelOffset.y = baseY + Mathf.Cos( sinScale ) * 5;
  for ( i = 0; i < iPhoneInput.touchCount; i++ )
  {
    if ( iPhoneInput.GetTouch( i ).position.x > 400 && iPhoneInput.Get-
Touch( i ).position.y < 100 && timeStamp + 2 < Time.time )
      Application.OpenURL( "http://www.amazon.com/iPhone-Game-
Programming-All-One/dp/1435454782" );
  }
}
function Start()
{
  thisGUIText = GetComponent( GUIText );
  thisGUIText.text = "iPhone 3D Game \n Programming \n All in One";
  baseX = thisGUIText.pixelOffset.x;
  baseY = thisGUIText.pixelOffset.y;
  timeStamp = Time.time;
}
```

This code is very similar to the code driving the touchToPlayText object on the title screen. The biggest difference is that this code contains a timeStamp that won't allow it to open the URL unless the touch is sensed two seconds after the game is loaded. Then there's the `Application.OpenURL()` call, which accepts a string and opens a Web browser to display the Web page indicated by the string.

In addition to the GUIText for iPhone 3D Game Programming All in One, I also think it would be nice if we added a book image to give a solid indication of exactly what the words mean. We'll grab a piece of free clip art called Red Book Clipart from the public domain clip art site ClipartPal.com (also included in the Tropical Tailspin project). Next, we'll create a new GUITexture game object and rename it Book. We can then either use the import settings to scale down the book image or use the image editor. Then we'll position it at 92, −156 using the Pixel Inset fields and scale it to 92 × 128. We'll create a new script called `bouncingButton.js` and place that inside the GUI Scripts folder. This code is located within the Tropical Tailspin project under Tropical Tailspin > scripts > GUI > bouncingButton.js. That script should contain the following code:

```
private var baseX : int;
private var baseY : int;
private var baseWidth : int;
private var baseHeight : int;
private var sinScale : float;
private var thisGUITexture : GUITexture;
function Update()
{
  if ( !thisGUITexture.enabled )
    return;
  sinScale += 5 * Time.deltaTime / Time.timeScale;
  if ( sinScale > 360 )
    sinScale = 1;
  var adjust = Mathf.Sin( sinScale ) * 10;
  thisGUITexture.pixelInset.x = baseX − adjust / 2;
  thisGUITexture.pixelInset.y = baseY − adjust / 2;
  thisGUITexture.pixelInset.width = baseWidth + adjust;
  thisGUITexture.pixelInset.height = baseHeight + adjust;
}
function Start()
{
  thisGUITexture = GetComponent( GUITexture );
  baseX = thisGUITexture.pixelInset.x;
```

```
    baseY = thisGUITexture.pixelInset.y;
    baseWidth = thisGUITexture.pixelInset.width;
    baseHeight = thisGUITexture.pixelInset.height;
}
```

Now we have animating text indicating the title of the book, and viewers will know that it is, in fact, a book. In the process, we also learned some neat 2D animation tricks that we could apply to a whole 2D game.

Another problem that pops up during the last-minute testing sessions is the controls. Since we have not implemented a tail rudder (onscreen foot pedals that respond to touch would work), it's difficult for beginners to grasp the concept of roll and then pitch to change heading. The flight model changes heading with a bank, as we discussed earlier, but it's too slow. To fix this, simply increase the drag coefficient in the equations on the left and right wing force points from a 0.001 to 0.0025. Try adjusting this value to see what effect it has on the plane. This code is located within the Tropical Tailspin project under Tropical Tailspin > scripts > flightModel > flight004.js.

```
thisRigidbody.AddForceAtPosition( thisGravity + ( −thisRigidbody.
GetPointVelocity( forceWingLeft.position ) * 0.25 ) + ( ( thisTransform.up
* 2 * −accelY ) * wingFriction ) − thisTransform.forward * re-
lativeLeftWingPosition.y * thisRigidbody.velocity.magnitude * 0.0025,
forceWingLeft.position );

thisRigidbody.AddForceAtPosition( thisGravity + ( −thisRigidbody.
GetPointVelocity( forceWingRight.position ) * 0.25 ) + ( ( thisTransform.
up * 2 * accelY ) * wingFriction ) − thisTransform.forward * relative
RightWingPosition.y * thisRigidbody.velocity.magnitude * 0.0025,
forceWingRight.position );
```

One last huge problem is that, although the night scene we set up in Chapter 9 is neat and solved a technical problem, the game just doesn't really look that good, or tropical for that matter. To fix this, we're going to create a daytime scene with a blue sky, clouds, and lighting more in line with the concept.

With a few changes, the alpha-blended water effect we employed for the night scene can also be used for day scenes. To do this, we'll create a new white image and add an alpha channel to it (see Figure 10.27). Afterward, we'll add the contents of the old spotlight image to the alpha channel of the new image. Save this image as waterFade.png. In fact, let's create a daytime scene that looks

White Image   Alpha Channel

Figure 10.27
The `waterFade.png` white image with fade-out alpha channel.

convincing as well. This is one of those times when being creative to circumvent a technical issue has actually sparked a total solution.

First, let's adjust the lights. Change the intensity of the high light to 0.8 and change the intensity of the low light to 0.3. Then take the Bluesky left, right, front, and back skybox images from the Star Trooper project located under Hard Drive > Users > Shared > Unity > Star Trooper > Assets > Skyboxes > Source Images and import them to the image-editing tool. Select the bottom portion of the image that contains a large black section of pixels that's rounded on top. Expand it by 2 pixels and then paint it cyan. Increase the contrast on all of the side view images by 35%. Increase the contrast of the Bluesky Up image by 35% and lower its brightness by 10%. Increase the contrast of the Bluesky Down image by 35% just for thoroughness (see Figure 10.28).

Figure 10.28
Paint the black bottom area cyan and increase the contrast.

Figure 10.29
It's a beautiful tropical day, technically and figuratively.

After exporting and importing all of the images into Unity, create a new skybox material called blueSky and attach the new images to it. Adjust the Repeat field on the textures in the Inspector to Clamp. To finish it off, change the water material to use the new `waterFade.png` image. In fact, let's create two water materials (waterBlue and waterCyan, with their main colors set accordingly) just for kicks. In the end, I think that using waterBlue for the scene works great because with the alpha-blended image, it creates a very convincing Caribbean look running from blue to cyan. At this point, we're beginning to get away from the simple sequencing naming convention, so let's save this scene as tropicalDay (see Figure 10.29).

Conclusion

It looks like we made it. We've gone from conception to completion of an entire game. We've programmed physics, modeled islands, rigged propellers, added sound effects, and programmed a scavenger hunt game mode. The biggest question right now is what are we going to do next? There's so much we could do with the base we've built here that it could fill another book. There's so much that didn't quite make it into the game we have at this point. The lesson to be learned is that game development is always like that. At some point, you have to draw a line in the sand and decide if your product does what it's supposed to do. *Tropical Tailspin* is an example game for this book. Its job is to help convey knowledge of all disciplines involved in creating a game. With the base we have created, at this point you should be capable of adding new features to the game. In fact, expect new features to be added before it hits the App Store. We've covered the concepts behind making a game; take those concepts and extrapolate upon them. Take the code base and modify it until you feel comfortable beginning a new project from scratch. Now let's move on with *Tropical Tailspin* and get it ready for App Store deployment.

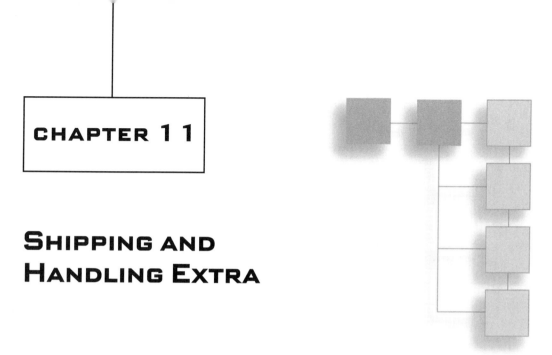

CHAPTER 11

SHIPPING AND HANDLING EXTRA

You have come a *loooong* way! *Tropical Tailspin* began as an idea, became two simple sketches, moved on to digital concept art, morphed into a working prototype, and emerged as a game with all the standard components. You have covered all aspects of 3D game development on some level, and you should be familiar enough with the general concepts to develop a game of your own. Of course, it doesn't pay to develop a game if you can't share it with the world. In this chapter, we will cover the deployment process and watch as our example game joins the App Store.

Back in Chapter 2, we covered the bare essentials of setting up an Apple developer account and getting the provisioning files for development and distribution. Now we're going to cover the iTunes Connect Web site.

When you first log into the iTunes Connect Web site (iTunesConnect.Apple .com), you're greeted with a Terms of Service Agreement. Accept the agreement and move on to the primary control panel.

In the primary control panel, select Manage Applications. You're shown a message stating that you haven't uploaded any applications. Click Add New Application.

The next screen allows you to choose a primary language and the name displayed to the public. Use English and iPhone 3D Game Programming All in One.

The next screen queries about encryption. The game does not contain encryption, so choose No.

The next screen is the game information. It's here that you'll choose the title the public will see. The game will be called *Tropical Tailspin*. Now, you'll see the Description field. Here, you'll try to convince the public that the title is indeed a good and valuable contribution to the community. The next option is the check for whether or not you want to limit the devices that the game will run on. You don't want to limit your options, so choose No. Then choose the categories the game will appear under. Go with Games as the primary category, with the subcategories Racing and Simulation. The next few fields are Copyright, Version Number, and SKU. I developed this game over a number of months between 2009 and 2010, so we'll set it to 2009–2010 Jeremy Alessi. The version number is 1.0, and the SKU will be 1 because it's our first game. The final fields are Application URL, Support URL, and Support Email. The official Web site for this book is iPhone3DGameProgrammingAllinOne.com for the first two fields, and the support email address will be mine for this project: jalessi@iPhone 3DGameProgrammingAllinOne.com. Then choose Continue and move on.

Next is the Upload screen. This is where you upload the game binary, the large icon, and the screenshots. Check the Upload Binary Later box for now and choose Large App Icon and Screenshots. The Large App icon must be a 512 × 512 JPG (or JPEG) file. The screenshots can be 480 × 320, 320 × 480, 320 × 460, or 480 × 300 in pixel dimensions. The screenshots can be JPG (JPEG), TIF (TIFF), or PNG files. Both the Large App icon and the screenshots must be 72 DPI (dots per inch) and be in the RGB color format.

Choosing the appropriate screenshots for the game is an art unto itself. The approach we're going to take is first to show a clean but descriptive shot and then move on to a more visceral, exciting shot showing the plane doing a barrel roll with the strong exotic clouds and mountain in the backdrop. The third shot is the somewhat boring but obligatory gameplay shot. I refer to it as *boring* because it's handed to the potential player so there's no element of surprise or discovery (as there would be if he were playing), in addition to the fact that most of the shot consists of text. The shot is obligatory, though, because people need to know what the goal of the game is.

The fourth is another exciting shot again aimed at the clouds, and the final one is similar to the first, in order to create symmetry. The layout of the screenshots should present a bit of a roller coaster ride of emotions for the player and ultimately make him want to play the game (see Figures 11.1–11.5).

The next few steps include localization, pricing, and a summary. We're going to skip localization for now and set the price to Free. If the application summary checks out, we'll click Submit Application. For future reference, *localization* is what we'd use if we were going to translate the game description into multiple languages so that the descriptions would better target the specific countries the game is released in.

Figure 11.1
Screen 1, clean yet descript.

Figure 11.2
Screen 2, exciting and wide open.

Figure 11.3
Screen 3, kinda boring but necessary.

Figure 11.4
Screen 4, again into the wild blue yonder.

Once you complete the submission, you can move on to building the final binary. Make sure that the Bundle Identifier inside Unity's Player Settings matches the Bundle Identifier you set in the provisioning portal, com.iphone 3dgameprogrammingallinone.tropicaltailspin.

After the Bundle Identifier is set properly, build the project in Unity (use Build, not Build & Run). The project will pop up in Finder. Open the project

Figure 11.5
Screen 5, a dive clearly showcasing the locale.

with Xcode, and the first thing you'll do is click the Breakpoints button. The Build & Run icon should turn green. Next, double-click on the Unity-iPhone collapsible tab on the upper-left side of the screen to open Project Info (see Figure 11.6).

Figure 11.6
Project info.

When the window opens, click on the Configurations button at the top. The two configurations you begin with are Release and Debug. To deploy the game to the App Store, you need a Distribution build. To do this, highlight the Release setting and click the Duplicate button on the bottom left. Change the name of the duplicate Release to Distribution (see Figure 11.7).

Click on the Build button at the top and use the Configuration drop-down menu to set the configuration to Distribution (see Figure 11.8).

Close the main Project Info window and set the current build to Distribution with the drop-down menu in the main Xcode window's upper-left corner (see Figure 11.9). Note that the Distribution build setting is for App Store submission, the Release setting is for development or ad hoc testing, and the Debug build is for specialized bug testing.

Now it's time to expand the Targets tab on the left side hierarchy. Double-click the Unity-iPhone item within the expansion to bring up the Target Info window. Set Xcode to use the distribution provisioning profile. To do this, expand the Code Signing tab and then choose Code Signing Identity > Any iPhone OS

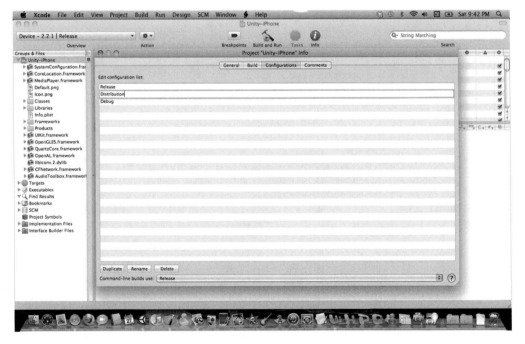

Figure 11.7
Duplicate Release and rename it Distribution.

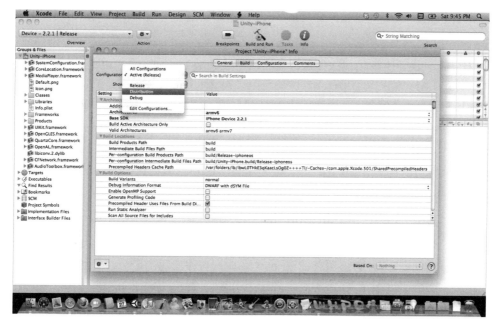

Figure 11.8
Distribution configuration.

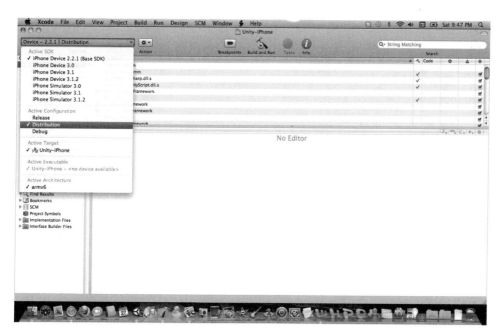

Figure 11.9
Distribution device configuration.

Device > iPhone Distribution > *whatever your name or company name is* (see Figure 11.10).

Choose Build > Build from the main menu to build the app. Xcode will prompt you to allow the application to be signed with the distribution certificate. Obviously, you want to allow it (see Figure 11.11). I personally just choose Allow from the dialog box so that I know when I've built a distribution build instead of just a release build.

Expand the Products tab on the left side, right-click on `tropicaltailspin.app`, and choose Reveal in Finder (see Figure 11.12).

When Finder pops up, right-click on the app and choose to compress it. Finder will create a ZIP file. This is what you will upload to iTunes Connect.

Now it's time to go back to the iTunes Connect Web site. Choose to manage your application. *Tropical Tailspin* should still be sitting there, just waiting for its binary to come along.

Figure 11.10
Code signing identity.

Figure 11.11
Allow code signing.

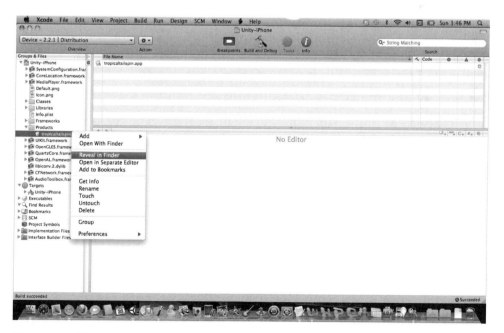

Figure 11.12
Reveal in Finder.

Click on the Tropical Tailspin icon to open its management page and then click on Upload Binary.

The next screen contains a Choose File button. Navigate to the tropicaltailspin. zip folder and choose it.

Click on Upload. A checkbox will appear, asking if this app has been tested on OS 3.0. Check it and then press the Save Changes button in the bottom-right of the screen, assuming that you have version 3.0 of the iPhone OS installed on your test devices. If you haven't tested with iPhone OS 3.0, your app may experience a crash if it's only been tested and built for iPhone OS 2.2.1 or below. At this point, iPhone OS 3.0 is nearly obsolete, and version 4.0 will be arriving very shortly (and there'll probably be a new checkbox for it). The best thing to do is always stay up-to-date with the latest iPhone OS once it has cleared beta form.

The next screen says that the app is awaiting review. Congratulations! You've made it through to the end. Now you just have to sit and wait three to seven agonizing days, wondering if Apple will approve the game.

When Apple approves the game, you'll receive an email letting you know. When that email arrives, log into iTunes Connect, manage your application, and then navigate to the pricing section. Change the date within the pricing section to match the date of approval. If you don't, whatever date it was set to is how the app will be sorted. The App Store moves quickly, and if an app doesn't get on the new list, it's very difficult to gain attention. Changing the date immediately ensures that your app will appear in the new list.

If the app is rejected, Apple will send an email with an explanation. Once the problem is fixed, you can go back to the game's profile on the iTunes Connect Web site and upload a new binary; there's no penalty for resubmitting an app, other than the time lost. Each submission will take three or more days to process. Apple rejects apps mostly due to crashes, conflicts with the Terms of Service, or business model conflicts. Generally, games don't cause offense beyond a crash caused by low memory or a programming error. Avoid these types of crashes by having as many people as possible play test your game.

Conclusion

It's been a really long road, but you made it. You learned the ins and outs of basic programming, covered math and physics principles, navigated the complex process of provisioning files through Apple's developer portal, learned Unity's interface, dissected the iPhone's unique hardware, created concept art, programmed a flight simulation prototype, modeled 3D shapes, rigged propellers, wrote landmark descriptions, and tied it all together and submitted a playable game to Apple for approval.

I hope you enjoyed the ride. Now by all means grab the flight yoke and take the world on a ride of your choosing. Thank you for reading and playing!

INDEX

YOUR ULTIMATE RESOURCE

Course Technology PTR is your ultimate game development resource. Our books provide comprehensive coverage of everything from programming, story development, character design, special effects creation, and more, for everyone from beginners to professionals. Written by industry professionals, with the techniques, tips, and tricks you need to take your games from concept to completion.

License Agreement/Notice of Limited Warranty

By opening the sealed disc container in this book, you agree to the following terms and conditions. If, upon reading the following license agreement and notice of limited warranty, you cannot agree to the terms and conditions set forth, return the unused book with unopened disc to the place where you purchased it for a refund.

License:

The enclosed software is copyrighted by the copyright holder(s) indicated on the software disc. You are licensed to copy the software onto a single computer for use by a single user and to a backup disc. You may not reproduce, make copies, or distribute copies or rent or lease the software in whole or in part, except with written permission of the copyright holder(s). You may transfer the enclosed disc only together with this license, and only if you destroy all other copies of the software and the transferee agrees to the terms of the license. You may not decompile, reverse assemble, or reverse engineer the software.

Notice of Limited Warranty:

The enclosed disc is warranted by Course Technology to be free of physical defects in materials and workmanship for a period of sixty (60) days from end user's purchase of the book/disc combination. During the sixty-day term of the limited warranty, Course Technology will provide a replacement disc upon the return of a defective disc.

Limited Liability:

THE SOLE REMEDY FOR BREACH OF THIS LIMITED WARRANTY SHALL CONSIST ENTIRELY OF REPLACEMENT OF THE DEFECTIVE DISC. IN NO EVENT SHALL COURSE TECHNOLOGY OR THE AUTHOR BE LIABLE FOR ANY OTHER DAMAGES, INCLUDING LOSS OR CORRUPTION OF DATA, CHANGES IN THE FUNCTIONAL CHARACTERISTICS OF THE HARDWARE OR OPERATING SYSTEM, DELETERIOUS INTERACTION WITH OTHER SOFTWARE, OR ANY OTHER SPECIAL, INCIDENTAL, OR CONSEQUENTIAL DAMAGES THAT MAY ARISE, EVEN IF COURSE TECHNOLOGY AND/OR THE AUTHOR HAS PREVIOUSLY BEEN NOTIFIED THAT THE POSSIBILITY OF SUCH DAMAGES EXISTS.

Disclaimer of Warranties:

COURSE TECHNOLOGY AND THE AUTHOR SPECIFICALLY DISCLAIM ANY AND ALL OTHER WARRANTIES, EITHER EXPRESS OR IMPLIED, INCLUDING WARRANTIES OF MERCHANTABILITY, SUITABILITY TO A PARTICULAR TASK OR PURPOSE, OR FREEDOM FROM ERRORS. SOME STATES DO NOT ALLOW FOR EXCLUSION OF IMPLIED WARRANTIES OR LIMITATION OF INCIDENTAL OR CONSEQUENTIAL DAMAGES, SO THESE LIMITATIONS MIGHT NOT APPLY TO YOU.

Other:

This Agreement is governed by the laws of the State of Massachusetts without regard to choice of law principles. The United Convention of Contracts for the International Sale of Goods is specifically disclaimed. This Agreement constitutes the entire agreement between you and Course Technology regarding use of the software.